memoir
of an
independent
woman

memoir of an independent woman

AN UNCONVENTIONAL LIFE WELL LIVED

Tania Grossinger

Skyhorse Publishing

In memory and honor of Art D'Lugoff whose encouragement, love, and support made everything possible.

Skyhorse Publishing books may be purchased in bulk at special discounts for sales promotion, corporate gifts, fund-raising, or educational purposes. Special editions can also be created to specifications. For details, contact the Special Sales Department, Skyhorse Publishing, 307 West 36th Street, 11th Floor, New York, NY 10018 or info@skyhorsepublishing.com.

Skyhorse® and Skyhorse Publishing® are registered trademarks of Skyhorse Publishing, Inc.®, a Delaware corporation.

www.skyhorsepublishing.com

10 9 8 7 6 5 4 3 2 1

Library of Congress Cataloging-in-Publication Data is available on file.

ISBN: 978-1-62087-615-2

Printed in the United States of America

Contents

Introduction   vii

1 Natasha   1

2 Karla and Max   3

3 Beverly Hills, 1939 to 1945   9

4 Introduction to Grossinger's   17

5 Adolescence   27

6 Life at the "G"   37

7 The Brandeis Years   41

8 My Year with the City of Hope   59

9 Not a Good Time in My Life   73

10 The Man I Was to Marry   77

11 Marriage and Its Finale   89

12 Getting My Life Together, Bits and Pieces   97

13 Love in the Early 1960s   105

14 Finding My Professional Niche   109

15 Betty Friedan: Up Close and Personal   113

16 The Playboy Years   125

17 Playboy Highlights: Ayn Rand, Tim Leary, Jean Shepherd,
Hugh Hefner, and the Playboy Mansion   135

18 Puerto Vallarta: A Fantasy Come True   149

19 Christy Brown's *Down All the Days* and Malachy McCourt   163

20 Mother's Last Decade: Montecatini, Italy   171

21 Death Takes Its Toll   177

22 After My Mother Died   183

23 Running Away from It All   191

24 Karla's Letters Discovered   195

25 Seeking Professional Help   203

26 *Growing Up at Grossinger's*   205

27 Publication   213

28 The Literary Years   219

29 Psychics, Seers, and the Supernatural   225

30 Life as a Travel Writer   237

31 Travel Writer Disappears in Jamaica   245

32 Israel   251

33 Love with a Married Man   261

34 Art's Death and Aftermath   273

35 Post-Art   279

36 Trying to Reconcile with Mother   283

37 Looking Back: Childless by Choice   287

Acknowledgments   295

Introduction

My life, by many standards, can be described as unconventional. I grew up as the daughter of a single mother at the famous Grossinger's Hotel in New York's Catskill Mountains; married early, briefly, and disastrously; beach bummed in Mexico; spent the best part of the swinging 1960s doing public relations for *Playboy*; wrote four books and numerous travel articles; had a long-lived affair with a married man; crossed paths with Ayn Rand, Jackie Robinson, Hugh Hefner, Betty Friedan, Tim Leary, and Elizabeth Taylor; and survived more dramatic escapades than I probably deserve. What I didn't have, by choice, was a child.

As a teenager I assumed, as did most girls my age, that I would grow up, marry, raise a family, and, of course, live happily ever after. Real life intervened. It was not that I didn't have maternal feelings, that my career came first, or that I never loved a man profoundly enough to bear his child. My decision was based on intuitive knowledge, a deep-seated, almost molecular awareness that even as my biological clock gave me the choice, not having a child was the wisest path to take. The reasons run deep, as do most things of value in life, and only now am I beginning to understand how complicated they were.

As I reach the age where there is more to look back at than forward to, I can't help but reflect on how different my life would have been had it gone in another direction, had I not been so dreadfully afraid, despite my many accomplishments, of not being good enough to raise a real daughter, of passing on to her the detritus of my emotional past. But that was years ago.

Things are different now, and though I proudly stand behind all the choices I've made, I'd be less than honest if I didn't admit to moments when I find myself starved for an emotional connection that only a child can bestow. That, of course, I will never have. As an alternative, however, I have Natasha—the daughter who exists solely in my imagination and heart.

1

Natasha

It occurs to me that before our odyssey begins, you might want to know how I came upon your name. I could be melodramatic and say that it was in honor of a beloved relative or romantic literary heroine. But I named you Natasha because I've always loved the way it sounds. Natasha! Strong! Proud! I also believe you to be open, sensitive, bold, thoughtful, fearless, tolerant, decent, kind, loyal, proud, generous, slightly bawdy, trusting, and trustworthy. You have a delicious sense of humor.

How old are you as I write this? I'm not sure. Old enough, I hope, to have experienced enough of life to accept at least some of mine. The color of your hair escapes me. Are you short or tall? I have no idea. I don't know whether you are single, whether you have a family, or what kind of life you lead. You are the child I might have wished for, the daughter who, in another life, might have shared some degree of happiness with me.

2

Karla and Max

I was born in Evanston, Illinois, on February 17, 1937. My mother, Karla Seifer Grossinger, had, in her seventh month, been hospitalized for observation. The pregnancy, her first, was not going well. My father, Max, had been admitted to a separate wing ten days earlier with a second heart attack. She overheard two nurses speaking outside her door. "Isn't it a shame that Mr. Grossinger is dying." My mother told me this story when I was six years old; it was one of the rare times she ever mentioned my father. She begged the nurses to let her see him but was warned she might lose the baby if she left her bed. Two minutes later they picked her up from the floor. My heartbeat was undetectable, and a caesarean section was performed, ostensibly to bring out a dead fetus.

Such was my introduction to the world!

My father, who had just turned forty, died six months later.

A friend brought my mother a gift, a baby diary, which I discovered many years later. My birth certificate, Number 252, was filed at the county clerk's office in Chicago, where we then lived. I weighed 5 pounds, 1 ounce. Color of hair: blonde. Color of eyes: blue. I doubled my weight at three months. "Saw for the first time on Easter Sunday," my mother wrote, "while I listened to a radio concert of Parsifal. Later in the evening, her first tears. Smiled for the first time on March 31 when she was six weeks old."

Considering her husband was near death and she would soon be a thirty-eight-year-old widow with a baby and no family support, the fact that she kept a record of my early months was likely the most maternal gesture she ever made.

My father was the eldest of four children; he was born in 1896 in a small village called Balnicz on the Austrian side of the Hungarian border. His father, Solomon Grossinger, had a general store on the outskirts of town that sold a bit of everything—clothing, pig feed, tools, and groceries. His older brother, Herman, escaped the Holocaust, barely, and settled in Montreal with his wife, Binka, and young daughter, Rose. There were also two sisters, who I believe died with their families in the concentration camps.

I have a few frayed photos of my father together with my mother, and from all appearances, he was a snappy dresser and attractive man. Relatives who knew him say I bear a strong resemblance; those who never met him say I look more like my mom. They could all be correct. In each of the pictures, my parents look like twins.

I know nothing about his young life, what he studied in school, what sports he liked, what ambitions he might have had. My mother was always uncomfortable when I asked, and early on, not wanting to make her sad, I knew to keep such questions to myself.

At some point he left Balnicz for Vienna, where he met and became engaged to my mother, a philosophy major at the city's prestigious university. In one of the many journals she kept at various stages of her life, she describes what happened when she told her father of her desire to get married. "My father was very disappointed when I wrote him about Max. Max was a businessman, but he didn't have a college education, and because of that, my father was against the marriage. When I brought him home to Poland to meet my family, Max insisted on renting a big car so we could arrive in style. My father and mother, both unassuming people, were not impressed. But it did not take long for him to win them over, and they grew to adore him."

They married in 1924 and shortly after that came to America and settled in Chicago, where my father had family who had emigrated earlier. They rented a small apartment on the city's north side. My dad worked for cousins who owned a car dealership, while my mother pursued her studies at Northwestern University. At some point my father went off on his own to start a small automobile oil company. It had just begun to turn a profit when, twelve years after they were married, my mother became pregnant. He died shortly after I was born.

A few years ago I met a professional handwriting analyst who agreed to look at the one letter from him I found in my mother's papers after she died. "Your father," she relayed in part, "was bright, elegant, showy, precise, and self-conscious over the fact that he wasn't a finished product. Circumstances prevented him from doing what he could have been doing very well. He was in awe of your mother, always tried to live up to her, very loyal, wanted very much to be seen as a go-getter, very persevering, very unforgiving of dishonesty, consumed with doing the right thing."

And, so, you now know almost as much about him as I do.

My mother was a most complicated woman.

There were a number of different Karlas, I was to discover. Somehow she managed to keep each separate from the other, which made it very confusing for me as a daughter; I still struggle to figure it out.

Here is how she describes her early life:

I was born in a little town called Horodenka in eastern Poland. It was my father, of course, who was the handsomest, proudest, most dignified man I knew. He came from a well-to-do family who owned a lot of land, which went to the

5

oldest son. My father was director of the only bank in town, which was a very special honor because he was an Orthodox Jew, and no Jew had been appointed a director of the bank before. My mother was small, kind, sweet, very intelligent. She read a lot, mostly about medicine, as she had five children. I was the oldest.

I could never play with the children in the neighborhood; they did not belong to the aristocracy. I was very proud in my childhood not to belong to a family of business people, shopkeepers. There was a caste system among the Jews in Poland. Family meant more than money; the most important thing was learning.

My father adored me; he was proud, as I was to him the most beautiful, the most intelligent child in town with A grades always. I was supposed to go to a girl's school, but I rebelled. I wanted to attend a university later on, to prepare for a profession, which was an unheard of thing for a girl at the time (the early 1900s). In order to be admitted, one had to attend the Gymnasium, a combination of high school and college with an eight-year foundation of Latin and five years of Greek. It was a classical education.

There was one school of this type for boys, but none for girls. It was a private school and very expensive. The family was against my being educated as a boy, so I went on a hunger strike. My mother helped with food in secrecy. And I won! (You didn't know your mother was a suffragette, an organizer!) I went to the home of some wealthy people who had girls of my age and sounded so convincingly that they agreed. We were finally ten girls, we had our class, wonderful professors, and I got my first taste of learning, of exploring the beauty of literature, of thought.

Speaking of her adolescence she writes:

I never liked boys my own age; they did not interest me. There were quite a few in love with me; they used to throw flowers and letters unsigned through the window. I used to be very vain and sit for the longest time in front of a mirror, trying to copy the hairdo of some heroine I read about and admired. I was always very romantic and dreamt a lot about a wonderful man whom I would meet someday and love forever. I never wanted to compromise. I did always the most and best I could in my work, but I would not compromise with my soul. I never gave up my ideals. I wanted to be an ideal woman, and I was that to many wonderful men who loved and idolized me and have never forgotten me.

I would have liked to be a famous courtesan, a beautiful, brilliant woman having around her the most distinguished men of the time. When I read French history about the life at the court of the French kings, about their brilliant mistresses, about famous French women who had "salons" where the greatest minds would meet at that time, I am sorry I did not live in that period.

This was not the Karla I knew; it was certainly not the mother I grew up with. I read this as if I were reading the diary of a stranger. Something must have happened along the way.

3

Beverly Hills, 1939 to 1945

My mother had never been close to my father's family in Chicago, even though they lived in the same neighborhood. She loved the opera, had a subscription to the Chicago Symphony, and led a weekly book club. She was much more comfortable with her non-Jewish friends from Northwestern, where she was studying for her Ph.D., than at family gatherings, where conversations revolved around the automobile business and memories of the "old country."

My father, it seems, shared few, if any, of her cultural interests, and it's still hard for me to get a sense of what they had in common. "He always looked up to me," my mother once said. Maybe the handwriting analyst was on the right track?

Everything changed that terrible day in August 1937, when my father succumbed to his third and fatal heart attack. The reasons my mother left Chicago aren't clear, but two years after my father's death, after sorting out his business affairs and paying off his debts, she did. So that's how, in 1939, we ended up in Southern California—a forty-year-old single woman with limited funds and her two-year-old toddler. What she lacked in contacts she made up for in confidence.

The first two or three years were the most normal we would ever have. It was just the two of us. We had a series of apartments in Los

Angeles, each nicer than the last as my mother's various jobs became more responsible and remunerative. We spent all of our weekends together—sightseeing, going to the beach, visiting neighbors. We were a real, albeit small, family.

Then my mother got a position as managing director of the John-Frederics millinery salon on North Rodeo Drive. Mr. John and Mr. Fred were the two most famous hat designers in Beverly Hills at a time when elegant "chapeaux" were the height of fashion. Their boutique catered to more society women, film stars, and celebrities than most of the well-known restaurants did.

We immediately found a new place to live at 121 South Elm Drive, just off Wilshire Boulevard, within walking distance of where my mother worked. It was a studio apartment, smaller than what we were used to, in a three-story, Spanish-style stucco building with a garden in the back. It had a modest kitchen with room for a round dining table, a slightly larger living room, and a Murphy bed that came out of a wall, which the two of us shared.

The changes in the beginning were subtle. She began to wear colorful turbans and hats and dressed up even at home. She made herself smell sweet and flowery when she went out at night—and she went out almost every night of the week. She bought gooey creams to put on her face, which she said would make her look prettier.

Then she took a new name, Madame Savonier, French, she said, for the name she was born with (it wasn't), and she rarely found time to be with me. She began, for the first time, to invite people to dinner, usually slim young men who didn't have wives or girlfriends and who gossiped about movie stars and said lots of naughty things I was instructed never to repeat. She referred to these conversations as her "education." I had to curtsy when meeting someone for the first time and wasn't supposed to speak unless I was spoken to. I was also told to say, "I don't know," if anyone asked how old she was, where she was born, or whether she had any boyfriends (not that I knew anyway!). "What I do and where I come from is nobody's business," she warned. "There are certain things that are private and meant to be kept secret. You are too young, darling, I know, to understand this, but someday when you grow up. . . ."

Shortly thereafter I was shipped off to boarding school. I must be careful here; it is too easy to misappropriate motives. "Shipped off" is how I felt. My mother, who as you may remember went on a hunger strike in Poland to get her parents to send her to a better school, had always placed high value on education. There was a prominent boarding school in the Hollywood Hills named Monsieur Hugo's, whose headmistress, Madame Hugo, was a new customer at John-Frederics. My mother, who by then had learned how business was conducted in Beverly Hills, paid her special attention. Madame returned the compliment, I was told later, by offering my mother the perfect financial arrangement. My tuition and room and board would be free; in return, Madame and her husband would be invited to all of the salon's star-studded events.

My being away during the week also afforded my mother privacy and a social life; sharing a Murphy bed with me could not possibly be what she had in mind. I'm sure this made sense at the time, but all I knew was that I was six years old and didn't want to sleep away from home, and, after all, wasn't I supposed to come first?

There were about thirty-five children in the first through sixth grades at Monsieur Hugo's, a number of them with fathers who'd been drafted to fight against Hitler's army overseas. The boys and girls lived in separate dormitories on the first floor and ate cafeteria-style on the second, and the third floor was set up as a one-room schoolhouse, something I imagined children from villages in the early nineteenth-century

Midwest had attended. We sat around large tables, instruction was given in both English and French, and whatever any one child was taught, the youngster sitting next to that child learned as a matter of course. Academically we were permitted to progress at our own speed. By the time I was eight years old, I was already in the sixth grade. Also, for the first time, I was encouraged to ask questions and speak out. After following my mother's admonition to not speak unless I was spoken to, it was as if I had just discovered the English language.

I never complained. I didn't want to get myself or anybody else in trouble. So what if I cried myself to sleep when they called me teacher's pet or smarty pants, hid my clothes, dowsed water on my bed sheets, or stole the Hershey bars my mother gave me? I concentrated on learning how to speak French and memorizing my multiplication tables, learned how to play piano, and wrote down whatever came to my mind. "Once Upon a Time" was my favorite topic. I still have a copy of what I wrote when I was seven years old:

ONCE UPON A TIME there was a little girl who lived very far away from everyplace else. She lived on an island with trees and cherries and the trees had long gnarled branches and she had long snow-white hair that sometimes got tangled.

Nobody else lived on the island but she didn't care because she didn't know there was such a thing as anybody else.

She ran across the island lots of times skipping and singing and shouting and she was never hungry.

I don't know if she ever slept.

ONCE UPON A TIME when I was a little girl, I was big and strong and smiled all over

ONCE UPON A TIME I ate glue. I ate it and ate it and ate it . . .
    until I got unstuck.
ONCE UPON A TIME I dreamt I was.
    But I wasn't.
ONCE UPON A TIME I made doughnuts
    and gave my mother the hole.
ONCE UPON A TIME I was free.
ONCE UPON A TIME
    I was dead.

As you can see, I was turning into your run-of-the-mill, well-adjusted child.

On Saturdays my mother would take the bus to Hollywood and pick me up, then take me to work with her at John-Frederics. There she charmed the customers in the front of the store while I watched the women in the back cut patterns out of felt, which they then fashioned into fancy hats. Sometimes they would make little ones for me, but I always felt they made me look stupid, especially compared to how elegant my mother looked when she was photographed wearing hats with film stars like Joan Crawford and Katherine Hepburn in *Silver Screen* magazine and *Photoplay*.

Once in a while we went to a movie. Ingrid Bergman in *Song of Bernadette* was my favorite. I must have seen it three times. Otherwise we stayed home and listened to classical music. I remember only the names Beethoven and Mozart, which were the two composers I loved most. My mother rarely spoke of what she did during the week. Sometimes I overheard snippets of phone conversations about someone who had taken a "shine" to her, but I had no idea what that meant.

Shortly after starting boarding school, my mother enrolled me at the Church of Christ, Scientist Sunday school, two blocks away. I loved

Sunday school, even if it took me away from my mom. I also loved that when it was over, she would make lamb chops (at least until they were rationed) and shoestring potatoes for lunch. I quickly memorized the prayers, learned the hymns, and dutifully got on my knees to pray each night, believing with all my heart that if indeed I died before I waked, my soul the Lord would surely take. I recited the Lord's Prayer so often that even now the words "Our Father, who art in heaven" sometimes hit my lips before my head hits the pillow.

I was beguiled by the concept of the soul, Jesus, and the power of God. Bible stories were like fairy tales, except in the end you got to go to heaven instead of living happily ever after. The Ten Commandments, the parables, and the Sermon on the Mount all appealed to me, especially the Beatitude that read, "Blessed are the meek, for they shall inherit the earth." Wow, someday I might inherit the earth—a heady thought for someone so meek! Miracles gave me something to hold onto—maybe my father wasn't really dead; maybe he just went away on a long vacation and would come back someday; or my mother would marry someone else who would love me like a daughter, and I'd have a real father to love. At school, every evening after dinner, the children whose fathers were overseas had to write letters telling them how much they loved and missed them. Some kids called me lucky because I could play instead of having to write. Some luck!

I was unusually sheltered from the world. There was no television, radios in the dorm were forbidden, and reading newspapers was something I rarely did. I hardly ever saw uniformed soldiers on the streets. Of course I wasn't oblivious to World War II, but it was taking place far away from me. To my knowledge my mother didn't know anyone who was drafted or killed, and she certainly didn't bring up the subject with me. What I remember most about the war was the rationing. I would often come home weekends complaining of being hungry, and though I understood it wasn't the fault of the boarding school, it didn't leave me feeling any less deprived. I hope it was not lost on my mother that she was being squired to fancy restaurants like the Brown Derby and Chasen's where, for a price, you could have whatever you wanted to eat.

It was also at this time that I declared I hated Jews. The kids at school said that if there were no Jews, there would be no war, and their fathers could come home and wouldn't have to fight any more. It was all the fault of the Jews!

4

Introduction to Grossinger's

When Selig Grossinger, my father's uncle, and his wife, Malka, opened Grossinger's as a small boarding house in 1914, their dreams didn't extend much beyond offering a haven for people on New York City's Lower East Side looking to breathe fresh Catskill Mountain air. No one could have anticipated that thirty years later it would have grown in size and reputation to become the most famous Jewish resort hotel in America. No one could have anticipated that their daughter, Jennie, my father's first cousin, would one day become the driving force behind the hotel's success and a celebrity in her own right because of her association with the hotel.

In the spring of 1945, Jennie chose to make one of her yearly visits to the West Coast. With the German forces about to surrender to the Western Allies, rumors were spreading that the war was finally winding down, and Jennie was convinced that the timing was right for Grossinger's, already famous in America, to expand its clientele internationally. She needed someone on staff with the skill to make Europeans feel at home. Someone well-traveled, elegant, who could converse in their languages. And if that someone also bore the Grossinger name. . . .

My mother's life at this time was in turmoil. She was no longer associated with John-Frederics. The departure was abrupt and never explained to me. She was now working for Gloria Bristol, an entrepreneur with a line of cosmetics that appealed to the rich and snobbish.

Mrs. Bristol had expected that the important people my mother knew from Rodeo Drive would follow her—but it hadn't quite turned out that way.

Jennie had always admired, not without a touch of envy, my mother's education, adaptability, sense of style, and ability to put others at ease, but though their paths had crossed periodically, they were not what one might consider friends. I once overheard my mother saying she didn't trust Jennie.

The two had dinner one evening, and Jennie made an offer to bring the two of us to Grossinger's. My mother told me that she would never have said yes had Jennie not added "and Tania will have a family." Neither of us could have predicted how that one "yes" would change our lives.

It was a long drive to the Catskills from New York City, four hours of torturous winding roads on the legendary Route 17 in what was called a "hack," a long black car that sat eight people—but on this day only sat my mother and me. Finally, looming high on a hill almost like a mirage, there it was, more majestic than I could ever have imagined. Grossinger's! I crossed my fingers, said a quick prayer, and took a very deep breath. A new life was about to begin.

It was late afternoon when we reached the Main House, a four-story, Tudor-style edifice that served as the locus for many of the hotel's activities. A man with a TRAFFIC pin on his shirt helped us out of the car and into the hotel. Up one flight of stairs and to the left we emerged into the largest room I had ever seen, a split-level bevy of wood-paneled walls, chocolate leather sofas and chairs, rugs so thick I ached to run over them without shoes, two fireplaces (one that actually worked), a grand piano, and Impressionist-style oil paintings on the walls. This, I was told, was called a lobby. Adjacent to the lobby was the dining room, easily a city block long and half-block wide, designed to serve close to 1,200 guests simultaneously. There were so many different things to familiarize myself with those first days. There was the service desk from which blue-uniformed bellhops zipped around carrying luggage, delivering messages, and performing other tip-rewarding tasks; the vast Terrace Room nightclub downstairs where guests danced, drank, and watched the evening's entertainment; an outdoor patio where they played games like Simon Says; the canteen that sold magazines, sundries, and snacks; a Tap Room that offered daily complimentary dance lessons; a writing room; a card room; a jewelry store; a beauty salon; a ping-pong room; a small synagogue; a dance studio . . . I'm sure I've left a few things out.

That wasn't all. Throughout the hotel's 850 acres were gardens with signs admonishing guests: PLEASE DO NOT PICK US. WE BLOOM FOR YOUR PLEASURE. THANK YOU. THE FLOWERS. There was also a lake where one could take out rowboats, a horseback riding stable, tennis courts, a baseball field, a golf course, a swimming pool, an ice skating rink, ski slopes, and a summer camp. It was quite an eye-opener for a sheltered eight-year-old, alternately astonishing, amazing, overwhelming, confounding, and confusing. Nothing had prepared me for this!

What made my adjustment viable was that there were two other girls close to my age connected to the hotel. My cousin Mary Ann was Jennie's niece. She was a "real" Grossinger. Not like me, a distant cousin. Patsy Kreindler, whose father, David, was the hotel's general manager, was also a Very Important Child. They could do things I couldn't—like ask the chef to prepare whatever dish they desired, even if it wasn't on the menu, get free ice cream sodas and candy from the canteen, ask someone to drive them into town if they wanted to go to the movies, or invite friends from school to the hotel. Little things, perhaps, but they made an impression as to where I stood. Fortunately, we focused on other things. We were the Three Musketeers: playmates, mischief makers, support systems, and, to this day, the most loyal and dearest of friends. I know my mother was relieved they were there.

My mother chose the long ride along Route 17 to confront me with another reality of my new life: I was Jewish!

Seemingly overnight I had become one of the people I hated. How could I be Jewish when I went to Christian Science school? I knew I wasn't a "real" Christian Scientist because my mother and I went to doctors when we were sick, a practice forbidden by the church. But Jewish? The reason why fathers of my boarding school friends were being killed? She took time to explain that soldiers weren't fighting because of the Jews; they were fighting because the United States was at war with Germany for invading Poland and other European countries and at war with Japan for the bombing of Pearl Harbor. She didn't tell me we were Jewish when we lived in California, she said, because all the children at my boarding school were Christian, and she didn't want me to feel out of place. But now that I was with my family, I could know the truth. I had no choice but to accept her explanation, especially because she said that she did it for me. She explained that Jews didn't believe in Jesus Christ, but that both religions worshipped the same God. She also told me that Jews were the "chosen people," which appealed to me more than I admitted. I was "chosen"! That alone made me happy that we came to Grossinger's.

It is curious, even now, how little drama I associate with having made the transition from Christianity to Judaism. I had a new home, new friends, a new school, and a new life—so why shouldn't I have a new religion? New protocols came with the package. Because the hotel was kosher, which I learned meant "according to Jewish law," there were certain dietary restrictions. Animals had to be be slaughtered according to ritual. Meat from a pig was not kosher. Neither was shellfish. Meat and dairy could not be consumed at the same time, and each was prepared at Grossinger's in its own kitchen. Sacrificing bacon at breakfast and milk with my chopped steak was no problem. I still had God, the

Bible stories from the Old Testament, and the Ten Commandments. All I did was trade Jesus and the Beatitudes (thought I did feel badly about being meek and now maybe *not* able to inherit the earth) for the privilege of being Chosen while I was still alive.

One snowy afternoon when I was ten and the guests were otherwise occupied, my mother asked me to come back to the room with her, as she had something to tell me. "I had two brothers and two sisters when I grew up," she told me. "I was the oldest. We were Orthodox Jews and always went to the synagogue on Friday nights and Saturday mornings. I deeply believed that if I was a good girl God would take care of me and everyone I loved." She then jumped to the beginning of World War II without mentioning intervening years, and I knew better than to interrupt her. "I was still in Chicago in 1938, the year after your father died. Jehoshua, my oldest brother, was already living in Israel. My younger sisters lived on the outskirts of Warsaw and were married with a boy and a girl each. Fabian, the youngest, was finishing high school in Horodenka, where our mother and father still lived. I was not in touch with them as often as I should have been. They were very sad when Max and I emigrated to America in 1924, even though they knew how excited I was, and I don't think they ever forgave me. When Hitler invaded Poland in the fall of 1939, it was the last time, with the exception of Fabian who managed to escape to Detroit where my mother had a cousin, that I heard from any of them. Through that cousin in Detroit I learned that my entire family was exterminated in the concentration camp at Auschwitz."

I couldn't help myself. I started to cry, even though I had promised not to. My mother held me close, and that's the last time she ever spoke of her family. I don't know if she ever attended a Jewish prayer service after that, but I do know that though the High Holy Days of

Rosh Hashanah and Yom Kippur at Grossinger's were magnificently presented with a Rabbi, Cantor, and twenty-five-piece choir, she always preferred to stay in her room.

It was on our arrival at Grossinger's that we discovered that Jennie had not arranged a place for my mother and I to live. It was only after eighteen months of being shuttled from room to room in a number of different cottages that we were permanently assigned to an attic room on the third floor of Pop's Cottage, named after my great-uncle Selig. We still had to share a room, just like in California, except in the cottage there was no kitchen, not even a private bathroom. Sometimes during the summers, if the hotel was overbooked, they would remove my dresser and put in a third bed to accommodate a guest. I had trouble understanding why my Aunt Jennie, whom I rarely saw once we arrived, wasn't treating us better.

I was also surprised that my mother and I would not be eating together. As part of her job as a "hostess," she dined with the VIP guests, while I ate an hour earlier at a table with staff from the front office. I had assumed that we would be eating with other members of the family. After all, wasn't becoming part of a family the reason we came to the Catskills? And didn't families eat at the same table?

My mother had to work at night; something else I hadn't anticipated, which meant we rarely saw each other. When I left for school, she was asleep. When she came home from work, I was asleep. In the afternoon I did my homework at the Main House so as not to bother her when she was resting. The staff had been advised, from the first day, that my mother was always to be introduced as Karla. There was only one Mrs. Grossinger: Jennie. As the hotel's official hostess, she was supposed to circulate wherever guests gathered, ingratiate herself with couples and families who returned year after year, introduce singles to each other (who knew she had such matchmaking skills?), and do her best to ensure that all who graced the Grossinger doorstep were made to feel they were the most important guests in the world. Karla would announce herself by strolling through the upper lobby where her "office" (desk) was located, chirping "Allo, Allo!" in her Viennese lilt, soon to become her trademark. She always wore a headdress, usually a colorful turban in the daytime. In the evenings she donned a hairpiece of plaited blonde braids, made of her own hair, which stood out strikingly from the beauty parlor coiffed "'do's" of the day. I can't believe she didn't feel demeaned, a woman with her education and cultural background reduced to playing second fiddle to a relative who hardly acknowledged her existence. I don't know what she had initially been promised, but if she ever felt betrayed by Jennie, she never showed it. "It's just the way it is," she would say when I asked why she didn't complain. "It wouldn't make any difference."

I didn't like that.

WHAT I (age 9) LIKE BEST ABOUT KARLA (age 47):
    She is beautiful.
    Everyone tells me how charming she is, how lucky I am to be her daughter.
    When everybody calls me "Karla's daughter."
    How she always tells me how much she loves me.

WHAT I (age 9) LIKE LEAST ABOUT KARLA (age 47):
    How she never takes me seriously when I am sad.
    How everyone always calls me "Karla's daughter." I have a name of my own. It is Tania.
    How she always tells me how much she loves me but never spends any time with me.
    How I don't think she likes being a mom.

A Friday night, 1947, Grossinger's: Malke Grossinger, Jennie Grossinger's elderly mother, affectionately known as "Mom," lives alone on the bottom floor of Pop's Cottage. My mother is taking her first vacation. I consider myself a grownup—after all, I am ten years old—but she is afraid to leave me alone and asks if Mom Grossinger will let me sleep in her room downstairs while she is gone.

Mom is an observant Orthodox Jew. She wears long dresses and a *sheitel* (wig) and prays in the synagogue every day. She is asleep by the time I come home, so I tiptoe quietly and turn on the light while I undress. I seem to have startled her, as she quickly looks up from her bed and starts to cry. "Why are you crying, Mom?" I ask. "Are you feeling okay? Is there anything I can do?" She remains silent, shakes her head, and falls back asleep.

A year later my mother plans another trip. This time Mom tells her I am not welcome in her room. My sin? I turned on the light, which is forbidden in Orthodox homes on the Sabbath, one of the Jewish proscriptions I was never told about. Instead of pointing out what I did wrong when I did it, so that I could have learned, apologized, and asked to be forgiven, my mother is now forced to send me to relatives in Jersey City when she goes on vacation. Mom is supposed to be the saint of the family.

I don't care what I learned in Sunday school. I no longer believe in saints.

My mother's closet in our room has a lock to which only she holds the key. Each night as she dresses, she unlocks the door and takes from the floor an oversized gray sock that holds her jewelry and other valuables. After making her selection, she returns the sock to the closet floor and locks the door. The routine never wavers. With me looking on, she then places the key under her scarves on the right side of her top dresser drawer. She knows I know where it is and has made me give my word I will never use it.

Why does she have to lock the door? Is she testing me? Can I be trusted? Will my curiosity overcome my sense of honor? Or will I be comfortable with secrets and locked doors the rest of my life?

When she was growing up, my mother loved to play the mandolin. In her diary she wrote that for her fourteenth birthday her parents took her to a concert starring a well-known mandolin virtuoso. She gave up the instrument the next day. "I realized I would never be perfect."

Am I my mother's mandolin?

Does she ever wish she could give me up because I'm not perfect?

It would explain a lot of things!

5

Adolescence

I entered high school when I was eleven years old (you may remember that I was three years ahead of grade level when we first moved to Grossinger's), and I entered what I considered to be my adolescence around the same time. I had accepted that I must be the good little girl and that guests always came first. Without guests, the hotel could not exist. Without the hotel, my mother and I wouldn't have a home. I did whatever the Grossinger family told me and never ever, as my mother made me promise, expressed anger, even when they said or did something I knew wasn't nice. I also tried to follow my mother's directive: "You must never show people how you feel."

I showed them anyway. To start, I developed a weight problem. In a setting where physical appearance counted almost as much as how much money someone had, even being five pounds overweight was a cardinal sin, and I was probably twice that. A day didn't go by without guests pinching my cheek and telling me I had such a pretty face, if only . . . or whispering behind my mother's back, "How could Karla let her daughter. . . ." I didn't fit my clothes well, and my mother wouldn't buy new ones until I lost weight. Stubborn to a fault, I spent part of one entire summer dressed in dungarees because I refused to wear dresses that didn't fit properly. I looked so sloppy and caused her such embarrassment that she was forced to give in and take me shopping!

Then there was the time I decided not to speak. If my mother wouldn't make time to talk to me, I wouldn't talk to her—or to anyone else for that matter. My mother thought it was a game. She would smile and tell anyone who asked, "Isn't it nice to finally have some peace and quiet?"

Instead of talking, I read every periodical from the canteen I could lay my hands on: *Life* magazine, *Saturday Evening Post, Reader's Digest, Today's Health, True Confessions.* "What to do about menstrual cramps." "What it takes to succeed in the business world." "How to add years to your life." "Ten ways to keep your husband happy at home." I learned about mulching and douching and making stuffing with Ritz crackers. I didn't have to speak in the dining room, as the waiters knew what I liked. Four days, five days, and the novelty was beginning to wear off. Six, seven, and then something scary happened. It was as if I had ceased to exist. No one seemed to care if I spoke or not. Nobody acknowledged my presence; it was as if I wasn't there. I remember the overwhelming fear of being dispensable. For what it's worth, I talk a lot now!

Two things in the next year gave me a new lease on life. I turned into quite a good ping-pong player (which later led to a long-lasting friendship with Jackie Robinson), and I learned to play the trumpet. One night I made an offer to Carlos, the lead trumpet player in the Latin band. I would teach him how to play ping-pong if he would teach me the trumpet. He considered the deal fair, so three times a week he lent me his horn. I would practice scales in an underground tunnel that connected the laundry to the pantry's storage area, where I could blow out my frustrations with no guests being disturbed.

My late afternoons were now filled with homework and trumpet lessons, the early evenings were filled with ping-pong and trumpet practice, and later on I would be in the Terrace Room analyzing musical arrangements the band played for guests to dance to.

I also was paying attention to the piano player, Eddie.

Sex was not as mysterious to me as it might have been to others my age. It was one of the facts of life at the hotel, sometimes subtle, usually not. It was the magnet that drew many people and part of my daily existence.

I remember, at age eleven, running to my mother with news that one of the single guests we knew was getting married. "Isn't it wonderful?" I exclaimed. "Now she can sleep with the bartenders!" My mother was nonplussed. "That's what a lot of the ladies do during the week while their husbands work in the city," I explained. How could she not know that?

Once, a guest who was assigned to our room because the hotel had overbooked brought a man back with her very late at night. We were awakened by the sound of his voice. My mother said he had to leave; there was a child in the room. The guest insisted that she was paying for the bed. The man, pulling down his pants, said he didn't care. For sure, I didn't care. I had never seen the "thing" that a man had between his legs. This was going to be exciting! My mother and I ended up huddled in the bathroom next door until they were finished.

In fact, the summer before we moved into Pop's Cottage, we were living in a shabby, rarely occupied cottage desperately in need of renovation behind which porters, often drunk, congregated after dark. It was facetiously nicknamed the Little Ritz because it was hidden from sight down a dark path behind the elegant Ritz Cottage. Sometimes the porters yelled bad words at me, and I told my mother I was afraid of going home alone. She arranged for a bellhop to accompany me whenever I asked. There was never a problem, until the night one bellhop came into the room with me, which he wasn't supposed to do. He grabbed me in a way that I knew was wrong, and I screamed. It was one of the inebriated handymen who actually came to my rescue. I was still crying when my mother returned to the room. The bellhop's father was a majordomo on staff, and I thought I would be the one in trouble. My mother assured me that I did nothing wrong, that the bellhop was the one who made a mistake, and that she would make sure that he'd never walk me home again. I had to promise not to say anything to Patsy and Mary Ann and forget it ever happened. But it had happened, and because my mother told me it was his fault, I wanted to know why he wasn't going to be punished. She told me, not for the first time, that one day I would understand. I wondered when I would finally understand things that didn't make sense, and why she wouldn't stand up for me. If I had a kid, I certainly would have stood up for her!

As I approached puberty, and despite the many admonitions from my mother and even some guests to "stand up straight," I began to slouch to the point where I was forced to wear a cotton shoulder brace. I knew full well why I was doing it, even if nobody else did. I slouched so that no one would see my tits. It didn't work. My budding maturity attracted the attention of one of my older cousins, who used to be a favorite because he would take me for rides to the nearby towns of Monticello and Loch Sheldrake. One afternoon he wanted me to sit closer so that he could put his arm around my shoulder. Then he asked me to put my left hand in his right pants pocket while he drove. He told me he had a surprise for me, and if I found it, he would give me ten dollars. All I had to do was move my hand closer below his belt. It didn't take more than a few seconds to realize what the surprise would be. This time I spoke up for myself. I threatened to tell his wife and everyone else in the family if he didn't take me back immediately. I didn't even bother mentioning it to my mother. I knew she would have never have confronted a member of the family, not even on my behalf.

Alan L. was my worst experience. Alan's parents had been guests at Grossinger's for years. They spent and tipped so lavishly that, boorish as they were, in the eyes of the family and staff they could do no wrong. Alan was perhaps fifteen years old, a Jewish "prince" who never let anyone forget how important he thought he was. He was so good looking that all the younger girls, myself included, had a crush on him. One evening, he asked me to go for a walk to the tennis courts.

What happened next was the last thing I would have expected. He pushed me down on a bench, unzipped his fly, and demanded, "Pull down your pants and take off your undershirt!" I wasn't even old enough to wear a bra! "If you don't, I'm going to tell everybody you did." I was terrified. I didn't think anyone would take my word that he made me do whatever it was I would end up having to do, and for all I knew my mother would have wanted to kill me because I had humiliated her. Fortunately, before anything could happen, a night watchman came by and shooed us away. When I told my mother about it, she didn't believe me. Years later, when Alan became a fairly well-known comic and our paths crossed professionally, he would hug and introduce me as his "girlfriend" from Grossinger's.

The thought that my mother would ever confide in me about her first sexual experience is as surreal as my thinking I could tell her my own. It's been said that for many women, the first sexual encounter sets a pattern for the rest of their lives. In my case, it most certainly did. I lost my virginity just three weeks before I turned fifteen. He was ten years older, and I was a willing participant. By then I had had sex education at high school, read novels like Madame Bovary, and listened to many Grossinger staffers and guests brag about their sexual exploits. As much as I professed to know about sex, when it came to personal experience, I doubt there was anyone as dumb as I was. I had never gone beyond playing Post Office and Spin the Bottle, and had only once been seriously kissed. The only comment my mother made on the subject was that sex could be a beautiful thing, but without love it was meaningless. I took her at her word.

Eddie, the piano player in the hotel's mambo band, was the room-mate of Carlos, my trumpet instructor. The son of Puerto Rican immigrants, he was a graduate of the High School of Music and Art, had gone to Colgate University, and had served two years in the Army Air Force. He was different from the other musicians in that he was low-key, didn't smoke, drink, or do drugs, and seemed to enjoy spending time by himself. I also thought he was handsome. I would often find him in a corner reading while I was doing my homework. A quiet friendship—and that's all it was at the start—blossomed slowly. I was in my junior year in high school, and he would start quiet conversations about what I was studying or things that were going on in the world, topics about which not too many people at the hotel indulged me. Innocent. No innuendo. Nothing that ever made me uncomfortable. To the contrary, it was exciting to find an older man who didn't laugh when I'd say in my "mature" teenage way that I was seeking to "find" myself. I could talk to him about whatever came to mind. Friends, family, fears, dreams. He was a fine listener and seemed to find me interesting.

I'm sure it comes as no surprise that I was the only one at the hotel happy about our budding attachment, and it would be disingenuous to say I didn't savor the intrigue. Gossip had already begun. My mother, knowing how needy I was for male attention, was particularly disturbed. Her dictum that sex without love was meaningless quickly turned into, "You can never trust a man. Men only want one thing," but she never took her concern to Eddie or the band leader directly. (Relieved as I was then, I now find it stunningly offensive that she didn't act in a more aggressive manner and speak to either one directly.) Members of the family were equally upset. How could Tania, supposedly so intelligent, spend so much time with a Puerto Rican musician? Wasn't she aware it didn't look good? The fellows in the band had reason to be edgy. They could lose their jobs if there was any hint of scandal involving one of their own with a Grossinger, an underage Grossinger at that. They begged Eddie to stay away from me, but he maintained that there was no reason to. For the first six months we had never been alone together in a room, much less intimate. It never dawned on me that he had any interest in me other than a platonic friendship, and I didn't dare flatter myself that he might think of me any other way.

It was New Years Eve, 1952, when everything changed. I celebrated as I did every year, with early moonlight ice skating and sleigh rides with Patsy and Mary Ann, dressing up in new clothes for the fancy champagne and filet mignon five-course midnight supper, multicolored lights, glittery banners, streamers, balloons, noisemakers, "Auld Lang Syne," and numerous Happy New Year hugs and kisses. I suddenly remembered that Eddie was headed to Manhattan early the next morning and had promised to bring me back a book: *The Psychopathology of Everyday Life*. I wanted to make sure he didn't forget. I went to the Terrace Room, caught his eye, and motioned for him to meet me backstage at the end of his set. When I opened the door, he was standing alone in the shadows. He surprised me with our first kiss. A very long first kiss.

Was I taken by surprise? It was the biggest, unexpected, most incredible surprise of my young life! Three weeks later, instead of ping-pong after dinner, he looked at me in a curious way and whispered me to follow him through the empty Terrace Room, past the bandstand, and into a backstage dressing room that was rarely used. The room was barren except for a large mirror, sink, dressing table, chair, and wastepaper basket. The memory is still vivid. Our arms intertwined. Standing up. Leaning against the large chair for balance. Kisses, grabbing, fumbling with clothes, letting him do whatever he wanted, happy to let him do it. I felt no pain. When he was done, he held me close, kissed me more, and told me either how wonderful "it" was or how wonderful "I" was; I don't recall which word he used. It was only when I couldn't fall asleep that a curious thought occurred to me. Was this what people meant by *sleeping* together? *Going to bed* together? Maybe we had done it the wrong way?

The next morning arrived too soon. I was smiling from the inside out. Was I now an adult or still an almost-fifteen-year-old? I quickly stared in the mirror. Did I look any different? Was that a sly smile I saw? Was my mother looking at me in a peculiar way? Could anyone tell I was no longer a virgin? How long could I keep it secret from Patsy and Mary Ann? Would Eddie ever want to see me again? How could we make sure not to get caught?

I wasn't sure if my own enthusiasm was because of the sex; I wasn't even sure how sex was supposed to feel. I loved being held and touched and kissed and petted; even that would have been enough. If I had had an orgasm the same way he did, I'm sure I would have known, so I guess I didn't. One thing was certain: There was no way I could confuse myself into thinking I now had a traditional boyfriend. If anything, we saw less of each other, at least in public. We never once spoke about it. In private, we still managed to sneak backstage after dinner two or three times a week. The word "love" was never part of the equation. That would be asking too much. Our liaisons were quick and furtive, every meeting clandestine, a pattern repeated with curious comfort many times as an adult. Drawbacks notwithstanding, we managed to see and enjoy each other off and on (the band only played at the hotel on a seasonal basis), until my sophomore year in college.

I mentioned the relationship to a psychiatrist twenty years later. His first question, "Did it ever occur to you that he loved you?"

prompted my immediate answer: "Are you out of your mind?" Even two decades later, the thought hadn't occurred to me. The psychiatrist pointed out how much Eddie had at stake had we been caught. Statutory rape was a felony, and he was smart enough to know that. I had already mentioned that a number of young women on staff had shown interest in Eddie, but he had chosen to be with me. Couldn't that, the psychiatrist asked, have meant he had feelings for me? Maybe I was selling myself short?

I still can't seem to acknowledge the possibility.

6

Life at the "G"

I don't want to give the impression that I spent inordinate amounts of time feeling sorry for myself. Despite the unconventional atmosphere at the hotel, I had no trouble finding normal kid activities. At summer camp I dabbled in arts and crafts, went on nature hikes, played tennis and basketball and learned to swim, participated in songfests, campfire events and color wars, and played tricks on fellow campers and counselors. I donned costumes on Halloween and trick-or-treated through the lobbies, and on Memorial Day, in full Girl Scout regalia, asked for a moment of silence to play "Taps" in front of hundreds of guests. I went to all the classical music concerts, dramatic readings, and lectures by writers and self-help experts, and along with the other kids served as co-writer, producer, director, and star of silly shows we put on for the staff. I was thriving in many ways.

I had always been a curious child, ever seeking the "how's" and "why's" behind the "what's" and looking for role models to emulate. I was fortunate in that I probably met more people in my teens than most do in a lifetime. Especially celebrities! In the heyday of the Catskills, the 1950s and 1960s, Grossinger's was a celebrity watchers' paradise. There was hardly a big name entertainer or athlete of note who didn't visit or perform at some point; Eddie Fisher (who got his start and then married Debbie Reynolds there), Elizabeth Taylor, Milton Berle, Eddie Cantor, Danny Kaye, Buddy Hackett, Sammy Davis,

Jr., Alan King, Red Buttons, Harry Belafonte, Jan Peerce, Joel Grey, Jerry Lewis, Rocky Marciano (who once took cha cha lessons at the dance studio so that I'd have someone to dance with at cocktail hour), Mickey Mantle, Kim Novak, Jayne Mansfield, and, as I've mentioned before, Jackie Robinson. Not to boast, but I got to know them all on a first-name basis.

Famous entertainers headlined variety shows at least three times a week, but what appealed to me most was the opportunity to discover how seriously they took their work and watch them rehearse away from the madding crowd. In those days celebrities didn't travel in posses. There was no such thing as bodyguards or paparazzi. Everything, including rehearsals, was done on an informal basis, and I still can't quite get over how patient the stars were with having me witness their every move and flub. Only one performer ever took affront. Zero Mostel refused to rehearse when I was there. Why? Because every other word out of his mouth was off-color. He gave in only when he was assured by the band leader that he likely couldn't say anything I hadn't already heard! For a youngster like myself, watching what went on behind the scenes and seeing how talent behaved when the spotlight was off was more exciting than sitting in any front row.

Funny recollections come to mind: Jerry Lewis taking me to the dentist and making him laugh so hard he was asked to leave. Holding up cue cards for Eddie Fisher with the lyrics to "Oh, My Papa" in case he forgot the words. Buddy Hackett paying me to make lists of jokes comics told earlier in the week so that he could make sure they weren't stealing his material. Of course there were celebrities who were not so funny: stars who refused to tip and treated staff as indentured servants. Dr. Jekylls who, away from the spotlight, turned into Mr. Hydes. It was painful and disillusioning, because I was still at the age when I wanted to believe the best of everybody. Now, of course, I know better. But at least they had talent. And the one named Jackie Robinson had so very much more!

I was Jackie's ardent fan even before we met, the only celebrity I ever begged to be introduced to. My dream came true in 1951 on his first visit to the hotel, when our PR person singled me out as a champion ping-pong player. Jackie immediately challenged me to a game later that day, to which I didn't show up at first (Jackie had to call and remind me that we had a "date"). "Why did you think I wouldn't be there?" he asked after graciously letting me beat him two games in a row. "I thought you were just making polite conversation because of my last name." "Aren't you a bit young to be so cynical?" he responded. "You *can* trust some people, you know." It was the first and last time I was to underestimate him.

He was invited back with his wife and children often; everyone had fallen in love with him. Each time, no matter how people fought for his attention, he made a point of carving out personal time for me. He once asked me to explain my relationship with the family. Struggling to put feelings into words, I finally blurted out, "Jackie, I don't think you understand what it's like to be on the outside looking in." (Can you believe I actually said this to Jackie Robinson?) Very quietly, he took my hand and said, "Yes, dear, I think I do." What was it that Jackie Robinson, so deeply admired throughout the world, saw in me that impelled him to offer so much time and love? I'll never know, but I am eternally grateful that he did. When he was on the road, the thirty-two-year-old baseball star and his chubby 14-year-old protégé became pen pals. I tore open my heart to him. Every adolescent insecurity he experienced vicariously. His faith in me gave me faith in myself. At low moments, I reminded myself that if Jackie Robinson liked me, there must be something. . . .

During my sophomore year of college, there was a horrible fire at Grossinger's in which many staff members died. Jackie was with the Brooklyn Dodgers in Vero Beach, Florida. Two days later I received a letter from him. *"Dear Tania,"* it read, *"I was so shocked about the tragedy and I can only imagine how terrible you must feel. I immediately interrupted spring training to write and tell you how much you are in my thoughts. At least we can thank God that there were others who were lucky. Tania, I hope nothing ever changes your ideas about God and his doing. I know how horrible it was and sometimes when disaster strikes near we want to question but, Tania dear, we must always understand. Please, for my sake, try. Love, Jackie."*

Because of Jackie Robinson, I am a better person.

7

The Brandeis Years

By the time I turned fifteen, four months shy of graduating high school, I was ready for college. My mother and I agreed that I would be happiest at a campus university. Because my grades, my College Boards (the equivalent of the SATs in 1952), and recommendations were exemplary, neither of us doubted I'd be admitted to the school of my choice. We were wrong.

My first application was to Albany State, because it was tuition-free. That school rejected me, as did four other colleges, all for the same reason: I was too young. They would reconsider once I turned sixteen. As you can imagine, the possibility that Jennie might suggest I hand out guest room keys while adding another year to my life mortified me.

Fortunately, I didn't have to wait long. Alice and Jan Peerce, friends of the Grossinger family whom my mother and I had met in Los Angeles, visited the hotel frequently. Jan was a world-renowned opera star, and his wife, Alice, was the woman I periodically turned to when I was upset because my mother was too busy, which was almost always. Alice always had time to talk to me, to ask about school, friends, and anything else I felt like talking about. (I remember at twelve confiding that when I grew up, I wanted to be "a happily married psychologist.") Her brother, Walter, handled the insurance for Grossinger's and, as luck would have it, also for a new university called Brandeis in Waltham,

Massachusetts, to which they had strong personal ties. Together, they volunteered to make my admission problem theirs.

I was probably the only student in the young university's history whom the administration chose to spy on. Shortly after I had received and filled out my Brandeis application, I noticed a portly man (curiously sporting a suit and tie during the day) who seemed to show up wherever I went. I finally asked why he was following me.

To my surprise, he burst into a most ingratiating smile and introduced himself. His name was Saul Elgart, and he was the director of development at Brandeis University. He was sent to observe me, he explained, to see how I interacted with others and whether I was mature enough to adapt to a college environment. The university had received my application, along with letters from Alice and Jan, and was disposed to act favorably. Brandeis, he went on, was a dynamic institution in the early stages of its development, and it was prepared to take chances on students who were young and motivated, both of which I was. The administration just wanted to make sure I would be comfortable.

I accepted his story but couldn't help wondering why, if Brandeis was so interested in whether I would fit in, they didn't send someone from Admissions. It didn't take long to connect the dots. "Mr. Elgart," I said, "if you think for a moment that my family is going to make a contribution to Brandeis in return for my being admitted, you don't know my family!" At this point his smile turned into a laugh. "I admire your chutzpah!" he said. That was the end of our conversation.

Not only did Brandeis accept me the following week; they gave me a partial scholarship.

The highlight of that transition summer was learning about alcohol. My mother absolutely hated it when people got drunk. She grimaced when she said the word. One steamy summer evening at a staff party, a dance teacher handed me a glass of whiskey and dared me to drink it. Aching to be considered grown up, I took a deep breath and, on an empty stomach, downed a large double shot of Scotch. Vile! Within minutes my head began to swirl, and I was lucky to get back to my room in time to throw up. The next morning I realized how fortunate I had been. I had seen enough people at the hotel drink too much and later do things they were ashamed of. I didn't want that to ever happen to me. The entertainment director had hired a new Latin band for the summer. Eddie wouldn't be back until fall. I had buddies on the staff with whom I danced in the Terrace Room and went out for Chinese food or to movies, but I was always the friend, never the romantic interest. I was the "sister" guys confided in. I listened well and could keep secrets. I was trusted. I knew this trust was meant as a compliment, but I wanted more.

Two unexpected things happened at Brandeis the week of freshman orientation. I got a D on an essay titled "What Is a Civilization?" and a senior took me out for a drive and told me he had an "insatiable desire" to feel my breasts. Welcome to college life.

In 1952, my first year, I lived in the Castle, a dorm located high on a hill overlooking the town of Waltham. Assigned to the top of a bunk bed, I shared a room with two other girls, one from the Bronx, the other from Attleboro, Massachusetts. It was cramped, the bathroom and showers were at the end of a long corridor, and sixteen of us shared a single telephone. Who cared? It was my first time away from home since I was a child in boarding school, and I thought it was just fine!

I had already decided to work part-time so that my mother wouldn't have to give me spending money. My first job working for the university was making box lunches for the faculty and students who had early classes—which meant work started at 5:30 AM. I was fired after two months for pilfering an orange but quickly hired by the more interesting public relations department. What little free time I had after classes, work, and studying, I spent in the commons room, the only place where, because males and females had separate dorms, we could comfortably socialize with each other.

The D on my first college essay demonstrated that I was not as academically prepared as I had thought. I had never been intellectually challenged in high school and was now about to pay the price. I was surrounded by super-smart students and demanding professors, and, knowing I had to maintain a B average to keep my scholarship, I applied myself by spending more time in the library than I probably did in bed and enjoyed every minute. The challenge paid off in a grand way. After a year I made Dean's List, and my half-scholarship was expanded to a full one.

Socially, at least in the beginning, I had a built-in advantage. Many of the Catskill hotels during the summer hosted basketball teams made up of male college students. A few members of the Brandeis team played for a small hotel in nearby Swan Lake. They had heard that a girl from Grossinger's had been admitted, so they made a point to meet me before school started. By September, I was like their unofficial mascot.

Girls had curfews in those days, and the university insisted on sign-out sheets at night on which we had to write where we were going, with whom, and when we expected to return. The guys I knew on the basketball team were the "big men on campus." They adopted me and took me to movies or pizza in Waltham and gave special waves from the court when they were playing against another team. I sometimes wished one or two would take me more seriously, but, alas . . . at least my sign-out sheet made me look popular. One evening I returned to find my sheet missing. When it mysteriously reappeared the next day, it had smudges not there the night before. This happened again the following week. The last time there was a note attached instructing me to see the dean of women who, once we met, accused me of making all the names up in order to impress everyone else in the dorm. "There is no way that (she mentioned the names of two of the more attractive athletes) are going to take you out almost every other night. I just don't believe it!"

My first stab at independence sabotaged! No one else in my dorm had their sign-out sheets checked. I was furious and refused to give her an explanation. The next day I marched angrily into the office of Saul Elgart. He assured me that this was the first he had heard of it and would make sure it never happened again.

I made friends slowly. Many of the girls in my dorm came from Jewish enclaves in New York or Boston. Some had been Grossinger guests whose goals centered around marrying rich men and re-creating their parents' penchant for conspicuous consumption without giving anything back to society. I wasn't exactly unpopular; I just wasn't "in," but it was OK because these were not girls I wanted to be "in" with. I engaged in dorm activities when I had time, helped start a women's basketball team, was invited when classmates took study breaks at the local pizza parlor, and never, unless by choice, ate alone in the cafeteria. I was just so grateful to be away from home, to be able to wear sweaters with a large "B" on the pocket, to feel part of a place as prestigious as Brandeis, that when I was left out of certain get-togethers, I hardly gave it a thought. The truth is that only as I write this am I able to acknowledge that I didn't quite belong as much as I would have liked to or as much as I pretended that I did. At the time, I guess, I was too busy writing everybody at home telling them what they wanted to hear: how happy I was.

And the senior I met orientation week who had the insatiable desire to feel my breasts? I let him. I had an insatiable desire to be accepted. I figured one insatiable desire deserved another!

Not too long ago, Ina, my roommate the last two years at Brandeis, dropped by on a visit to New York. We hadn't seen each other in fifteen years, yet time stepped aside as we spent a joyous afternoon in a French café on the Upper East Side catching up, reminiscing, and reminding each other how alternately nutty, impetuous, responsible, earnest, impractical, thoughtful, foolhardy, passionate, considerate, caring, intense, and sometimes dumb beyond belief we used to be. And what good friends we had been! Ina personified the kind of girl I had wished to be. Cute as a button, she was vivacious, emotionally secure, popular with the boys, and from a stable family in Elkins Park, a suburb of Philadelphia. Whenever her parents visited, they made sure to include me when they took Ina out to dinner in Boston to such historic restaurants as Durgin Park or the Union Oyster House. Who else but a good friend would lend me her boyfriend so that I'd have someone to take me to my senior prom?

—⁓—

Tania y Sus Mamboleros: My trumpet, my metal security blanket, was the first thing I packed before leaving for Brandeis. Making music had continued to give me great pleasure, and I had progressed to the point that I was sometimes invited by the various Latin band leaders who alternated seasons to sit in with their musicians at night. One day I had the idea to form my own mambo band at Brandeis. Our campus photographer, who often arranged student entertainment at the nearby Fort Devens Army Camp, helped put together a bongo player, singer, saxophonist, drummer, and piano player from different dorms. What a merry group we were, not as good as the professionals, but surely one of a kind. I like to say, with no sense of modesty whatsoever, that we were the only band for which the soldiers, when they heard that "Tania y Sus Mamboleros" ("Tania and Her Mambo Fanatics") were coming to entertain, screamed, "Ship us out!" Actually, we were better than that, and were soon hired to play for dorm and fraternity parties at many colleges in the Boston area.

—∞—

Tania the amateur hypnotist: Grossinger's had a hypnotist/entertainer on staff who taught me how to put people in trances. Attempting to make an impression my first week at school, and with her permission, I put one of my roommates in a trance with the "suggestion" that once she came out of it, whenever she heard me say the word "strawberry," she would stand up and sing the National Anthem. During a lecture given by Dr. Abe Maslow, the founding father of humanistic psychology and chairman of the Department of Psychology, I whispered the word "strawberry." My friend stood up and sang. Dr. Maslow was understandably furious and tracked me down at the Castle, where he castigated me like I had never been dressed down before. Didn't I know how dangerous it was? Hypnosis was not a game; in the wrong hands, considerable damage could be done. In vain I tried to explain how I had learned to do it and that there was a point beyond which I knew never to go. I knew I had screwed up. I would never do it again. What could I do to make up for it? Dr. Maslow must have realized how frightened and genuinely remorseful I was, because once I calmed down, he suggested that I come to his office the following day. I got lost on my way to his office. Brandeis was only five years old in 1952, and so much new construction was going on that the signage hadn't always caught up. I was surprised that Dr. Maslow's office was so small. Maybe it was because he was so tall and his desk and bookshelves were so cluttered. I thought he might still be upset, but his smile convinced me otherwise. "Have you given thought to what you would like to major in?" he asked. "I'm considering psychology." His next question, sensibly, was, "Why?" I came up with the most erudite, semi-adult reason

I could think of. Having met so many different kinds of people at the hotel, I became fascinated by what goes on "behind the scenes of one's emotional facade." At least I got him to laugh! By the time the session ended, he not only forgave me for playing amateur hypnotist; he volunteered to be my faculty advisor. One of the great honors of my life!

—⁕—

Tania the political demonstrator: This didn't come easy to me. At the hotel, politics was not part of my life. I knew I was a Democrat, siding with the underdog, the minority, the outsider, the dispossessed, all of whom I vicariously identified with. At Brandeis, I began to find a voice. I campaigned in Waltham for Democratic presidential candidate Adlai Stevenson, circulated petitions demanding mercy for Ethel and Julius Rosenberg, and spoke at a rally at the student union insisting that it not show the racist film *Birth of a Nation*. My first experience, a liberating one, in speaking up for what I believed, without caring what anyone thought!

—⁕—

Tania the volunteer worker in the psych ward of Metro State Hospital: As part of a course in abnormal psychology, I was assigned to observe a children's ward—a putrid, overcrowded, mostly unattended unit where they warehoused the most unresponsive boys and girls. One young girl, who seemed to have difficulty responding when given a direction, was particularly singled out for what seemed to me to be unnecessary punishment. I was only there a few hours a week, but I remember her being denied water when others were served or bathroom privileges when everyone else went. At the hotel I had learned sign language in order to better communicate with a relative who was deaf. One afternoon at the hospital, struck by the strange way she stared at people when they spoke, I had a curious hunch. I looked at the frightened youngster and used sign language to introduce myself. "Hello, my name is Tania. What is yours?" She immediately responded and signed back. I ran for the supervising nurse. The kid didn't respond to orders because she couldn't hear what anyone was saying. She was deaf and maybe didn't even belong at Metro State. What kind of hospital was this? I was immediately ordered to leave. Not leave the room—leave the premises. The professor who assigned me got a call later requesting that I not return. He informed the local authorities but was never able to find out whether they had followed up. I was so frightened and disgusted by the experience that I almost changed my major.

—ᴡ—

Tania the lover: Well, not exactly. I went out on dates, but there was no one special person. I still couldn't shake the suspicion that some of the guys were more interested in the "Grossinger" than the "Tania." For most students the social rush began right after the school year began. In my case it started after spring break, when the conversation on the second or third date went something like this:

Him: "Gee, Tania, I can't believe it took me so long to ask you out. I mean, I really like you and wish we had more time to spend together. It's such a shame the semester is coming to an end and we'll be separated for the summer."

Me: Silence. I knew what was coming next.

Him: "I have a terrific idea." Pause. "If I could get a job at Grossinger's as a busboy or something, we could make up for lost time. Do you think you could put in a good word for me?"

I wouldn't, couldn't, and didn't.

And then, in my junior year when I was seventeen, I fell in love. I was introduced to Gerry by Ina, who was in an English Literature class with him. He was a pre-med student from Philadelphia, where his father was a judge, and he had been president of his class, an honor student, and an all-city basketball star. He was on a full scholarship at Brandeis where, at six-foot, six-inches tall, he was the starting center of the basketball team. I began to drop his name in letters I wrote home—what a bright student he was, what good times we were having, and finally how we were beginning to mean something to each other. My mother couldn't have been happier. At last I was attracted to someone closer to my own age, someone who wasn't a Puerto Rican piano player, a male model who ran off to join a carnival, or a staff singer with the band (regarding the last two, Natasha, you can see that I haven't told you everything). When asked for a photo of the two of us, I said yes, of course, but it might take time.

One day in mid-December, my mother mentioned to a guest who had a daughter at Brandeis that she had a daughter there as well. "Oh, everybody knows who your daughter is," the guest replied. "She's the one going out with the Negro!" My heart sank when my mother called to ask if it was true. I knew how much pain I was about to cause. In the 1950s, African Americans in many circles were still considered second-class citizens. Certainly, especially among many Jews (for reasons I still don't understand, especially because they themselves had been so often discriminated against), interracial dating was abhorrent, a proscription, and, according to some, akin to sin. I don't recall overt hostility to black people at the hotel, because there were none on the staff and very few guests of color. Discrimination didn't need to be discussed to be practiced, however, and I imagine it was understood by all concerned that they might be more welcome elsewhere. It was different, of course, with entertainers and athletes like Sammy Davis, Jr., when he was still part of the Will Mastin Trio, jazz artist Lionel Hampton, and Jackie Robinson. They were celebrities and treated as such. How I thought I could keep the truth about Gerry's race a secret escapes me. I assured my mother that we weren't sleeping together (yet) and certainly weren't thinking of marriage, but the damage was done. She told me in no uncertain terms that I had humiliated her, that I had no pride. She couldn't care less about how I felt about him. She was wrong. This had nothing to do with her. I did have pride. And I wasn't going to give up Gerry because of her prejudice

We continued to see each other, not giving a damn what anyone else thought, but when I went home, my mother and I barely spoke. Thanks to the guest with the big mouth, my relationship with the "Negro" was the talk of the hotel, and my mother had to bear the brunt of the "How could you allow Tania . . . ?" questions, and the comment from certain members of the family, "Doesn't she understand she has *our* reputation to live up to?"

In desperation I called the one person whose advice I knew I could trust: Jackie Robinson. Self-involved to a fault, and his friendship with my family notwithstanding, I never gave thought to the uncomfortable situation I was putting him in. He graciously invited Gerry, who was very excited to be meeting him, and me to his home in Stamford, Connecticut. He lived there with his wife, Rachel, and their children Jackie Jr., Sharon, and David, having recently moved there from the racially mixed neighborhood of St. Albans in Queens. Having been rebuffed from living in Westchester County because of their race, they settled on North Stamford, where they had close friends. The country atmosphere that they wanted for the kids was also close enough for Jackie to commute to Brooklyn where, as the first African American to integrate into organized baseball in 1947, he was still leading the Brooklyn Dodgers to victory. I was expecting a lovely house but certainly nothing like the sprawling estate we visited, which included a lawn large enough for children to play baseball, a lake where they could swim and ice skate, and a baseball mitt–shaped swimming pool. Jackie greeted us at the car when we arrived and led us to a small, freshly painted, wrought iron table on the back porch overlooking the garden, where, after bringing us soft drinks and cookies, he got down to the business at hand. He began by asking about Gerry's family and gently questioning us about our feelings for each other. I asked if he would intercede with my mother, who was still furious with me. I wanted him to tell her what a wonderful young man Gerry was so that she would understand why I felt so strongly about him. "Maybe you could even hint that she consider inviting him to the hotel and see for herself," I suggested. I wanted Jackie's involvement to make her ashamed of her prejudice. Wisely, he sidestepped my request. "This has nothing to do with racial differences," he said. " You're both so young and have so much to learn about each other before you even start to consider a future." And then he made a promise: "A year from now, if you are still together, come back, and I'll see if there's something I can do." Four months later, having nothing to do with race and everything to do with another girl, Gerry and I broke up.

Understandably a good deal of my senior year was spent pondering what to do from then on. I would be nineteen years old at graduation, a very old teenager and a very young adult.

Brandeis had taught me many things. There was a history professor who would end lectures with a wry smile and the admonition, "Just because I say it, doesn't make it so!"

In my junior year I took a course in the 20th-century American novel. We were assigned to read *A Farewell to Arms*, *For Whom the Bell Tolls*, *The Great Gatsby*, and *Moby Dick*. In the final exam we had to identify an excerpt from the book and explain how the passage represented the author's point of view. I realized only after walking out that the paragraphs I thought were from *Gatsby* were not from *Gatsby* after all. Goodbye scholarship—I'd have automatically failed the course!

The exam was returned with a B+ and a note to see the professor after class. She acknowledged my mistake but added that I had rationalized my answer in such a way that for a moment she, herself, almost believed the passage had been written by Fitzgerald. That being the case, she couldn't possibly fail me. One didn't always, she said ever so slyly, have to "go by the book."

My last term I had a class titled "Readings in Psychological Literature," a personal tutorial given by an eccentric professor whose office hours were whenever he felt like it. My instructions were to read anything I was curious about, and we'd discuss it at a time to be determined. I chose paperbacks by George Orwell, Graham Greene, Aldous Huxley, Ray Bradbury, and Isaac Asimov. Two weeks before the end of the semester I requested a meeting—it would be our first. As I opened my thick pad of notes, he leaned over, picked it up, and threw it away. I was almost in tears. How could he grade me if we didn't go over what I'd written?

"You're graduating at the end of the month," he bellowed. "Who gives a damn if you get an A or a D? What did you learn from what you read? Don't give me literary prattle or academic bullshit. It's not important what I think. It's not important what the author thinks. The only thing that counts is what *you* think. So tell me what you think!" For the next two hours I did exactly as requested. His last words to me were very much to the point. "Now go out and get a life!" When I checked my report card, I found that he had given me an A.

Lessons I learned at Brandeis:

1. Just because someone says it, doesn't make it so.
2. Rules are made to be broken.

3. What I think counts.

An education doesn't get better than that!

I grew up in an atmosphere dominated by public relations. Everything was set up to impress and please the public. If it wasn't for brilliant public relations, Grossinger's would have been just another Catskill hotel. Instead, it was a world-famous resort. The job of a PR person, as I understood it, was to disseminate information, and, if there was no information to disseminate, to create it. I saw this firsthand when I realized that the so-called "discovery" by Eddie Cantor of Eddie Fisher at Grossinger's in 1947 was a myth. The story was that Mr. Cantor was so taken by Fisher's talent after hearing him sing with the house band, he told the audience that if, by the show of their applause, they agreed with him, he would take Fisher under his wing and make him a star. Of course the guests went wild. They wanted to be part of the action! It was a publicity stunt mapped out by the PR director of the "G" months before. Cantor had already signed a contract to take Fisher on the road. As Fisher's reputation grew, so did the hotel's. I noted how reporters and columnists at the "G" were coddled and given free accommodations in return for favorable mentions. I found it all fascinating and asked to become part of the PR operation during college breaks. Along with licking stamps and stuffing envelopes, I learned how to write press releases and photo captions. I called reporters with updates on Rocky Marciano when he trained for his championship boxing bouts, set up interviews with entertainers, and gave tours to select VIPs. I watched how certain events that the media might perceive as negative could be turned into something positive, sometimes with care packages from the bar or kitchen, sometimes with something more appetizing.

I took much of what I learned back with me to Brandeis. In my senior year, I was actively involved with generating international media attention for the dedication of three interfaith chapels at the university, Catholic, Protestant, and Jewish. Their uniqueness lay in that they were built around a heart-shaped pool that symbolized their respect for each other, a first on a college campus. I helped put together press kits and gave tours of the campus to potential contributors, some of whom had been Grossinger guests. One time I was paid to tour a group of politicos led by then–Massachusetts Senator John F. Kennedy. My earnestness and heartfelt love for Brandeis, the beauty of the campus, the excitement of having such professors as Leonard Bernstein (music appreciation), Max Lerner (American civilization) and Abe Maslow (humanistic psychology), and the exposure to ideas and opinions in small classes where we were encouraged to participate must have impressed Kennedy, because he asked Dr. Abe Sachar, the president of the university, to have me assigned to him as his female tour guide whenever he returned. I was thrilled not so much because he was a senator but because it meant more hours and more money. Three years after I graduated, I was having a celebratory birthday lunch at Orsini's, a fashionable Italian restaurant on West 56th, with Allen Secher, my male tour guide counterpart chosen by Kennedy at Brandeis. Senator Kennedy walked in at the head of an entourage of six shortly after we arrived. He strode past us toward the stairs leading to the second-floor private dining area, then turned and said, "I know you!" in his signature New England twang. It was obvious he recognized us but wasn't sure from where. "We know you, too," I replied, and he laughed when we told him who we were. I explained that we were there for my birthday; he wished me a happy one, shook our hands, and went on his way. When Allen asked for the check, he was told that the bill had been taken care of by the senator.

What became obvious as I considered my next step in life was that I enjoyed public relations. From my mother I had picked up skills in tact and diplomacy. Always having to be the "good little girl" taught me to keep my emotions in check and make others think I was more interested in them than I probably was. I could write reasonably well. I had the background and probably as much experience as anyone else my age. The question now was how to make it pay off.

The first serious discussion my mother and I had about my future came as the result of a suggestion from my advisor, Dr. Maslow, who volunteered to recommend me for a master's program in the Department of Psychology at the University of Iowa. He said that he could arrange a scholarship, and my only financial responsibility would be room and board. I expected my mother to be thrilled, considering that one of the first things she did when she came to America was to sign up for a PhD. program at Northwestern. For reasons I never quite understood, however, she had strong feelings about my not becoming a "professional student." "It's time for you to get out into the world," she said. "If, after two years, you still want and can afford on your own to return to academia, I'll have no objection." I didn't take issue with what she said. I had never expected her to support me financially once I graduated.

In Los Angeles my mother and I had met Sam Golter, the man who almost single-handedly created a medical center in Duarte, California, called the City of Hope, through Jennie Grossinger's husband, Harry, who had grown up with Golter in Poland. My "Uncle Sam," as I came to call him, along with his wife Rose and daughter Irma, lived in the Hollywood Hills near my boarding school, and sometimes we spent holidays together. By the time I graduated from Brandeis, the City of Hope was nationally renowned as a leading medical research hospital that specialized in treating patients with cancer, heart disease, tuberculosis, and leukemia, regardless of their ability to pay.

I kept in touch with the family after we moved to Grossinger's. Irma took a job at the hotel the summer before I graduated, and when her parents came to visit, Sam casually mentioned that if I didn't have other plans, I might give thought to coming back to California and working for the City of Hope.

Once graduate school was out of the question because of my mother's objection, I thought back to that offer. I was still idealistic enough to think that I could make a difference in the world. I also wanted to get far away from home. What better venue than a medical institution that specialized in finding cures for people with catastrophic diseases?

I asked Uncle Sam if he had an opening for me. He said he'd be delighted to create one. He wasn't quite sure what it would be, but I was not to worry. "We'll figure it out as we go along."

My mother was in total accord. I graduated from Brandeis on a Sunday, said goodbyes at Grossinger's on Monday, and the next day my friend Patsy drove me to Idlewild (now JFK) airport. There, I boarded an airplane for the very first time, armed with a phonograph record player, Frank Sinatra's *In the Wee Small Hours*, cast albums of *South Pacific*, *Damn Yankees*, *Guys and Dolls*, and *My Fair Lady*, and my "You can do it, kid!" manila envelope stuffed not with photos but with snippets of treasured letters from Patsy, from my beloved Jackie Robinson, from professors at Brandeis confirming their pride and confidence in me, and from hotel staff members saying how much they'd miss me.

8

My Year with the City of Hope

"And I sought for the man above them, that should make up the hedge, and stand in the gap before me for the land, that I should not destroy it. But I found none." —Ezekiel 22:30

This was a quote gifted to me by one of the most important surgeons at the City of Hope. He had determined, within a very short time of meeting me, that I was to become that "man," one of the profound and many challenges I was unprepared for that summer of 1956.

My living quarters in Duarte, twenty miles from downtown L.A., consisted of a small studio without kitchen facilities in a courtyard complex shared primarily with scientists who rarely acknowledged my presence. The hospital and dining facilities were a short block away. The first anyone at the medical center heard of me was through a memo sent by Uncle Sam to the directors of the medical, surgical, and research divisions a few days before I arrived. They were told I was being trained for a position in either public relations or fundraising and that he would personally appreciate every courtesy extended. His mandate included having me trail physicians on grand rounds, attend board meetings, witness surgeries, and be present at sessions with patients, social workers, therapists, and families. It was to be a total immersion process.

I was so out of my league. Other than when I had my tonsils removed, I had never set foot in a hospital. Within a week of graduating college, I was surrounded by people with life-threatening diseases, by death and the dying. I was overwhelmed with inadequacy. I followed the doctors like a little mouse, taking pages of notes, not daring to say a word. To their credit, they did their best to explain what they were doing in terms they hoped I could understand. It was an awkward situation for us all, but in the end it paid off, at least for me. I was totally motivated by everyone's dedication, devotion, and commitment to the art of healing. It was exactly what Sam had wanted me to experience, to bear witness so that I could define the City of Hope to the outside world.

There was a price to pay, however. Being present where extraordinary medical procedures were performed was often unbearable. Evenings were spent going through medical journals trying to process what I observed during the day. At night, my subconscious took over in the form of horrendous dreams.

Such was my frame of mind the first time I was assigned to follow Dr. C, one of the leading lights of the surgical department. He was the person I, having bought into the stereotype that surgeons were arrogant, brusque, and self-centered, was the most uncomfortable about meeting. When I met Dr. C, I was experiencing a severe sense of isolation. When he asked the first day of my "tutorial" if I believed in God, I answered truthfully that at the moment I wasn't quite sure what I believed in. I had unknowingly given him his opening.

Dr. C was an elder of his Presbyterian church and taught Bible classes on Sundays. I told him about my early Christian Science education and subsequent pride, when I moved to Grossinger's, in learning of my Jewish roots. He nodded in acknowledgment. I saw no harm when he invited me to pray with him before surgeries. "May God's will be done."

Spiritual seduction takes place in many ways. Before long Dr. C had given me a Bible and assigned texts for me to read. I recognized that they all came from the New Testament but didn't give it much thought, because discussing them the next day brought me as much pleasure as the observation of dying patients brought despair. As I wrote to Patsy back home, "Dr. C gives me the courage and confidence to face each day." When he presented me with the quote from Ezekiel with which I began this letter, he explained with great seriousness that he knew in his heart I was meant for even greater things than representing the City of Hope. He was convinced that I had been chosen by God, that I alone would be the "man" because of whom God would not destroy the land.

It was the most dramatic and astounding pronouncement that had ever been directed my way. I was vulnerable, and Dr. C's approval had come to mean more than I should have permitted. How could I possibly have lived up to what he expected from me? "All you have to do," he said ten weeks into my stay, "is stand before my congregation and accept Jesus Christ as your Lord and savior." "I'm Jewish," I sputtered. "I can't do that!"

Without missing a beat, he took back his Bible, told me that I obviously could never be the "man," and asked me to leave the room.

The word *devastation* doesn't do justice to the disheartenment I experienced. To compound my anguish, I learned the next day that Dr. C had called Sam Golter to say that he wasn't sure I would be a fit spokesperson for the City of Hope, that I was unhappy most of the time, that I had alienated many of his colleagues, and that it might be wise for my tenure at Duarte to be terminated.

I struggled with what he said all night. Was he angry because I was Jewish? He had known that from the first. Because I wouldn't convert? I never intimated that I would. My belief in God, my admiration for him, hadn't changed. What brought on such hostility? Why would he want to jeopardize my job? What had I ever done to hurt him? I was not naive when it came to acts of deceit and deception, but here in California, where I only wanted to do good and to be good, to be so falsely betrayed, by a man of God, no less!

Sam was very soft-spoken when he relayed the gist of Dr. C's call, but it was obviously a situation he didn't want to deal with. He assured me that he didn't believe a word the surgeon said, and from the gossip I'd heard from others at Duarte, this wasn't the first time the two had crossed swords. Sam would be furious if he knew the truth, yet I was also aware of the doctor's stellar reputation, which was responsible for many donations to the medical center. Sam didn't want a confrontation, and I was in no position to argue. Because my Duarte internship was already coming to an end, I suggested that it might be best to tie up loose ends right then and begin my new "education" a week earlier than planned in the Los Angeles headquarters. Neither of us ever mentioned the subject again. I was sorry to have to leave under a cloud. The bitter pill did not dissolve easily.

After a week in Los Angeles spent sleeping off my depression and swallowing my anger and pride at a friend's place, I moved in with the Golters and assumed a semi-normal life. While still at Duarte I had come up with a plan to involve college students with the City of Hope. The month I spent in the downtown Los Angeles office learning about public relations and fundraising was enlightening and gave me a foundation on which to grow. What I wanted in my personal life during this time was to go back to Beverly Hills and retrace the steps of my early childhood. The apartment building on South Elm Drive was still there but with different owners. Friends on the block had moved. My boarding school had long since closed. John-Frederics, the elegant millinery boutique my mother managed on Rodeo Drive, had gone out of business. The designer Lady Mendl (Elise de Wolfe) whose grand parties I had attended as a youngster had died. There were very few people left. My mother's indifference when I reported this to her came as a shock. "Let ghosts haunt other people!" How different the two of us were. Me, who clung so emotionally to my past. She, who wanted nothing to do with hers.

Sam had signed off on my college student involvement, and, with his blessing, I spent the next four months traversing college towns in upstate New York and New England convincing fraternities, sororities, and social clubs to create charity events that resulted in a new awareness and different kind of media coverage for the medical center. When that ran its course in early 1957, the directors in Los Angeles assigned me to the Chicago office as a troubleshooter for Keith K., the director of the Midwest region.

One of the first things Keith did was introduce me to the media and major players in the Jewish philanthropic community, so that they would know that "Tania Grossinger of the Grossinger family who owns the famous Grossinger hotel in the Catskills" was now working for him. It paid off in newspaper publicity and invites for me to speak at fundraising functions. Ambivalent as I was about my last name being used so blatantly, I rationalized that I wasn't the one who was doing it; the City of Hope was doing it, and the City of Hope deserved whatever donations might come their way as a result.

The three months I worked under Keith were the equivalent of a master's degree in fundraising. I had never realized how cutthroat and competitive the charity business was. The worthiness of the cause often had little to do with why people donated money. Reasons varied from the innocuous "if you support my charity, I'll support yours" or "I'll contribute if I can be the keynote speaker or if you let me sit at so-and-so's table" to intimations of blackmail concerning someone's personal or professional life if that someone didn't ante up.

That was the least of the surprises I was to discover in Chicago!

As you know, my mom and I left Chicago when I was two years old, so I never knew my father's side of the family. That was one of the reasons I was so pleased with my new assignment; I couldn't wait to meet his/my family. Unlike the Catskill Grossingers, my father's first cousins and their families were very warm and welcoming, but what was strange was that no matter how many times I asked, other than to say that my father was a very nice man and that everyone adored him, no one was able to give me an insight into what kind of person he was. He and my mother had lived in Chicago for thirteen years, but not one person could relate an anecdote about him. It was as if I had a phantom dad!

When I was about twelve, I surreptitiously overheard snippets of my mother's phone conversation. I picked up enough to realize that she was talking about the year before I was born. These are the pieces I tried to put together: "I was pregnant . . . Max's business starting to make money . . . someone trying to take over. . . (here she mentioned a man's name) . . . Jewish Mafia . . . bad argument with Max . . . I couldn't make out the exact words . . . (his) first heart attack . . .in hospital . . . baby born . . . Max maybe dying. . . threats get worse . . . second heart attack . . .nursing home . . . tracked down . . .third attack . . . murder."

My mother sniffled into the phone and switched to Polish, so that's all I could understand. Murder? What were the word *murder* and my father's name doing in the same sentence? When I asked what my mother was talking about, she said that I had misunderstood. I knew something was terribly wrong and vowed to one day figure out what she had been talking about.

When I got to Chicago, I asked the older members of my family, hoping that someone might verify or negate parts of the story. No one did either. Each, however, cautioned me against mentioning it to anyone outside the family and suggested emphatically that the questions be stopped. Their reaction only spurred me on. I had not forgotten the name my mother had mentioned. It was still listed in the Chicago telephone directory. I had to speak to that man, the man who may have been responsible for my father's death. "Max Grossinger's daughter!" I almost screamed when he asked who I was. After all the years at the hotel as "Karla's daughter," for the first time in my life I was able to acknowledge myself out loud as "Max Grossinger's daughter."

He confessed amazement at hearing my name. "And you're calling me because . . . ?" he asked gruffly. I said I'd gotten his name from someone I recently met in Chicago. "I understand you had some dealings with my father the year before he died, and maybe you could tell me something about him." "Your father was such a lovely man," he said, after pausing to collect his thoughts. "And shrewd in business, too. Such a terrible thing he had to die so young." He asked about my mother: Was she still so beautiful, how was she getting along, what was I doing in Chicago, and I mechanically answered his questions, all the time wondering how I might be able to find out if he was in any way involved with my father's death.

He finally gave me an opening, if not an answer. "You sound like an intelligent young lady," he said, "so much smarter than your mother." He did not permit an interruption. "I don't know if she ever told you this, but I was in the automobile business, too, and after your father died, I offered to buy his company for twice its value and give her a percentage of the profits for the next ten years. She told me she would rather burn in hell than have anything to do with me. Stupid woman! You would have been a rich girl right now if she hadn't been so stubborn." With that, he cut off the conversation and refused to answer when I called back.

Without any proof, I knew that the man I had just spoken with must have had something to do with my father's death—and that there must have been a reason why no one did anything about it. My family in Chicago must have known it. My mother knew it, too. If not, there would have been no reason to refuse his offer. Instead, when my father died, she made the decision that the businessman whose name I remembered for years was not going to make money off my father's dead body. After putting the pieces together, I was never as proud of my mother as I was that day! At the same time, and I'm still ashamed of this, I couldn't help but wonder, "Maybe if she hadn't been so stubborn. . . . " I quickly swallowed that thought. Brava Karla!

Brava Karla was furious. She was also frightened. Rarely one to raise her voice, she did so on the phone that night, telling me I had done something incredibly stupid and possibly dangerous. She made me promise not to contact the man again and pleaded with me to mind my own business. (As if why my father died when I was only six months old wasn't my business?) She reminded me, not for the first time, that there were certain things I was better off not knowing. I was never to raise the subject again. I was so frustrated that I sat down and scribbled the following:

WHAT IS IT LIKE NOT HAVING A FATHER?

I'll tell you what it's like not having a father.

It's like knowing you can never have what most other children have.

IT'S LIKE NOT FEELING NORMAL!

It's like everything you fantasize for yourself about happy families with a father and a mother is not true and can never be true.

IT'S LIKE BEING ALONE!

It's like being jealous of your best friend who has two parents because she's got something in her life you'd give everything to have in yours and then being angry at yourself for feeling that way.

IT'S LIKE KNOWING THAT NO MATTER HOW HARD YOU REALLY WANT SOMETHING, THERE'S ALWAYS SOMETHING YOU CAN NEVER HAVE!

IT'S LIKE NEVER KNOWING WHO YOU ARE!

It's like never understanding how some kids can hate their dads.

IT'S LIKE BELIEVING THAT MEN WILL DESERT YOU EVERY TIME!

It's like being punished because you must have done something bad.

It's like not having someone special to teach you how to dance.

It's like knowing there will never be anyone to protect you.

IT'S LIKE NOT BEING GOOD ENOUGH!

IT'S LIKE KNOWING YOU WILL NEVER BE GOOD ENOUGH!

The very next day, there was a brief story in the *Chicago Sun-Times*. The "gentleman" I had spoken with had been pinned between floors in a freak elevator accident at his office building two hours after our conversation. Spooky! Despite her warnings, I continued to ask my mother about the circumstances surrounding my father's death. The best I could get out of her was that she promised she would . . . at some other time.

I was running out of things to do in the Chicago office and recognized I was not pulling my financial weight. There were few things left for me to publicize, and I was too young to be taken seriously by the philanthropic heavyweights. Keith told me that he was sending me to create a moneymaking event in St. Paul and Minneapolis. He didn't have to explain that my job was on the line. I was to live at the home of Phil Birnbaum, the man responsible for raising money from labor unions, who would also explain to me how to get the City of Hope's volunteer women's auxiliaries to work with me.

Not having done anything like this before or having the vaguest idea how I was going to make it happen, I came up with the ambitious idea of putting together the first annual Minneapolis–St. Paul Mother's March and Motorcade on behalf of the City of Hope. Six weeks later, the night before the big day, May 3, Phil wrote a glowing letter to Keith and Sam Golter. "As of tomorrow, Tania has more than 1,300 door-to-door marchers ready to go. The money raised in these communities should exceed anything ever done here. She has all the radio and TV stations plugging the Minneapolis and St. Paul efforts. It is the most exciting charity event ever to hit the Twin Cities."

How did I pull it off? Chutzpah, support from the women's groups, naiveté, Jackie Robinson once again (he put me in touch with a columnist from the *Minneapolis Tribune,* who wrote an article about what I was doing and introduced me to other media people who were kind enough to interview me and publicize the march), and, never to be underestimated, the Grossinger name. Not having the time to observe protocols, much less knowing what they were, I worked the phones ceaselessly, miraculously convincing executives at Northwest Airlines to fly in, at their own expense, thousands of orchids from Hawaii for volunteers to hand out and also to donate plane tickets that we could raffle off, along with other gifts I had talked businesses into contributing. Explaining the miraculous work that the City of Hope was doing and how it had a history of treating patients without charge from the Twin Cities area, I actually managed to persuade the mayors of St. Paul and Minneapolis, and even the governor of Minnesota, to award prizes at various marching sites. It's amazing what not taking "no" for an answer will do! Even Keith, on his periodic visits, was impressed.

In his letter to my superiors, Phil continued, "Tania has gotten to people in all walks of life and pushed the City of Hope ever forward in the minds and consciences of the people in the community. She has often had to endure small-minded people, some of whom unfortunately are in charge of City of Hope auxiliaries, and also hostility on the part of some religious segments in the city, but she has come out on top, and the results in the next few days should be outstanding. She is a credit to you both for hiring and training her and is a credit to the City of Hope for having built up such goodwill for our medical center."

Two weeks later I was asked to return to California for the annual national staff meeting. Shortly thereafter I was fired.

I was understandably proud of myself when I returned for the California convention. After my success in the Twin Cities, I believed I had justified everyone's confidence in me and took for granted that Keith would have me reassigned to Chicago. Sam was initially tied up with meetings, and I was so full of myself that it never occurred to me that no one had mentioned my next assignment. I spent the downtime enjoying my California friends and let two weeks pass before I even bothered to ask.

Sam addressed my future in his living room by reminding me with a big hug that he had known and loved me since I was a child and wanted to make sure I understood that everything he was about to tell me was with my best interests at heart. He pointed out that I was extremely well liked and that his entire staff agreed I had done an excellent job, but he was not convinced that the life I was living was appropriate any longer. I needed to have a personal life, a social life, and not travel from city to city on a moment's notice. It was time for me to settle down and think about marriage and a family. I think he also said something like, "I know it doesn't feel like it right now, but someday you will thank me." Next, he was telling me that he thought it best that I return to New York and start anew surrounded by people my own age. In other words, I no longer had a job.

How did I respond? I reverted back to my ten-year-old self trained not to show anger. I sat ramrod-straight, forcing myself to silently repeat, "The guest is always right. The grown-up is always right. I have no power in this situation." Sam may not have been a guest, but he was certainly the grown-up. I was not allowed to be angry with him.

I tried to call Keith, confident he would come to my defense and change Sam's mind. We worked so well together, we were friends, and—this is where things get sticky—one time in Minnesota I slept with him. How to explain this? I'm not sure. I didn't drink at the time, so I can't blame being out of control. He didn't take advantage of me. I wish I could say that he made me feel special, but I knew all along that I was only one of his many conquests. He was married, and I know how bad this must sound, but because I wasn't in love with him and didn't even had a crush on him, it honestly didn't occur to me that there could be repercussions. There was no emotional involvement. It was fun. It was a human connection. It took my mind off work. I made a mistake; I have no excuse. But the repercussion was serious indeed.

Keith told me that his hands were tied; Sam had cut back his budget, and he could no longer afford to keep me. That alone should have made me suspicious; Sam had told me no such thing. It was only through a mutual friend weeks later that I learned the truth. Keith was desperate to get me away from the City of Hope. He knew Sam would terminate his contract if I ever let it slip that we had slept together. To ensure that wouldn't happen, he made up a story and told Sam I was complaining about being homesick and that I yearned for a more conventional life, knowing Sam would put his personal affection and desire for my happiness before business and arrange to let me go. For the second time in less than a year, my confidence in a man I respected took an emotional hit.

By the time this all became painfully clear, I was back at Grossinger's, where I was about to discover, not for the last time, that even things done for the wrong reasons sometimes turn out for the best.

9

Not a Good Time in My Life

I spent the summer back at Grossinger's. It didn't take long to realize how much I had missed the energy and excitement, but the life I
wanted to make for myself was in New York. Through a friend I met a
woman looking to share her one-bedroom apartment on Central Park
West in return for $90, half of what she told me was her monthly rent.
The rules were stringent: I couldn't have company if she was entertaining, she didn't want me coming home late at night, and I was forbidden
to use the kitchen if she had dinner guests. Though far from ideal, it
was affordable, and I didn't have to spend time looking for a place to
live.

I was quickly hired by a PR agency that, among other clients,
represented Revlon, which sponsored the TV quiz show *The $64,000
Question*. Each Tuesday night millions of viewers tuned to CBS to
watch contestants vie for the largest amount of money ever given out
on television. One of my responsibilities was to appear at the studio an
hour before broadcast to meet with the contestants and coax newswor-
thy "items" from them I could then relay to the press. At the end of the
show I called reporters all over the country with information about the
questions and answers, which contestants won how much money, and
any backstage gossip I thought they could use in their stories. Not long

after, the biggest scandal ever connected to television erupted. Headlines blasted the news: *$64,000 Question* FIXED! Some contestants had received the answers beforehand. You wouldn't believe the pandemonium. The public was enraged, and Revlon was furious because millions of dollars in advertising were at stake. Editorials cried out for heads to roll. I was probably the only individual who had dealt with contestants who didn't know the fix was in. One of the producers thought the crisis might be controlled by scapegoating someone to the press. Rather than jeopardize his own career or that of the host, Hal March, he leaked that a publicity person (thank God I wasn't named, and the reporters I'd dealt with didn't believe it anyway) had some knowledge about the fix but never reported it to him, and that they were fired on the spot. I was the last to know that the show was rigged and the first to be let go.

At the same time, through a friend of my roommate's who knew I was being taken advantage of, I learned I had been paying much more than half my roommate's rent. That deception I couldn't abide. Lousy timing, because I was out of work, but I finally found a tiny, furnished sublet on the Upper East Side, which I took on a month-to-month basis. Determined to shed the excess weight that had plagued me off and on since puberty, I was also paying weekly visits to a diet doctor who specialized in giving shots of what I later learned was amphetamines to speed up the body's metabolism and burn calories. I lost ten pounds in less than three weeks, was thrilled with the way I looked, and had only a few more pounds to go.

I was still making the rounds of employment agencies when my friends Alice and Jan Peerce invited me to their Passover Seder. It took less than five minutes for Alice to notice something was wrong. It had somehow escaped my attention—poor lighting in my bathroom, probably—but the whites of my eyes had turned a dull shade of yellow to match parts of my skin. She arranged for a car to take me back to

Grossinger's, where Jennie Grossinger's son-in-law, David, a physician in nearby Liberty, immediately admitted me to the local hospital. I had hepatitis caused, it turned out, by a dirty needle the diet doctor used.

I hated David's instructions: three weeks in the hospital, followed by three weeks of bed rest, with orders to regain the lost weight. When I looked in the mirror, I saw a fun-loving, intelligent, not unattractive twenty-one-year-old who should have been at the prime of her life, yet had no real place to live, was under medical "house arrest" at the hotel while her mother was on a preplanned vacation in Europe (which I insisted she continue), had no job to return to, had a diminishing bankbook, and, at the moment, was emotionally unattached. Not exactly a great place to be.

As I mentioned earlier, my mother's youngest brother, Fabian, came to America shortly after the war began and finally settled in Detroit, where he married my Aunt Edith and eventually took over a suburban dental laboratory.

Periodically Fabian and his family would stop by Grossinger's on their way to another resort in upstate New York (Jennie wouldn't give them a discount to stay at Grossinger's). Because of the geographical separation, I never had the chance to get to know them in the same way I did my father's family, which is why their phone call inviting me to recuperate for a week at their home in Michigan came as a pleasant surprise.

Recollections of my aunt Edith at the time were few but pointed. She always teased me about the importance of meeting a rich guest. "It's just as easy to marry a rich man as a poor one!" Knowing her inclinations to play matchmaker, I reminded her that I would only be visiting for a few days and wanted to spend as much time as I could with the family. She assured me that she understood. So why was I not surprised when she met me at the airport with a list of all the Jewish "catches" she had set me up with for every night the following week?

The first night's selection was a twenty-nine-year-old podiatrist named Neil Jacobs. I didn't need to meet any of the others.

Where to begin?

I've been grappling with this for days, Natasha. I question the wisdom of dredging up the pain of my marriage to Neil. I wonder, not for the first time, why even after so many years, the consequences of that heartbreaking, ego-shattering relationship influenced so many of my future decisions, including the one to not have a family of my own.

I hardly recognize the woman I intend to write about now. It didn't take me long to realize the road I was about to walk down was rocky. I just had no idea how rocky it would be.

10

The Man
I Was to Marry

Name: Dr. S. Neil Jacobs
Age: 29
Marital status: Single
Profession: Podiatrist, ski instructor
Attributes: Attractive, athletic, charming, engaging, confident,
open, easy to talk to
Family relationships:
Father, Joe, podiatrist; estranged from son
Mother; died when he was seven
Stepmother, Pearl; hostile to Joe's children
Older brother, Ray, also a podiatrist; competitive relationship
Younger sister, Luba; adored by Neil; kept him grounded
Interests: Jazz, theater, sailing, liberal politics, Latin music, Detroit
Lions
Passion: Skiing (the ultimate thrill)

It is still hard to make sense of the extraordinary week that followed—the intensity, elation, excitement, and sense of urgency in
what was supposed to have been quiet time with family. After our
first date, we asked my aunt to cancel whatever others she had set up.
For the rest of the week Neil and I were inseparable. Dinners at the

home of his devoted sister, Luba, sailing with their brother Ray, an evening with his childhood friends, one of whom confided that I was the first "girlfriend" he had introduced to them in years. Girlfriend? In five days?

Did I believe in love at first sight? For others perhaps, but certainly not for me. The concept of even having a serious boyfriend, someone with whom I could comfortably be seen in public (you are already familiar with some of my unconventional choices) was as far from my mind as was going to Detroit to meet the man who would upend my world. My Grossinger's friends Patsy and Mary Ann had had boyfriends since their late teens, as had my college roommate, Ina. I was, at age twenty-one, the late bloomer, the one who least expected to find herself dumbfounded, dazed, astounded, flattered, even giddy over a man she hardly knew.

Edith and Fabian were understandably alarmed. Neil was just one of the various friends Edith had selected to show me the town. She certainly didn't expect a relationship to come of it. They always assumed I "had a good head on my shoulders." What had Neil done to me? His reputation as a playboy, and not necessarily a considerate one, was their primary concern. (They needn't have worried; he hadn't touched me.) I told them I already knew his reputation, and he reassured me that I was very unlike the girls he was used to dating. To ease their concerns, we promised not to do anything rash. At the end of the week I'd return home as planned, and we would see what effect the separation would have. If our feelings didn't change, he would come to Grossinger's to meet my mother and we would decide on the next step.

On the drive to the airport Neil was uncharacteristically silent. "It's not you," he finally said. "I'm so afraid of what I may be getting you into. I don't want to hurt you. I love you."

I had always assumed I'd get married and start a family with the man I loved. I was in no rush, however, to do either. I was blessed in that my mother never subjected me to the pressures so many guests at the hotel put on their own daughters—marry early, marry Jewish, marry rich. There was a whole world waiting for me. I had a knack for public relations, and was confident I could make a living. I wanted to travel. I wanted to write. Everything would happen in its own time. In other words, I had never met the right man. Before Neil entered my life, even with the many dates I'd gone on, there was never a relationship where the rewards measured up to the affection I bestowed. That's why everything—the intensity of our emotions, dare I say the shock of it all—left me so stunned.

All I could hear were those three precious words: "I love you." No one, not even my boyfriend Gerry at Brandeis, had ever said them to me. After hearing them for the first time, nothing else mattered, even though it should have. Neil came from a dysfunctional family. I knew from experience what that was like. We would be each other's family and make up for the love we didn't have at home. Money was tight. He had recently opened a second practice, which cut into the limited income from the first, but I wasn't particularly concerned. Money, as long as my basic needs were met, was never important to me. At Grossinger's I saw how often it corrupted people, and I never envied it or them. That Neil never once attempted to touch me sexually? This I must say I found odd, but I imagined that having alerted me to his previous lifestyle, he was paying me a compliment by not coming on too strong. A sensible woman, of course, would have taken a reality check. When I returned home, I kept Neil a secret the first few days, afraid to speak of him on the off chance it wasn't real. His letters, which arrived almost twice a day, convinced me it was.

I can't begin to tell you how much I'm feeling my love for you. I am aware more each day of some part of me missing. As long as you're not here I'm wandering in a fog.

I prolong my coming home at night just so I won't have to think about you, though I really can't stop thinking of you at any time.

I'm waiting for the day I have you with me all the time—to guide me—help me and love me. I still can't believe you're real.

We are going to have such a wonderful life together.

I first broke the news to my mother, describing Neil as mature, a professional who made a good living, someone who came from a fine family (if I were Pinocchio, I would have tripped over my nose!), and someone with whom I wanted to spend the rest of my life. To my surprise, even after speaking to my aunt and uncle, my mother made no attempt to talk me out of seeing him. Her reaction took me by surprise, but by then I was used to not understanding her. It most likely occurred to her that if Neil was everything I said he was, it might prove providential for her as well. With me ensconced in a secure life somewhere else, perhaps she could leave Grossinger's and re-create her own.

Three weeks after I returned home we set a date for Neil to fly in from Detroit. There was a definite air of excitement at the hotel. Who was the "mysterious stranger" with whom Tania had so dramatically and hastily (was she pregnant?) fallen in love? The Grossinger family, too, was anxious to meet him (but not anxious enough, I might add, to offer him a room on the grounds; it was left to Patsy, who had a home in nearby Liberty, to extend that hospitality). We were all nervous about his visit. It was one thing for Neil to know *about* Grossinger's and quite another to be the center of attention when he arrived. And then there was Karla. . . .

We had arranged for the three of us to have dinner in a private area of the dining room the night he arrived. None of us knew what to expect, but Neil's reaction to my mother came as a jolt. He fell in love with her! Without overwhelming him with questions, the one thing I feared might happen, the chic, charming, charismatic Karla, the esteemed Madame Savonier from Beverly Hills, the elegant hostess from Vienna, held us enthralled with her pithy outlooks on life with a sense of humor I never knew she possessed. Neil was mesmerized. Even I fell under her spell!

Over the weekend I pointed out places at the hotel that had special meaning to me. (I was tempted to show him the backstage dressing room where I lost my virginity, but because my sex life was a subject neither of us had yet broached, I thought better of it.) We went for long walks, took a boat out on the lake, danced in the Terrace Room, and spent time with Patsy and others who shared so much of my life. It was quite an experience for him, trying to imagine what it was like for me to grow up in such a circus-like atmosphere, and I must say he handled it with aplomb and impressed all he met. Unfortunately, one aspect of our relationship hadn't changed. Though outwardly affectionate, he still managed to avoid intimate contact, and by this time I knew something was wrong. Against my better judgment, though fearful of what it might mean (the word "homosexual" entered my mind, but then I remembered his previous relationships with women and eliminated that possibility), I again turned a blind eye; I didn't want to spoil the otherwise perfect weekend.

After that visit a certain darkness began to creep into his mail.

I guess crossing the "finish line" is not as easy as I thought it would be. You probably knew I wanted to ask you to marry me when we were sitting by the Grossinger pool but then talking to your mother made me feel so inadequate and undeserving of you. I am just plain scared. Of what, I don't know, but I am.

I wish I could put on paper how mixed up I am—wanting you, wanting the right thing for you and me. I've asked myself how many excuses can I make—and why. I'm so scared of being happy. Sometimes I feel I want to destroy myself in your eyes just to avoid hurting you.

You know and I know we can't continue much longer like this—being apart. The least I can do is "do it" or free you. I tell everyone that I want to marry you and then—no guts. Do me a favor—marry some rich guy and let me be miserable!

Is it possible to want someone so very much, yet be afraid? I have no desire to be with anyone else yet I keep myself from having you. I find the need and desire for you in every phase of my life and yet I can't find an intense physical desire (this is very difficult for me to write). It is something we both know I have to find an answer to. It started shortly before I met you. I wanted to change my life. You know the reputation I have, always running, overindulging, not thinking of anyone but myself. I had to get away from the crazy life I led. My body couldn't take it anymore. I lost all interest in everything, including sex. Then you came into my life and made me look at myself differently. You had confidence in me and convinced me I could start over again. I realized for the first time how much I need someone's love, your love, to make me whole. The problem I have is that my body still doesn't seem able to respond. I'm sure with time we will be able to work everything out. Please, sweetheart, don't blame yourself.

I was relieved that Neil at least acknowledged that sexually things were not normal between us, and I thought I understood intellectually, if not emotionally, how complicated the situation might be. I couldn't help but remember my chubby adolescent days when boys were only interested in me as a friend. I no longer carried the excess weight, but the insecurity remained. Neil told me not to blame myself and that everything would turn out all right. I wasn't sure about either but decided to take him at his word. My only other choice was to back away, and there was no way in the world I was going to do that.

He loved me!

By quoting only certain parts of his letters, I've done Neil and the best parts of our relationship an injustice. There was so much more to him and our relationship than his insecurities. I wasn't alarmed by his flaws—I was in love, and his willingness to admit to and deal with his faults outweighed everything else. During that period of my life, denial was the place I felt most at home. When he returned to the hotel a month later, it was to ask for my mother's blessing, which she gave, and to officially announce our engagement. Then I flew back to Detroit with him for five weeks.

Our first appointment in Detroit was with a rabbi, a friend of my Aunt Edith's, who agreed to officiate at the wedding. It might seem strange to you that I wasn't getting married at my home, at Grossinger's. The reason was simple—no one there made the offer. I refused to make a big deal out of it. Neil's family was in Detroit. That was where we were going to live. I was already staying with Edith and Fabian, who graciously offered their home for a small ceremony. My mother would fly in a few days before the wedding. I'd invite the Grossinger family anyway. If they wanted to show up, fine. If not, I could live with that, too.

I genuinely adored Neil's friends, and they took me in as one of their own. By the end of my stay, I had lost whatever trepidations I had about moving to an unfamiliar and seemingly unexciting city. We had a wonderful time together doing everything courting couples normally do, learning about each other's pasts, sharing dreams and secrets, except that in our case evenings still ended with a platonic hug and kiss. I had come to accept that he was working on his problem his own way. It was something he was uncomfortable talking about in person, and we seemed to have come to a silent understanding that this was the way it was going to be until we married, at which time, as he promised, everything would change.

We began to accumulate presents. Neil's cousins and my aunt threw showers for us, and I was surprised at how many Grossinger guests sent checks for $100, or kitchen cookbooks, or appliances like toasters, coffee makers, and serving platters that I would soon need. Neil had been sharing a small duplex apartment in the Palmer Park section of Detroit. Because I was going to be moving in, his roommate, Hank, a professional photographer who gave an album of his photos as a wedding gift, moved out shortly thereafter. With him went most of the dishes, cooking utensils, blankets, and furniture. I had few possessions, outside of our wedding presents to contribute, having lived most of my life in hotel rooms and furnished apartments. Neil made light of it. We'd make do with what we had. "Love and laughter will make up for all."

He was acutely aware that he had to focus on work. One practice was located in the suburb of Farmington, where, as an associate of the American College of Foot Surgeons, he had applied for staff privileges at the community hospital. If accepted, he could finally do the type of foot surgery for which he was trained. It distressed him that most people associated podiatry only with bunions and toenails needing to be cut.

I used the time he was at work to find a job of my own. I used every Grossinger contact I could think of and secured a dream job with a gentleman who represented the legendary Shubert Theater and needed a PR assistant to promote Broadway shows when they came for preopening tryouts to Detroit.

Things were finally starting to fall into place. We opened a joint bank account, but I knew nothing about his income or debts, for which he had a separate account. In those days it was de rigueur that the husband handled finances. He assured me that thanks to much-appreciated wedding checks, as long as we were reasonably careful, we didn't have to worry. His apartment didn't need much work, and he was able to make the needed adjustments on his own, a very good thing because my experience in selecting home furnishings was as limited as my expertise in the kitchen.

What was most important was the emotional bond we had forged. That Neil allowed himself to be frank about his shortcomings and fears I found endearing; I had never known a man to do that. His honesty encouraged me to return the compliment. I made clear how difficult it was for me to express anger, my proclivity to mask feelings, the threat of rejection that always loomed. I shared my pain of having grown up without a father and how, until I met him, I seemed to select only men who would repeat my father's pattern and, through no fault of my own, leave me. I was careful discussing my mother because he was still slightly smitten, and I wanted that relationship to continue.

I finally felt comfortable enough, in case it made a difference, and so that he wouldn't be surprised on our wedding, to confess I was no longer a virgin. He didn't ask for details but, after a short silence, finally laughed and said he wouldn't have it any other way. By the time I went back to the hotel to pack my belongings and say goodbyes, I was as foolishly confident in our future as I'd ever been!

This trip back to Grossinger's caused confusion on his part once again. He was nervous. He missed me. He wasn't sure he could get past his playboy days. He needed me by his side. "Come home, already, damn it. Can't we just elope and tell everyone to go to hell?"

I honestly wouldn't have minded. Without a father to walk me down the aisle, I had stubbornly decided as a young girl to not ever have a large wedding. I was grateful to my aunt and uncle for volunteering their home, but it held no emotional attachment. We mentioned elopement to Edith, but she reminded us that we had already sent out the invitations. We agreed to a small family ceremony on October 19 and a larger reception the following Sunday hosted by friends. Factoring in the time Neil could afford to close his offices and my new job, we decided on a short honeymoon, three nights in Chicago, a city we both loved and where Neil could meet the other members of my father's family.

It was only when I tried on the classic scoop-necked tulle and chiffon wedding dress for the first time that the enormity of the responsibilities I was taking on became real. I was going to be a wife and someday somebody's mother. I could understand Neil's pre-wedding nervousness about the new life he was entering into (I was beginning to feel the same), but his misgivings and lack of desire for me were suddenly not as easy to dismiss. What if everything didn't change once we were married? Of the four months between our first date and wedding day, ten weeks had been spent apart. Why couldn't we wait? And then the terrible fear—could I possibly be making a mistake? I believed I could be understanding. I believed I could be patient. What if I wasn't able? What if I wasn't as smart as I thought I was? All considerations I should have taken seriously weeks before. I wished there was someone in whom I could confide. My mother, I imagined, or at least hoped, would have encouraged me to cancel the wedding, but I didn't want to put her to the test or complicate her life. My aunt and uncle had been against our relationship from the start. Patsy was less experienced and lived too far away. No, this was something I had to deal with on my own.

This is not easy to write. But I was mortified that if I backed out I would have to give back the gifts. It wasn't the possessions I was concerned about; it was the symbolism. I would be a failure before I even started.

That night it was Neil's turn to assure me that our fears were normal. And groundless. We just needed time together. We wouldn't let the past determine our future. "Happily ever after" would be more than a cliché. We would never let each other down as others had done. Little did I know that all along I was being held hostage by those six words: "With me it will be different."

11

Marriage and Its Finale

He was half an hour late to his wedding.

A stranger had a flat tire on the freeway, and Neil felt obliged to wait until help arrived. He called it his good deed for the day.

The wedding, when it finally got underway, was a lovely, low-key event, just as we had planned. Thirty-five people, including my very happy mother, gathered in my uncle's den for the ceremony. Everyone remarked on how beautiful I looked, and Neil added that he was the happiest he'd ever been. I couldn't shake the feeling that I was not *the* bride but a bride playing the role of a bride. The rabbi's counsel after we exchanged platinum bands was wise and taken to heart: "There is much you have yet to learn about each other. Be loving. Be understanding. And, above all, be patient."

The celebration buffet, catered by a friend of Neil's who owned a delicatessen, was accompanied by an inexpensive sweet pink champagne, and because the living room was so stuffy, I imbibed more than I should have. As the conversation, laughter, kisses, toasts, and congratulations ebbed, I excused myself to change into my traveling outfit. When the beautiful bride returned to the living room, she proceeded to throw up on her aunt's newly reupholstered couch. I was drunk for the first time in my life! I recall very little about the flight to Chicago, although before we landed, Neil told me that I kept repeating how happy I was and that we had to learn to "live and let live"!

When we finally checked into our hotel, the bellman led us to a room with twin beds. I was aghast, thinking Neil had requested them. After a few angry phone calls, we were transferred to a honeymoon suite, complete with everything he had ordered in advance—champagne (Dom Pérignon this time), chocolates, fresh fruit, and flowers. By this time we were both in better moods. I went into the other room and slipped into the silk negligee I prayed wouldn't let me down, and to our mutual relief the honeymoon was off to a joyous start.

It was a marvelous three days. Breaking the sexual impasse brought us together in ways I never thought would happen. We kept to our own time, caught up with friends, met my father's family, who hosted a cocktail party in our honor, and reveled in finally being together. This was the Neil I couldn't wait to spend the rest of my life with and the Neil I loved with all my heart. If only my mother hadn't called early, very early, our first morning to check on how I was feeling. Neil was indulgent but determined in his response. "Everything is just fine, Mom; you don't have to worry. She doesn't belong to you anymore. She belongs to me."

It didn't take long for me to realize that as much as I enjoyed being married and being Mrs. Neil Jacobs, I wasn't certain how to be either. Not for the first time being fatherless had consequences. I had never learned how to relate to a man on an intimate level. At the hotel there were few married couples I could look to as role models. My family certainly didn't qualify, and the guests I saw at Grossinger's were on holiday, certainly not a normal setting by which to judge behavior. I had no idea what their lives were like at home where the daily nitty-gritty played out. I didn't know what the rules were, and this later came back to haunt me.

Neil and I were rarely home at the same time. My job at the Shubert Theater often had me working nights. Neil had no problem with my entertaining VIPs outside of normal working hours—sometimes he even joined us—but his evening office hours usually lasted later than mine. He was often asleep when I left for work, and it wasn't unusual for me to be dozing off by the time he returned. We made fun out of it in the beginning, leaving Hallmark-type greeting cards on each other's pillows to show how much we loved each other. Weekends were when we caught up.

On Friday and Saturday evenings we went out together or with friends. It was almost impossible to entertain at what had been Neil's shared bachelor pad, which, though a duplex, didn't have much room for company. We hadn't considered moving to a new place because as soon as it was financially viable we expected to make a down payment on a house, most likely in the suburbs, and start the family we assumed would follow. That's what married couples did.

Other than spending time with Neil's sister Luba, we saw little of our respective families. My aunt and uncle were off traveling, and the conflicts Neil had with his brother, father, and stepmother made avoiding them our only choice. As the ski season began, we saw less and less of anyone. Each Saturday and Sunday morning, we drove the fifty miles to Mt. Christie, a ski area where Neil was an instructor. I never took to skiing but enjoyed the cozy atmosphere of the ski lodge and kept busy by playing with the kids while their parents took lessons, reading, or, as I did at Brandeis, writing letters saying how amazing my new life was.

There were clues though. There was something unsettling about our relationship that I couldn't quite put a finger on.

One evening Neil brought up the possibility of our taking a ski vacation in Utah. A second honeymoon, he called it, and even though he knew I probably would have preferred another destination, I was so touched by the thought that I was about to say, "Great!" when he added, "We can easily afford it if we sleep separately in same-sex dormitories." Something went "click," and I knew that the worst of my unspoken fears had come true. Even though as far as I could tell everything was perfectly fine, Neil obviously didn't find me sexually attractive enough. What else could I possibly think? He didn't even want to share a bed on a "second honeymoon." I didn't get angry. I didn't say, "Some honeymoon!" I said nothing other than that I couldn't get time off from work, but it he wanted to go by himself, I would understand. He didn't bring it up again. He didn't need to. He was restless. After only five weeks the foundation had begun to crumble.

Maybe the fault was mine. Maybe I wasn't as knowledgeable about pleasing a man as I should have been. What did I know about passion? For me, the highlight of sex was the kiss after the man was satisfied. Neil never complained about our love life. It never occurred to me that he was not fulfilled.

December 1, 1958. Sunday night. We returned from Mt. Christie earlier than usual to see *Li'l Abner*, a show that had just opened at the Shubert. We had plans for a post-theater supper with an actor who cancelled at the last minute. On our way to the parking lot and for no apparent reason, Neil suddenly became enraged. In the car the anger grew even more intense. I foolishly asked if it had anything to do with a heated argument I saw him have earlier with a woman at Mt. Christie. He told me to shut up and almost slammed into the car ahead of us. I breathed a sigh of relief when we finally got home and I went straight to bed. I was half-asleep when he bounded up the stairs, his breath reeking from Scotch, and forced himself on me with such ferocity that I couldn't breathe. I was so frightened that I ended up kneeing him in a place I probably shouldn't have. And then I screamed, or at least I've convinced myself I did, something particularly vicious.

"If you're so great, why can't you make me come?"

The next thing I knew he smacked me in the face.

Those are ego-shattering words. I can't believe they ever came out of my mouth. Words that in my entire life had never entered my thoughts. But how else could the terrible breach that was to come about between us happen if I hadn't instigated it? By putting some responsibility on myself, I couldn't hold him totally at fault. I am aware that victims of abuse find ways to blame themselves. Without realizing it, I was establishing another pattern in my romantic relationships. Blame myself.

Anyone who comes out of the raw end of a relationship knows that even years later, pain persists. It is still difficult for me to write about the six weeks that followed, and I'm sure I'm leaving much out. Neil and I never spoke to each other about that night, but there was no way to pretend it hadn't happened. Gone was the intimacy that makes a relationship special. Our communication bordered on ugly. We picked on each other. Arguments were magnified above and beyond what caused them. We could do no good in each other's eyes.

He belittled me for not cleaning the apartment or preparing meals to his satisfaction and for not even trying to ski. I, in turn, grumbled that I was tired of competing with the slopes for his love. I went to extremes to get his attention, pushing him to prove that he loved me. One night I made up a story that I almost got hit by a car. His reaction: "That's just great. One more thing to fuck up my life."

He began to come home at odd hours. Women who wouldn't leave messages called late at night. Condoms were missing from his drawer. Another primal fear realized. Desperate for any sort of reaction, I became petty and nasty, and accused him of the one thing I knew would crush him even more than what I'd said about his sexual performance. I told him he was incapable of giving love. With my back to the wall, I was not a pretty person. I regret how my words affected him to this day.

We separated for a week during the Christmas holidays. He placed a rambling letter on the dining room table the morning I left.

Tania, since I can't talk to you. I'll write. Maybe this can offer a solution to my getting through to you. I've become a machine in a sense because that is how I feel, numb. I don't sleep. Food doesn't agree with me. I can't get a hold on myself. If this is what you wanted, to break me, you've succeeded. I'm torn apart each time you pick a little. I cannot take it. You are a wonderful person to everyone—me you want to fight—the first person in your life. We've both got our problems and only by bearing with them will things work out.

   · I guess when you boil it all down in theory I know what I want but I just can't practice it. Maybe I never gave you a fair chance or you me. The things I thought I understood about myself suddenly are muddled. You are not a car I can drive relentlessly. You are not wood and metal and I can't drive you down a hill—possibly this is why I can't give to you what I apparently give to skiing. I can't escape to you, for if I do I must drive you—punish you as I do myself—drinking or cheating won't solve anything. How much of it is aggravated by your actions or problems, I don't know. I'm scared, I'm unhappy, I just don't know what is right or wrong. When you are away I know how much I'll miss you. I want to figure out a way to live. I do love you but if I have to jump from the Empire State Building to prove it, I quit!

I reread these words now and can't believe how unwilling I was to face reality. I still can't make sense of the decision I made. Call it the arrogance of youth or the drama of the challenge. A week later I returned.

We were pleasant and polite, waiting hopelessly for a miracle to revitalize our relationship—one that would never come, as we still weren't having sex or willing to talk about that particular night. The damage was irreparable. There was no final blowup. There were no fights, no arguments, no emotion, no anything. That was the worst of all. At one point we vaguely spoke about starting over and moving to Los Angeles, but the idea never went beyond conversation. It wouldn't have made a difference. Our problems were internal, not geographic.

When we realized we could no longer go on the way we were, we stopped being angry with each other. On a curious level we almost never felt as close. We both understood we had needs that neither of us could fulfill. We were not equipped to be each other's life raft. Neil was not a bad man, and I wasn't a bad woman. We were lousy marriage partners, not lousy people. We stayed together another month and a half, but the marriage had come to an end.

My departure was set for a Saturday, Valentine's Day. By then we were unaccountably again friends, carefree; the responsibility had lifted. The last night we went out for dinner and then to a jazz club where we had enjoyed happier times. We drank champagne. Neil had a present for me: his fraternity pin. If I couldn't be married, he told me, at least I could be "pinned." In bed later that night, free from obligations or expectations and a little bit high, we surprised ourselves by spontaneously reliving the first night of our honeymoon. Should we give it another chance? We talked about it for hours, but with overwhelming sadness agreed that lack of love was not what tore us apart; being married to each other was. We vowed that my departure didn't have to mean the end. We would keep in touch, and perhaps someday in the future. . . .

Our marriage had lasted four months.

12

Getting My Life Together, Bits and Pieces

The year 1959 was turbulent in unexpected ways. I moved to Greenwich Village, opened a PR agency, and had a health scare that hospitalized me for twenty-one days.

My mother's reaction to my homecoming came as an unwelcome surprise. It was easy for her to say, "I don't know, Tania doesn't confide in me," when asked about my breakup with Neil, because she never asked me. Each time, in desperation, I tried to open up to her, she changed the subject. The reason behind her attitude didn't become clear until a few weeks later, when I learned she had a more immediate problem of her own. Her situation at the hotel had become untenable and certain decisions had to be made.

Catskill hotels at the end of the 1950s were in a state of flux, with jet and cruise travel depleting much of their business. Grossinger's was by then obliged to cater to conventions and large groups, minimizing guests' need for the "personal touch," one of the hotel's signature strong points. Singles weekends attracted a different class of people, and unattached men and women didn't have to rely on someone like my mother to introduce them. Longtime guests no longer committed themselves to extended stays. Whatever minuscule pleasure the job once provided disappeared, and it was clear to my mother that her days as hostess were numbered.

The departure didn't take place overnight. I think Jennie wanted to make my mother uncomfortable enough to leave of her own accord so that she wouldn't have to take responsibility for her no longer being there. She never confronted my mother directly, delegating her son, Paul, the managing director of the hotel, as her surrogate. He apologetically, very apologetically, told my mother that though there was no immediate deadline, at some point she would have to give up her (our) room in Pop's Cottage. They needed it for guests. (As if anyone would ever pay to stay in that ugly garret, overheated in summer, freezing in winter, that didn't even have a private bathroom!) Perhaps, he suggested, she could rent a room in Liberty. My mother didn't drive or own a car and declared it out of the question. Another possibility was to cut back her workweek or salary, neither of which was realistic. My mother asked only one favor: time. She was then sixty years old. Whatever move she would make would likely be her last, and it had to be right for her. When this started, she was relieved that at least she didn't have to worry about me, because as far as she knew I was happily married. The shock of my divorce, along with her own circumstance, explained much of her inability to reach out to me when I first came back from Detroit. Now she had to tell me I was truly on my own. I could no longer consider Grossinger's my home.

Before I left Detroit, I withdrew from our joint account what I thought necessary to get me back on my feet and left enough for Neil to pay the lawyer and take care of his immediate obligations. There was no question of alimony, and of course no child to support. I unfortunately underestimated how much money I'd need to start over in New York—setting aside a certain amount for living expenses, the best I could afford was a room in a rundown hotel called The Bryant on

West 54th Street, off Broadway, where I stayed for almost two months. It came with a toilet at the end of the hall, forty-watt light bulbs, and a radiator that didn't work. On the positive side, it was cheap and located in a neighborhood I was familiar with, and I was robbed only once.

At Brandeis I had bonded with Naomi Parker, whose family owned The Concord, the other grand hotel in the Catskills, and who was now living in Manhattan. Uncomfortable being alone in my room, I spent most nights with her at clubs where we knew the managers or entertainers and could get in, eat, and drink for free. The bonus was that I would get home too late and tired to even think about how screwed-up my situation was. I found a job as a fundraiser for the Federation of Jewish Philanthropies, expecting to meet new people, but after three months, spent primarily in meetings and finding fundraising as a profession less than appealing, I put the money I had made in the bank and resigned.

Naomi put me together with a friend of hers from Brandeis who was also looking for a place to live, so we decided to move in together. Through an ad in the *Village Voice* we found a spacious, one-bedroom apartment on Christopher Street in Greenwich Village—central to public transportation, inexpensive restaurants, movie houses, pubs, and off-Broadway theaters. Not only was it rent controlled at $168 a month ($84 each); it came furnished with antique end tables, mirrors, marble-top dressers, couches, tables, beds, and chairs. I counted my blessings, because once again I had no possessions of my own. Everything Neil and I had received as gifts I had put in storage in Detroit. Three months later I discovered that he had taken most of them—so in the end I was left with very few things.

My new roommate provided all the additional furnishings we needed, so I felt I was in no position to complain when her friends camped out, raided the refrigerator, or kept the noise going late at night. But we did have fun. She wrote songs for off-Broadway revues, and there were lots of young talented performers like Mel Brooks and Joan Rivers traipsing in and out of our apartment. The downside was that because we shared the bedroom, I had no privacy and never felt my home belonged to me. I should have confronted her but didn't have the energy. Instead I prayed for the day when she'd meet a guy and move out.

When I lived in New York the first time and did PR for *The $64,000 Question*, I met a young man named Harvey Marks. We lost our jobs at the same time, and he had been successfully freelancing ever since. He was an excellent writer, and I had the necessary media contacts. We were both adept at coming up with promotion ideas, so we decided to join forces and open our own public relations agency, Grossinger Associates. Neither of us, unfortunately, had a head for business. Our first client was a singer who used to be on the staff at the hotel and was about to come out with a record. He promised to pay when it "hit big." Our second account was an Indian restaurant whose owner considered free meals (which we used to entertain media people) fair trade. With both we were able to accumulate impressive press clips. Our most successful account was a Village nightclub called Trude Heller's on Sixth Avenue and West Ninth Street, which featured jazz artists, comics, and folk singers. Trude, too, claimed lack of funds, explaining she had many investors who insisted they be paid first—she forgot to mention they were associated with the mob. Her best offer was to give us a 50 percent discount at the bar, which, because she assured us she could steer new accounts our way, we accepted. As the new accounts failed to materialize and she terminated our bar discount, due to what she called a slow period (the room, thanks in part to our publicity, was busier than ever), we realized we'd been had. Harvey's freelance writing kept us going until we finally picked up more commercial accounts—a wig maker, funeral parlor, beauty salon, and amusement park in Queens—but the writing was on the wall.

—⁓—

These are the words I added to my vocabulary in early 1960: biopsy, hematoma, lesion, Butazolidin, Darvitron, thyrotopic micopathy, osteochondrosis, osteochondritis, Disipal, Sigmagen, Tietze syndrome, Timeral, Arthus phenomenon, and keloids. What began as sensitivity to touch on my chest quickly progressed to pain at the slightest pressure, even that of a bra. Over-the-counter medication didn't help. The first two doctors I saw—after personal interviews where the subject of my divorce was discussed but no blood tests or X-rays taken—diagnosed the problem as stress. But I knew intuitively that whatever was wrong with me had nothing to do with anxiety. My dear friends Alice and Jan Peerce sent me to their personal physician, who in turn referred me to specialists who were equally puzzled. Checking in to a New York hospital for more intensive tests was out of the question. I didn't carry health insurance, and the cost would have been prohibitive. Meanwhile, I was still in pain.

I finally turned to Sam Golter and the City of Hope Medical Center in California, where patients were never charged for care. Sam immediately made the necessary arrangements.

I was in and out of the hospital for the next three weeks. Ward One, Bed Five became my new headquarters.

At any medical institution, the difference between working there and being a patient there is staggering. It was one thing, the summer I worked there, to sit in on medical meetings and follow physicians as they attended patients, and another, as a patient, to share a ward with incredibly sick people, many critical, for whom the City of Hope might indeed be their last hope.

Other than my childhood bout with scarlet fever and German measles and recent hepatitis, I had never had a serious illness. The moment I was admitted to Ward One, my frame of reference changed, especially when my first biopsy was bungled by a surgeon who didn't remove enough tissue from my chest, and I had to have the procedure repeated. I was at the mercy of white-jacketed strangers who prodded and poked, mumbled words I didn't understand, and told me to be patient (never one of my virtues!). I couldn't understand what was taking so long. City of Hope was one of the most prominent research centers in the country; why couldn't they find out what was wrong with me? The chest biopsy had ruled out cancer. I was assured I didn't have leukemia. My blood pressure was high, but other than that my heart appeared fine. A number of blood levels, however, were abnormal and presented a challenge that the doctors took very seriously. I was advised to have faith.

Faith was difficult to come by. I didn't know what was going to happen. Friends came to visit and sometimes even took me home for an overnight, but they couldn't provide answers. Neil refused my calls. I was lonely, and I was very scared.

Where was my mother, you might ask? Why did I end up in so many traumatic situations by myself? This time it was by choice. I got sick six months after her troubles at Grossinger's began. The last thing I would do was add to them. Before she made the final decision to quit the hotel, she embarked on a series of cruises. The one she was on during this particular time included stops in the Far East. I had a mailing list for each port so I could write to her. Rather than give any clue to my hospitalization, I first sent the letters to my business partner Harvey, who in turn resent them to her from New York in preaddressed envelopes so that they wouldn't bear a Los Angeles postmark. I made up stories about what I was doing in Manhattan, and she never had the slightest idea what was going on. I'm not even sure I mentioned it when she returned.

Her maternal instincts, as you know, were barely evident when it came to mothering me. She was a very decent person, and I never doubted that she loved me; she told me so all the time. She just didn't love me in the ways I needed to be loved, and I never felt comfortable turning to her when that's what I needed most. I always hoped that if I ever had a daughter, I would do better by her than my mother did by me.

One evening during my third week at the City of Hope, my attending physician decided that I needed a break from hospital food. He suggested that he bring in some appetizers from the local Chinese restaurant. Spare ribs! The highlight of my stay! Who knew that it would also be the turning point in diagnosing what was wrong with me? It took only two succulent ribs for a multicolored growth the size of a golf ball to bulge from my right arm. The doctor immediately drew blood for a test no one had reason to consider before. The results came back the next morning. I had trichinosis, a parasitic disease caused by eating raw or undercooked pork, which must have been caused by a dinner I had in New York's Chinatown weeks earlier. Its symptoms were an exact match for what I was experiencing. At the same time a pathologist came up with the name of a relatively rare disorder called the Tietze syndrome, a form of arthritis that was causing a swelling of the cartilage between the rib cage and diaphragm, and which matched the results of my blood test and was causing my pain. Though both chronic and painful, neither was life-threatening, and periodic medications would be able to keep them both under control.

With two diseases under my belt, I was ready to get back to New York!

13

Love in the Early 1960s

It was bound to happen sooner or later; I fell in love again. Not surprisingly, I could have made a better choice. The thought of emotional commitment was as frightening to me as was being readmitted to the hospital, but that doesn't mean I didn't have an active social life. When I look at the daily appointment books I kept, I'm astonished I found time to sleep. It was a heady time to be living in the city. I doubt there was a performance on or off Broadway I missed. Theater was relatively affordable in those days, as were restaurants, clubs, and films. My diary is filled with names like the Russian Tea Room, Copacabana, Lindy's, and, closer to where I lived, the Village Gate, White Horse Tavern, San Remo, and Cafe Figaro. There was no lack of something fun to do and someone fun to do it with.

Unfortunately, a part of me still belonged to Neil; I found it impossible to let go. After the divorce, I continued to reach out to him. Some issues were trivial; possessions we had in storage (not knowing he had emptied most of them out). I thought I left something in the apartment; could he please look for it? I misplaced so-and-so's address; would he please send it to me? "How are you doing?" I asked, hoping to hear back, "Not too well. And you?" The letters went unanswered. After my bungled first biopsy at the City of Hope, I left a message in hopes that he might fly out to see me. He didn't respond. It wasn't my desire to get back together; it was my wrenching need, using any ruse, to apologize in person for having hurt him as terribly as I knew I did. I wanted to make things right between us. He wanted me to stay away. Involvement with another man was the furthest thing from my mind.

In April 1961, I was working as public relations consultant on a special welfare medical care project for New York Hospital. Grossinger Associates was still bringing in some money, and by spring I had saved enough to treat myself to what I considered a well-deserved vacation. I had never been to the Caribbean and easily succumbed to the allure of ads heralding sparkling turquoise waters, dazzling sunsets, soft sandy beaches, fancy rum drinks, and cool trade winds whispering through the swaying palms. A friend told me about the carnival in St. Thomas in the U.S. Virgin Islands, which sounded like exactly what I was looking for. I made reservations for the entire ten days.

I met Steve my second night at a waterfront bar called Sebastian's. He was from New York and knew St. Thomas well. He graciously offered to show me around "his" island. We met for cocktails the next day at Smith's Fancy, a charming hillside hideaway where everyone seemed to be friends. Cocktails led to dinner, which led to breakfast the next morning, which led to everything the travel brochures promised—moonlight walks on the beach, champagne breakfasts, swimming, sailing, steel bands, calypso music, dancing in the streets, and always a nightcap or two or three at Sebastian's, where Steve often played piano and sang (one of his many talents). All was so glorious that if I hadn't been falling in love with Steve, I'd probably have fallen in love with myself!

Steve was not the first man I'd slept with since Neil. It's amazing what the body lets you do after a few drinks. Not being found sexually attractive by the man you marry can lead to a strange disconnect between right, wrong, and not giving a damn. I didn't give a damn. I didn't screw indiscriminately, but after the few times I did, I rarely cared if I ever saw the man again.

With Steve it was surprisingly different. How much of it was the romantic St. Thomas setting, that my heart had been closed for more than two years, that I'd slept with enough men to prove that at least some found me desirable, I'll never know. I wasn't going to be duped again by the fantasy of love at first sight, but Steve was definitely a man I was interested in seeing the next day. I deluded myself once again. In my heart it was already more than a vacation fling, and not for the first time I ignored clues that all may not have been as perfect as it seemed.

Our relationship when we first returned home was as passionate as it had been on the island. We saw each other two or three times a week, met each other's friends, went to concerts and operas, befriended cabaret spellbinders Bobby Short and Mabel Mercer, and hosted dinner parties together (he did the cooking). In spite of my initial trepidation, it wasn't long before I began to think of us as a couple. Yes, he had an eclectic group of friends, but so did any interesting person in New York. As well as giving private piano lessons to wealthy socialites of a certain age, he also entertained in clubs catering to gay clientele. So what? I also knew he had been married before and had trysts with some of his female students. With the exception of that one night during Carnival when, thinking I was asleep, he slipped out of our bed in the wee hours and came up with a cockamamie excuse that a drunken friend had knocked on our door by mistake, whom he had then taken back to his room (for two hours), I had no reason to doubt his sexual preference. But there came a point. There always does.

Fewer and fewer women were invited to parties he gave. Dick Boehm, a chef we met in St. Thomas who catered some of his gatherings, warned me more than once to "go slow," advice I didn't take seriously because I knew he had a personal interest in me and thought that was the reason for his counsel. One afternoon, six months into our relationship, I left work early and decided to surprise Steve at home. Flinging open the bedroom door, I shouted, "Surprise!" and what a surprise it was! There he was, buck naked, in a very creative position with an equally naked Frank, a dance teacher who had befriended us in St. Thomas and was by now a guest at some of our dinner parties. I leave it to you to imagine my embarrassment, anger, sense of betrayal, and hurt. Steve's last words as I ran out the door were classic: "It's not what you think it is!"

It was four months before I saw him again. He gave another party and asked Dick, who still catered for him and with whom I had developed a closer but not yet involved relationship, to bring me along. I rationalized that it was only curiosity on my part; I wanted to see mutual friends, and I no longer had feelings for him—but of course I ended up in his bed. We went on and off like this for a number of months, until I finally came to realize that I would be as sick as the situation if I continued.

Postscript: My mother first met Steve in New York and then later when they both found themselves at the Salzburg Music Festival in Austria. They shared a devotion to classical music, enjoyed each other's company, and my mother openly approved of our seeing each other. When, after we went our separate ways, she insisted on knowing the reason (something she never did regarding Neil), I told her the truth: He was gay. She couldn't understand why I was so upset. She told me that she knew it all along. "Why was it so important?" she said. "At least you wouldn't have had to worry about his sleeping with other women. That should come as a great relief!"

A strange sense of priorities my mother had!

14

Finding My Professional Niche

Some people dislike looking for a new job. I was not one of them. I found going on interviews and making new contacts to be its own reward. After my tenure at New York Hospital had come to an end, and we closed Grossinger Associates because clients stopped paying, I made the rounds of employment agencies, answered help-wanted ads, and asked advice from everyone I knew. Never quite sure what I was looking for but open to whatever might intrigue, I ended up meeting people at the Ford and Rockefeller Foundations, *Time* and *Newsweek*, Planned Parenthood, the Anti-Defamation League, various publishing houses, the National Foundation for Mental Health, and, of course, public relations agencies. It always came back to public relations, the area where I had experience and felt very much at home. Despite my disillusionment with practices I had observed in the past, I realized that as long as I adhered to my own standards (never knowingly mislead a professional associate; do not betray a confidence; my word is my bond; take notes, keep notes, make sure those in power know I have notes; challenge a client immediately if what he suggests is immoral, illegal, or goes against my sense of propriety; be prepared to walk away and never look back), it could provide a fascinating and rewarding career.

A friend at the Brandeis University public affairs office suggested that I contact Bert Barkas, a partner in the midtown PR firm Barkas and Shalit (Gene Shalit, to my delight, later became the entertainment critic for the *Today* show on NBC and interviewed me when my first book was published). One of the firm's major accounts was *McCall's Magazine,* and timing was in my favor. A staffer had just left, and they hired me on the spot.

It didn't take long to carve out a professional niche. I became a specialist in broadcast promotion. My job involved placing authors who had written articles in the *McCall's* issue I was promoting on the many radio and TV talk shows in New York. Having been interviewed so often when I was with the City of Hope, I was quite aware of what made someone a good guest. I knew all about sound bites. I understood how crucial it was to communicate one's message early on, and, if the host digressed, how to politely bring him or her back to the central point, and when not to interrupt. I taught writers how to converse, not pontificate, and how to dress for TV appearances. Most important, because that is what I was paid for, I made sure that the writers mentioned that their articles appeared in the current issue of *McCall's.*

I would get an advance copy of each issue two months before publication and then contact the authors of articles I felt most promotable. I was offering them a remarkable opportunity—free of charge they could publicize their books or areas of expertise. In return, the talk shows got guests whose names were likely familiar to millions of listeners, and *McCall's* potentially attracted new subscribers.

The guests I placed ran the gamut from best-selling authors to psychiatrists, Jackie Kennedy's hairdresser, sex therapists, financial advisors, jewelry designers, political reporters, and celebrated doyennes of Café Society like Elsa Maxwell, "the hostess with the mostest," and Perle Mesta, former U.S. Ambassador to Luxembourg and inspiration for Irving Berlin's hit Broadway musical *Call Me Madam*. Ms. Mesta loved that I lived in Greenwich Village and used to enlist me to show her the "scene." She so enjoyed the folk singers she met on Bleecker Street that she recruited me to put together a hootenanny for her in Washington, D.C., which she hosted and arranged for *McCall's* to sponsor. The media coverage was extraordinary, my relationship with Barkas and Shalit solidified, and not long after I unwittingly struck career gold!

15

Betty Friedan: Up Close and Personal

In the 1950s and early 1960s it was generally assumed that men worked to support their families, while wives served as caretakers of the children and home. The financial, social, and gender inequities were many, though I must admit that until Betty Friedan came into my life, I never paid them much heed. I considered myself fortunate that I was raised by a working mother who, by words and example, taught me from an early age never to be dependent on a man. Quite a few educated women, single and married, worked at Grossinger's, a number in responsible positions. I always intended to work after marriage. I never believed the words "career woman" needed justification.

I didn't take umbrage that the *New York Times* listed job opportunities under separate sections, "Help Wanted, Male" and "Help Wanted, Female," nor did I have complaints about what I was paid. Most of the young women I associated with felt the same way. We were single, solvent, and so full of ourselves that the frustration felt by the housewives Betty Friedan reached out to so earnestly with her book *The Feminine Mystique* was far removed from our real lives.

I had a lot to learn!

Periodically *McCall's* would publish an excerpt from a book that would not be available to readers until months after the issue came out. Such was the case with *The Feminine Mystique,* written by a relatively unknown writer named Betty Friedan. In mid-January 1963, I received a call from Ann Gorman, a publicist at W. W. Norton, the book's publisher, who came directly to the point. Ms. Friedan was a demanding and difficult woman to get along with. She was convinced she knew better than all of the editors, PR people, and marketing experts at Norton and was not shy about voicing her opinions. Thank God for *McCall's,* Ann said. "Now you will have the pleasure of being on the receiving end of her rants."

Our first meeting took place at a lovely French bistro on the Upper East Side. Over cocktails and a bottle of wine, Betty was quite specific, if not exactly restrained, about what she expected of me— nothing less than being interviewed by Barbara Walters on *Today* and Johnny Carson on *The Tonight Show* the first week "her" issue of *McCall's* came out. I found her fascinating. I had never met a woman so magnificently passionate about a message—in this case, to put it simplistically, that there was more to a woman's life than just marriage and children. She wanted to transform their lives. She wasn't out to promote Betty Friedan; she was out to change the world! I was going to help her do it, she declared, and that was that.

My work was cut out for me. To say Betty needed media training belies the reality of the situation. Her intensity did not serve her well. She was, according to Western standards, relatively unattractive. She was about to address a subject that was sure to make men and many women uncomfortable. Talk show hosts were primarily male, and men in the media had the same biases as men everywhere did at the time. For the most part, they preferred their women at home and certainly weren't looking forward to more competition in the marketplace. Betty spoke too rapidly. She repeated her mantra—there must be more to women's lives than just being wives and mothers—never changing cadence or tone. She monopolized conversation. She antagonized who-ever disagreed with her. She was rude. Worst of all, she had a temper that, if it ever got the best of her on air, would kill the possibility of any additional appearances.

She also, as you can imagine, didn't like being told what to do, but I was finally able to convince her that if she was going to get media exposure, she would have to trust me and put herself in my hands. She had to speak distinctly, carefully measure her words, and think before she spoke. She had to be more respectful of those who disagreed with her. And she had to show the sense of humor I had just begun to catch glimmers of. What she must avoid, at all costs, was becoming a media caricature, a shrew, a woman whom those who needed to hear most would be frightened to identify with.

We went through practice sessions until we were exhausted. I played the thoughtful interviewer, the obstinate interviewer, the in-terviewer who realized that she may have a point, and the interviewer who thought she was out of her mind. The more I questioned her, the more I began to understand how important professional, financial, and sexual equality was not just to suburban housewives but to me person-ally. I worked overtime promoting that issue of *McCall's* and found myself overjoyed when I noted my efforts paying off. Betty was finally relaxing and becoming more flexible. She even made self-deprecating remarks about her compulsive earnestness. Best of all, she was begin-ning to enjoy herself. She was ready!

There was one nationally syndicated show called *Girl Talk* hosted by a woman with whom I had a special relationship. Virginia Gra-ham was a well-known television personality who used to visit Gross-inger's often and always treated guests I brought to her show respect-fully. Because we were friends and her viewers, primarily women who stayed at home, were our target audience, I thought Virginia would be sympathetic to Betty's message. I was so wrong. The studio where the show was taped a week in advance was located at the Little Theater on West 44th Street, directly next door to Sardi's, Broadway's well-known theater gathering place. The afternoon of her appearance on *Girl Talk*, Betty insisted that we stop there for "good luck" drinks. I should have paid more attention. Actually, I should have said no. The show's panel included a noted Chicago newspaper columnist and the actress Hermione Gingold, a mainstay on Jack Paar's late-night TV show. I don't remember Virginia's opening question—I was too transfixed by the ugly smirk on Betty's face. It seemed there was something about the bejeweled, flamboyantly outfitted Virginia Graham that set her off. The alcohol had gotten the better of her, and, inhibitions diminished, she interrupted every time the host and panelists tried to have their say, and at times everyone was babbling at once.

Betty, in her memoir *Life So Far*, retells what happened in her own words:

> This horrible host . . . kept telling the viewers how much more fulfilling it was for "girls" to be housewives than to have a career . . . So I turned directly to the camera and said, "Women, don't listen to her. She wants you out there doing the dishes, or she wouldn't have the captive audience for this program."[1]

And it got worse. Frustrated at being interrupted every time she tried to make a point, when the taping stopped for a quick break, Betty faced the studio audience and screamed at both them and her host, "Virginia Graham, if you don't let me have my say, I'm going to say the word 'orgasm' on television ten times!" (You can see how long

---

[1] Betty Friedan, *Life So Far*. (Simon and Schuster, 2006).

ago that was. In 1963, the word "orgasm" was a no-no on talk shows.) The next voice belonged to the host. "Tania Grossinger, get your ass up to my office immediately." The only thing I could think to do, mortified though I was, was laugh. Virginia said that if I couldn't control my guest, she would kick her off the show and blackball any further authors of mine. I countered that nobody could control Betty Friedan (especially after a few drinks) and that the interplay between everyone on the panel, as crazy as it was, made for great television. I suggested that because there were only ten minutes left to tape, she should consider letting all of the women, including herself, have a go at each other. Her producer agreed. He later told me it was the most replayed *Girl Talk* show ever broadcast.

Betty pretended to be contrite afterward, but I knew she wasn't. She was also aware that her performance would get the attention of the press. She was becoming media savvy. After a number of carefully selected radio interviews, we were ready for the next step, *The Merv Griffin Show* on NBC. Merv was a mild-mannered, much-beloved host, who was always open to my suggestions and sometimes let me bypass his producers. This time, he explained, he was compelled to turn me down. Controversy was not his strong suit, and he had heard about the *Girl Talk* fiasco.

I tried every justification I could think of. "*The Feminine Mystique* is going to have a lasting influence. It will change history; you will be able to say you were the first to give her exposure on network television." (*Girl Talk* was syndicated and didn't appear on as many stations as Merv's show did.) "She really can be charming, trust me." "I've never let you down, have I?" Finally, I came up with the deal maker: "Look, you know you periodically end up booking a *schlub* [a Yiddish expression often used in showbiz for someone who's not quite up to par]. It's never done you serious damage. I've brought you so many interesting people in the past; please, do me the biggest professional favor of my life. Book my *schlub!*" I promised he wouldn't regret it. This time there were no preshow cocktails. Betty was forthright, intelligent, soft-spoken, a hit! I can only imagine how many women—and men, too—she influenced that day.

My six weeks with Betty were coming to an end—I had a new issue of *McCall's* to work on. I apologized for not having enough time to place her on the *Today* or *Tonight* shows, but hopefully Ann at Norton would be able to pick up where I left off once the book came out.

A month later I received my second call from Ann. She was effusive in her praise for everything I had accomplished. *The Feminine Mystique* was to be published sooner than expected, and she had a favor to ask. It was obvious that Betty and I had bonded. The entire staff at the publishing house was impressed not only with the many interviews I arranged but also with the fact that I was someone Betty would listen to. Ann could not face dealing with her for the three-month period it would take to launch the book. In fact, she had told her boss that she would quit if she had to. After a number of meetings, the publisher had come up with an offer rare in the business for a book that had an initial print order of only 5,000 copies. (It has since sold over 4 million!) W. W. Norton wanted to hire me to handle Betty and *The Feminine Mystique* on a freelance basis. I could name my price.

I just so happened that I had been let go the week before from Barkas and Shalit. They had lost their major account and could no longer afford to keep me. It was in no way reflective, I was assured, of my ability or contributions to the firm but was strictly a financial decision. Such was the PR business.

I accepted the offer to be Betty's publicist, and Ann Gorman kept her job!

I first met Betty's husband, Carl, at a cocktail party in their Manhattan penthouse apartment shortly after I began Betty's media training. I imagine that if I knew the Betty Friedan whose champagne I was sipping would become *the* Betty Friedan, I would have paid more attention to how she was interacting with the people around her, including her husband. I do recall that a great deal of alcohol was consumed, and serial flirtations took place, many instigated by Carl himself. I also noted that Betty and Carl hardly spoke a word to each other.

One of Carl's curious contributions to what would be known as Women's Lib was to see to it that I remarried and would no longer have to work. To this end, and because I was too polite to insist that he desist, he took it upon himself to introduce me to what he considered available men in his advertising agency, one more coarse than the other. He couldn't understand why I finally asked him to stop. "They're single, and they're rich. What is your problem?" I couldn't help but wonder if that was how little he thought of me, how little he thought of women in general, and how little he seemed to think of his wife's mission.

One time I went to pick Betty up for a TV interview and noticed that, for the first time, she was wearing dark sunglasses. She told me I had to cancel her appearance. When asked why, she removed them with great care and obvious pain. Her swollen eyes, black, purple, and blue, spoke for themselves. I quietly assured her that the studio make-up artist could cover them up so that it would look like nothing had happened. A number of years later she revealed that her husband, Carl, periodically beat her. I was probably one of the few who was not surprised.

I'll explain shortly how I came to be working for Playboy. For the moment I only need you to imagine how apprehensive I was to realize that while I would be representing Betty Friedan's *The Feminine Mystique*, which deplored women being seen as sex objects, I would also be representing Playboy, whose success was largely based on promoting just that. I approached Betty first, explaining that our contract for the book launch would run out shortly, and I had always intended to take a full-time job. Her reaction was typical Betty: "I don't care what you do with your time. Just get me the publicity now!" (NOW, appropriately, was to become the acronym for a group she and others would set up called the National Organization for Women.) Vic Lownes, who hired me for Playboy, thought *The Feminine Mystique* was a bunch of hogwash, but he too didn't give a damn, as long as it didn't interfere with my work for him. All that was left was for me to find time to sleep.

I'd laid the groundwork by promoting Betty's excerpt in *McCall's* and broadcasters were even calling me to set up interviews. My next target was to expose Betty via the media in cities other than New York.

The "book tour," as it came to be called, was a most uncommon way of promoting books at the time, and I became one of the pioneers of this specialty. It was an expensive proposition for the publisher, who would have to pay for transportation, lodging, and meals and also for escorts in each city to drive and accompany authors to interviews. W. W. Norton was not keen to take this on. This did not please Betty. It did not please me, either. Betty needed to get her message out to women all over America, and I was ready to do everything I could to make it happen. After a few calls to ensure that I could deliver on what I was about to promise, I came up with a proposal. If Carl, her husband, would pay for the transportation, I personally knew enough broadcasters in different cities who would interview her (some had already promised to do so), and I would ask friends to serve without pay as her escorts. The publisher would be responsible only for lodging and meals. Everyone agreed that it was worth the gamble.

I wish I had saved the letters Betty sent from the road, the "Jewish Mother dispatches" as I came to call them. In Los Angeles, San Francisco, Chicago, Detroit, and Boston, many of the escorts I asked favors of were young men I had dated. "What did you see in Seymour?" she wrote from Chicago. "All he thinks about is sports!" From Los Angeles: "I don't like Andrew at all. He's much too egocentric for you." And her impression of Keith in Boston: "Why have you stopped answering his letters? Now that's a young man I like!" Finally, from Detroit: "I was going to look up your ex-husband (your friend Patrick who interviewed me still sees him, if that is of interest to you), but I wouldn't have done it without asking you first, and I was afraid you would tell me to mind my own business." All from a woman who, in the six months we had worked together, had rarely asked a personal question.

When I relate this side of Betty to people who worked with her in the Women's Lib Movement, most find it hard to believe.

My friends also found it hard to accept that Betty loved coming to the Playboy Club. After her road trip, which was so successful that her publisher ordered a second printing of the book, we agreed to extend my contract so that I could place Betty on shows that had passed on interviewing her the first time around. *The Long John Nebel Show* on WNBC, which broadcast at 11:00 PM, was one of them. Knowing I had to be at the Playboy Club earlier that evening, Betty suggested that she meet me there for dinner. I did not consider this a good idea, especially knowing that she would be exposed to the Bunnies waiting tables while scantily clad in revealing costumes with hot pink bunny ears, corseted waists, voluptuous breasts, and white fuzzy bunny tails on their rear ends. Once I made it clear that the Bunnies came of their own free will, were well protected by management, made more money than most of their colleagues, and could leave whenever they wished, she would not be deterred. As hard as it may be to believe, she loved it! That's what she told me, and she came back more than once!

By the time I finished working with Betty, *The Feminine Mystique* was on its way to becoming a national best-seller. Betty, who had written for a number of magazines earlier on, was a member of a professional organization called the Society of Magazine Writers. Each month the group held dinners at a private club where members and guests heard editors speak about their craft. The procedure was for members to introduce and relate something personal about the person they brought shortly before the speeches began. Betty invited me almost every month, hoping I would be able to pick up some freelance work. Her introduction never changed. "My guest is Tania Grossinger. If it hadn't been for Tania and her PR efforts, 90 percent of the women who bought *The Feminine Mystique* would never have heard of it. Much of my success belongs to her!"

On November 29, 1970, an article about Betty appeared in the Sunday *New York Times Magazine* quoting me as having said, "Sometimes I look back and can't believe the monster I created." I was mortified. Of course I never had said any such thing! It was the first time I had ever spoken publicly about our association and was complimented to be asked. I told the journalist much of what I have written here, absent the references to Betty's husband, Carl, and her impressions of the Playboy Club, both of which I felt were hers to address. Everything I said in the interview was laudatory and true.

I immediately called Betty, who, not surprisingly, was furious. In between her cursing me out, I tearfully tried to explain that she had to know me well enough to know that I couldn't possibly have said anything like what she read. She was not a monster—I didn't create a monster— I never created anything. Everything I told the interviewer gave credit to the woman I was honored to consider a friend. Hadn't she herself been misquoted many times? To no avail. We didn't speak for a number of years. I wrote letters to the author and the editor of the *New York*

Times Magazine asking for retractions. Neither responded. I later learned through a third party that Betty didn't believe me because, according to her, I was no longer on "her side."

Betty had wanted me to take an active role in NOW, but from previous experience I'd found large committees unproductive, especially when complicated by conflicting agendas, competing egos, and personal rivalries. I was not surprised to have my reservations justified at the few meetings I attended as a favor to her. It's not that I didn't want or wasn't able to work with others; it was that with so many factions battling for attention, I didn't believe anything would get accomplished. (I was wrong; much did get accomplished, and bravo to all involved!) Betty was not shy in letting me know that I had let her down, and her attitude was reinforced by what she read in the *New York Times Magazine*. Adept as she was, however, at holding a grudge, she did mellow as time went by, and we shared a number of rewarding conversations toward the end of her life.

16

The Playboy Years

Despite my success with *McCall's*, no woman's magazine I approached in April 1963 would hire me. My specialty, broadcast promotion, was too special. I approached Playboy on a lark. I didn't know a soul connected to the organization, and even though my physique didn't exactly conform to the Playboy image, I was convinced this was one organization that could benefit from my expertise.

The Playboy Club, whose primary appeal was the skintight-costumed Playboy Bunnies who served as waitresses, had opened in New York the year before, to the great glee of potential members and consternation of conservative political and religious leaders. The press had a field day. Sex and controversy sells, and they made the most of it, not necessarily to Playboy's advantage. The Playboy organization itself was headquartered in Chicago, where founder and publisher Hugh Hefner made his home. There was an advertising sales office in Manhattan, as well as a small public relations operation on Central Park South headed by Victor Lownes, a major investor and marketing genius behind Hefner's initial success. "What do I need you for?" was his opening salvo.

He needed me, I planned to say when we would meet the following week, to counteract the negative publicity Playboy was receiving. It would be ludicrous to pretend that what attracted most men to the magazine wasn't the celebrated Playboy centerfold, the lushly photographed beautiful young woman sensuously posed semi-nude as the Playmate of the Month. There was also the "Dear Playboy" column, often written anonymously by a middle-aged woman, that gave tips on dress, vacations, how to decorate bachelor pads, what kind of music to play to get a girl "in the mood" (Sinatra and cool jazz were good, but liquor was invariably quicker), and what to do once she got there (use your imagination!). But to the surprise of many, and this is what I wanted to focus on, the publication also included a feature with intellectual appeal called the "Playboy Interview." The magazine's editor at the time, A. C. Spectorsky, was highly regarded in literary circles, and through his influence able to secure celebrated opinion makers and noted authors as subjects of penetrating and often controversial Playboy profiles. It was this side of *Playboy Magazine*, one that might attract upscale advertisers and balance sexual titillation with a sense of class, that I wanted to ballyhoo. So what were my first words when Victor opened the door to his penthouse apartment at the St. Moritz hotel?

"Could you please go back inside and put on your pants?"

It was three o'clock in the afternoon, and I could hear the soothing sounds of Dave Brubeck and a woman's voice behind him. He had at least been thoughtful enough to wear a towel. He listened carefully to everything I had to say, and, to my surprise, made an immediate offer. An insulting offer. He would pay me much less than I earned at Barkas and Shalit. In addition, I would be on probation for two months. If, after that, I met his expectations (which had not been specifically spelled out), I would be given a raise and permanent status. With no other option, I agreed.

My first day at work almost changed my mind. The PR office was located down the hall from Victor's apartment at the St. Moritz. It was run by Barbara Harrison, a woman even younger than me (I was 26 at the time). She was not happy to share her small office and break in someone new again (three previous hires had already quit). Incredulous as it seemed at the time, each of us was to end up being the other's best, lifelong friend.

I was then notified that in addition to doing broadcast promotion for the magazine, I would be responsible for coordinating media events with Barbara and arranging TV appearances for Playboy Bunnies and performers who entertained at the Club. Double the work for half the salary I deserved.

The first week was confusion incarnate. Barbara's responsibilities left little time to teach me what I needed to know, so after a quick tour of the Club and introduction to the general manager, it was up to me to make my way.

The Playboy Club was located off Fifth Avenue on East 59th Street, a block from our office on Central Park South. It was a dazzling operation. One had to be a member (fill out a form and pay a fee for the privilege) and produce the membership card in the shape of a key to gain admittance. Members were greeted in the lobby by the Door Bunny, who directed them, when necessary, to the Coat Check Bunny. The level below the lobby featured an intimate bar, cocktail tables, a small stage for musical groups, and a midnight breakfast jazz buffet. Cocktail tables on a higher level overlooked the lobby. The lights were dim, the atmosphere seductive, the clientele predominantly male. Two upper floors, the Playroom and Penthouse, served steak dinners at moderate prices and featured nightly entertainment. A more elegant restaurant, the VIP room, was located on the second floor. The sixth and seventh floors were set aside for management offices and Bunny dressing rooms. Bunnies knew from the day they were hired that they were not permitted to date a keyholder (member) or give out their last names or phone numbers (except to select VIPs and top management). I can't tell you how many patrons would return two or three nights in a row, fantasizing each time that their favorite Bunny would give them her phone number and risk her job for the "privilege" of going out with them.

Nothing was left to chance. There was a rule book called the Bunny Manual, which spelled out exactly how Bunnies were to behave at the Club and when representing Playboy at outside promotions. They were instructed in what order to put on their iridescent colored costumes, how to greet their customers, how to set up their drink tray, and how to do the Bunny Dip (a very coquettish way of serving drinks). The entire sixth floor was given over to their dressing rooms, lockers, showers, seamstresses, and hairdressers. Regulations were overseen by the Bunny Mother, a combination mother hen, disciplinarian, confidante, and demerit giver-outer. Infractions such as showing up late or not having Bunny ears on straight or tails fully fluffed (I'm serious!) resulted in demerits. A specific number of demerits got a Bunny fired. Bunnies who did PR promotions were rewarded with double merits. More merits got them assigned to stations where they could make better tips. Bunnies reported to room managers, who reported to day or night managers, who reported to the general manager. It was run like a military operation.

I sometimes wished Grossinger's had operated with such efficiency.

My First Months at Playboy

My first months at Playboy set the stage for the years to follow. Barbara had already set up a series of events for which I then arranged media coverage—a Bunny softball game that competed as part of the Broadway Show League in Central Park, Bunny water polo at Motel City, Bunny touch football (what television station wouldn't want to cover that?), golf tournaments, charity events, and assorted other promotions. Periodically we held celebratory events at the Club's VIP room to thank the Bunnies, in street dress, and the press—most of whom were disappointed that the girls weren't spilling out of their costumes!

How the tables had turned! In previous jobs I had to almost beg media people to share a meal with me. Entertaining was a standard way of doing business in the 1960s, a perk I particularly enjoyed because it gave me the opportunity to meet media professionals on an informal basis and make new contacts. I immediately sent out handwritten notes announcing my new association with Playboy and invited every broadcaster I could think of to join me for lunch, cocktails, dinner, or the midnight jazz breakfast buffet. The response was overwhelming. Even talk show hosts such as Arlene Francis, Barry Gray, and Long John Nebel, people I thought might not go out of their way to be seen at the Playboy Club, responded. One such occasion was particularly memorable.

"This is Johnny Carson," said the voice on the phone. "I'm here with my brother, and if you're free, we'd like to come by and have dinner with you tonight." Right! Johnny Carson wanted to have dinner with me at the Playboy Club. Johnny Carson was a celebrity, and there was no reason he needed me to visit the Club; all he had to do was show up. Someone was putting me on, and I was about to let my annoyance show when Johnny said that his brother wanted to speak to me. I had known his brother, Dick, for three years. He had been the director of Merv Griffin's TV show (and had helped convince Merv, as a favor to me, to interview Betty Friedan) before he joined Johnny at *Tonight*. I recognized his voice immediately. Of course it was all right if he and Johnny came over for dinner. It couldn't have been more all right!

They asked for no special treatment. They didn't even want the VIP room. Before they arrived, I had a meeting with the night manager and Bunny who would serve our table. Johnny's affection for the young ladies and alcoholic spirits was well known. I reminded the Bunny once again that under no circumstance was she to divulge her last name or phone number and insisted that she pass the message on to all the Bunnies on the floor. I suggested to the manager that he cover our table carefully. No autograph seekers, unless Johnny specifically agreed (which he graciously did after he had finished his meal). If I had to leave the table, I asked the manager to please keep Johnny company, and when Johnny had to go to the men's room, I suggested that the manager not be far behind. Johnny should never have been left alone—the temptations for him and for the Bunnies was too risky. Should a liaison occur and become public knowledge, it could create a press backlash that would not be appreciated.

Johnny's brother Dick departed early, which left just the two of us. I was concerned about what we might find to talk about, but I quickly discovered that I had no reason to be. Johnny turned out to find my experiences at Grossinger's as fascinating as I found his tales as a mischievous budding magician in small-town Nebraska to be. It was no surprise that the Bunnies had never been as attentive as they were that evening. "Is everything all right, Ms. Grossinger?" "May I offer your guest another drink?" Johnny never said no. Not surprisingly, he became more flirtatious as the evening wore on. Then it became a challenge. He was convinced that he could get any Bunny he wanted to give him her phone number. Knowing how easy it would be, I told him that my job was on the line, which was not exactly true but could have been. As midnight approached and we had both downed an ample number of beverages, I suggested that we call it a night. I had already witnessed a Bunny standing outside the men's room waiting for him (the manager hadn't been paying attention). I didn't want to take any chances. Kai Winding, the great jazz trombonist and Playboy's musical director, was preparing to go on. Of course, Johnny couldn't miss that. 1:00 AM passed, then 2:00 AM. I remember what happened next as if it were happening now: I've had my fill of coffee. Johnny is semi-sloshed. The Club is clearing out. The Bunnies don't care if they get caught cozying up to him. The manager has disappeared. Johnny is enjoying every minute. Nothing good can come from it. Johnny has a terrific idea! He will summon his chauffeur, who will take me home to Greenwich Village, then return to pick him up and take him to his apartment on the East Side. In a pig's eye! I counter with my terrific idea. He will call his driver, who will take the two of us in his car, drop him off first, and then take me home. By then the Playboy Club will be closed, and our game of "never let Johnny Carson out of my sight" will be over. He can hardly stand on his feet. He gives up reluctantly. I breathe a sigh of relief.

The next morning a dozen roses appeared at my office with a card: "To my charming babysitter. It was a smashing evening. We'll do it again sometime! Your friend, Johnny." And he turned out to genuinely be "my friend, Johnny." First he wrote a letter to Hugh Hefner declaring what an asset I was to Playboy. Six years later, after Hefner had me fired, he wrote to my next employer and said, "You better be good to Tania, because if not, you'll have to answer to me!" When he passed away, there were those who were quoted saying that Johnny was a loner, a very cold man who only came alive when he was in front of a camera. I was privileged to know better.

It was a good thing Johnny hadn't hooked up with a Bunny on my watch. A month later I learned I was being monitored at the same time. Shortly after being hired, I had been contacted by someone who did interviews for the Armed Forces Radio Network and made it a point to invite him to the Club frequently. He returned the courtesy by interviewing Bunnies, the Bunny Mother, entertainers, and anyone else connected to Playboy I suggested. I never sensed that he was anything other than what he seemed. One evening when we were having a nightcap, a Bunny brought over a note that she said came from a key-holder at one of her tables. It read, "It will be worth your while to give me the last name and phone number of Bunny _____." Without even turning to see where it came from, I sent it back. The second note came with a $100 bill attached. "There's more where this came from." The night manager was on a break, so rather than show it to him, I shared it with the fellow from the Armed Forces Network. To my surprise, he encouraged me. "Bargain with him. Why not? Maybe you can pick up some extra cash. No one will know the difference." I would know the difference. I called the evening to an end and left the building. I discovered the next day that I had been set up. The guy from Armed Forces was also moonlighting as a private detective hired by Playboy to check out new staff members. Because I had access to personal information about each of the Bunnies, the management paid someone to see if I could be trusted. Rather than be offended, I admired the company's professionalism.

I did most of my work for the magazine during the day, but much of what I did for the Club involved being there at night. Without being able to play "host" to my friends in between entertaining business contacts, it would have been difficult to maintain any kind of social life.

When Victor Lownes, the man who hired me, left to set up the Playboy Club in London, Barbara and I moved to the Playboy sales office at 405 Park Avenue. From there I embarked on two projects for the magazine simultaneously. The first was to promote a panel featuring prominent science fiction writers Isaac Asimov, Fred Pohl, and Ted Sturgeon. I couldn't have asked for a more fascinating, congenial, and cooperative group with which to make my Playboy debut. Each agreed to give me whatever time I needed, and, as a result, I was able to flood talk shows in New York with interviews highlighting much of what they discussed in the current issue of the magazine. Newsstand sales improved considerably, and the PR director in Chicago to whom I reported was impressed.

My second project was more lighthearted. It had to do with a nudist colony. Shel Silverstein, who contributed frequently to Playboy along with fellow illustrators, cartoonists, and artists Jules Feiffer, Harvey Kurtzman (who headed *Mad* magazine), and LeRoy Neiman, had written and illustrated a feature about a colony in New Jersey led by a middle-aged, heavy-set woman named Zelda. As part of the feature, Shel caricatured Zelda in all her naked "splendor." Her signature trademark, which she never removed, was a string of pearls. "I am too shy to walk around naked." I knew she would be a hoot on television. And what better show than Johnny Carson's? Johnny never booked his own guests, so I sent the article to one of his talent coordinators who, as I expected, was interested enough to arrange a pre-interview. A pre-interview was mandatory if potential guests were unknown to determine whether they could conversationally hold their own with Johnny. I brought Zelda over the next day. She was wearing a demure black dress with, of course, her string of pearls. The talent coordinator, when we arrived, was in another meeting. We were asked to wait in his office. I went to get some coffee and left Zelda there, and I returned in time to see him open his office door and then scream, "What the hell is going on?" Zelda had decided to remove her dress and everything else but the pearls. She thought, she said, that Johnny might want to see her as she had originally appeared in *Playboy*. Not only was she nuts, she also got to make her appearance on *The Tonight Show*. Johnny's first question: "I understand you threw my office into an uproar the other day. Are you planning to do the same tonight?" She gave him an innocent, "Who, me?" and lifted her arm as if to unzip the back of her dress. The audience went wild!

After the agreed-upon two months, I received my new contract, along with a commendable raise, though there had once been a moment when I wasn't sure I'd accept it. One evening when Victor was still at the St. Moritz, he decided to throw a party and asked me to invite certain Bunnies. He had his own reasons, it seems, for not wanting to extend the invitations himself. Barbara had declined a similar invitation shortly after being hired and warned me that the gatherings often became raucous (with drugs and sexual shenanigans). I followed her lead and was emphatic that I wouldn't get involved. I added something about not wanting to be a pimp and that if that was one of the reasons I'd been hired, I'd quit. He threw me out of the office, and it was never mentioned again.

The night before he left for London, however, he threw another shindig and this time personally invited me to attend as his guest.

He also suggested that I leave by midnight. He didn't want to insult my "sensitivities." In truth, my sensitivities would be both insulted and toughened during my remaining years at Playboy. But that's another letter!

17

Playboy Highlights: Ayn Rand, Tim Leary, Jean Shepherd, Hugh Hefner, and the Playboy Mansion

It never occurred to me when I started with Playboy that I would witness history in the making. With the Beat generation, hippies, sexual and cultural revolutions, civil rights and antiwar demonstrations, and political assassinations, I was working for an iconic magazine at a time when civilization often seemed to stand on its head. The best part was discovering unexpected facets of people who were involved!

Ayn Rand Has a Sense of Humor!

I was intimidated at the thought of meeting Ayn Rand, the first subject of a Playboy interview I was asked to promote. I had dutifully read *Atlas Shrugged* and *The Fountainhead* years earlier, and, along with millions of others, I was beguiled by her heroes. Strong, courageous, never wavering. Her indomitable men and women never lost confidence in themselves and never once compromised their ideals. I also skipped hundreds of pages where Ms. Rand pontificated her world view. My perception, after reading her books, was that the author was intolerant, judgmental, unforgiving, and not the kind of woman I would care to spend time with. How mistaken I was!

Our first meeting took place in February 1964 at her snug Murray Hill apartment on East 36th Street. She welcomed me with a warm smile and the words, "Behold Ayn Rand, eminent philosopher, who can't get the refrigerator to work." Her husband, an artist named Frank Connor, stayed in the background nuzzling their cats. I liked them immediately!

Rand turned out to be a broadcaster and publicist's dream, un-expectedly soft-spoken, polite, and tactful. We worked beautifully to-gether. I scheduled her for a St. Patrick's Day interview with Barry Far-ber on WOR Radio. I usually accompanied Ayn (by this time we were on a first-name basis) to the station, but this time, as she had errands to run, she suggested that we meet at the studio. She hadn't arrived at 4:30 PM, the appointed time, nor was she there by 4:50 or 4:55. No one answered her phone at home. It was a talk show host's nightmare (not to mention one of my own). "Have you ever been interviewed on radio before?" Barry asked me. I nodded, thinking back to my City of Hope days. "Good," he said. "Now you're the guest!" What neither he nor Ayn knew at the time was that I took issue with almost every-thing she stood for. "Objectivism," she had explained in the *Playboy* interview[2] with Alvin Toffler, "holds that reason is man's only means of perceiving reality and his only guide to action. . . . The pursuit of his own happiness is his highest moral purpose." She also mentioned her proclivity to view the world in terms of black and white.

---

2 *Playboy*, March 1964

5:00 PM. The red light in the studio began to blink. Barry and I were on the air. Part of me hoped that Ayn wouldn't hear what I was about to say. That she might be offended when I had such affection for her concerned me. After a brief introduction explaining why I, not Ayn Rand, was behind the microphone, Barry goaded me into saying what I really thought. "I live in a world of grays, faults, and indecisions," I started out, "a world where doubts and imperfections coexist with kindness, empathy, and generosity of spirit. Compromise does not have to be a nasty word, much as Ms. Rand wishes otherwise. Civilization depends on people caring for one another." With every word, the hole I was digging myself deepened. Had my ego not interfered, I realized quickly that I should have answered Barry's questions with the words, "Ms. Rand believes . . ." but by that time it was too late. I was not surprised that the first call into the control room when the broadcast ended was from her. The last words I expected to hear were, "You sound very lovely on the radio. You should do it more often!" She explained that she'd been stuck in traffic and thanked me for covering for her. She did express surprise at some of the things I said but didn't belabor the point and went on to discuss our next appointment as if nothing had happened.

A few nights later we had dinner at the Playboy Club (which she found "most interesting"). She asked about the work I did, how the Bunnies were hired, trained, treated by management, and so forth. By the time I finished, I jokingly said that she could now do my job. I was then told that a group of Italian journalists were in the lobby asking for information about the Club—and Ayn rose from the table to head me off. "Good evening, gentlemen," she greeted them, edging me aside. "My name is Tania Grossinger, and I'm on the public relations staff. Welcome to the Playboy Club. I'd love to give you a tour. Did you know, incidentally, that in order to keep their job, each of the Bunnies has to sleep with the boss?" She then went on to describe Hugh Hefner as a sexual pervert. I stood there like an idiot. "And you should see the parties that go on upstairs after the Club closes. If you're not busy later, perhaps. . . . " By that time she only had to look at my face to know she had punished me enough and started to laugh. "I'm sorry to disappoint you lovely gentlemen, but as I hope you have figured out by now, I don't really do public relations for the Playboy Club, and I'm not Tania Grossinger." She invited them to join us for a drink, where she explained that I had recently caused her some chagrin and that their arrival provided her the perfect opportunity to surprise me as I had surprised her. At least I can say that I had the last word. Would the journalists like to know who their "guide" really was? "Don't you dare," she said. I dared. So the writers left with an unexpected bonus. In addition to interviews with two Bunnies, they also had one with the famous Ayn Rand. But, alas, to their dismay, no invites to the "party" upstairs!

Al Toffler, the writer who interviewed Ayn Rand for *Playboy* and who would go on to write *Future Shock*, was so impressed with the media coverage I arranged that he wrote a letter to Hugh Hefner and the magazine's PR director. "Tania seems to know everyone in radio and television. She knows their program needs, and she is energetic and resourceful at finding ways to fill those needs with material about Playboy. It's a pleasure to watch a pro at work." That, along with the letter Johnny Carson had written earlier, served to solidify my status with Playboy. In addition to my unlimited privileges at the Club, I was also given an expense account.

Jean Shepherd

My friendship with humorist, author (*A Christmas Story; In God We Trust, All Others Pay Cash*), and radio personality Jean Shepherd began on two levels—one as a talk show host with whom I talked about upcoming *Playboy* interviews and the other as a writer who contributed to the magazine. His late-night radio show on WOR drew an audience similar to Playboy's, and with my prodding he mentioned the magazine—which published a number of his short stories for which he later became famous—quite often. He was described by many of his peers as an oddball, detached and downright bizarre. I, on the other hand, delighted in his idiosyncrasies. Our relationship was platonic from the start and unusual to the end. I never knew when I would hear from him, but when I did, I knew the outcome would be unforgettable.

One very late night at the Club, I received a call. Jean had just finished his show—did I want a lift home? Had you been on East 59th Street that night, you couldn't possibly have missed me. Straddling Jean and hanging on for dear life, there I was, hugging him and screaming my head off as we careened down Fifth Avenue, the first time I had ever been on a motorcycle. It was late summer, and Washington Square Park was bustling. As we approached the famous Arch on lower Fifth Avenue, I let out a cry. Someone in a nearby apartment house had flung a raw egg at my head (helmets were not mandatory at the time). Jean turned to check that I wasn't injured, then two blocks later he pulled up to a local diner. "I'll be right back." He returned, a container in his outstretched hand. "Some bacon to go with your egg, Madame!"

In the 1960s certain neighborhoods in Manhattan were safer than others. Greenwich Village was relatively secure, though there had been periodic street disturbances that bordered on dangerous. Jean lived four blocks from me. One night at a ridiculous hour he appeared at my door. He had heard something about scuffles on Christopher Street and wanted to make sure I knew how to protect myself. How I wish I had taken pictures of him, crawling on my carpet, guessing where rocks might land in my seventh-floor living room, should they ever be thrown through my window from the sidewalk below. He moved chairs to a far wall so that I could use them to hide behind—and he left specific instructions as to when I should hide under the bed. On the way out he gave me his unlisted phone number "just in case."

All of my friends should be so idiosyncratic!

To quote his radio sign-off, "Excelsior!"

Timothy Leary

Tim Leary will forever be remembered for six words: "Turn On, Tune In, Drop Out," the mantra and rallying call of the psychedelic movement that affected an entire generation. In his *Playboy* interview of 1966, Leary declared that "LSD is the most powerful aphrodisiac known to man,"[3] adding that most women were capable of several hundred orgasms during a trip. Is it any wonder he attracted so many followers? The interview he did with *Playboy*, along with the attendant publicity, turned him into a media celebrity almost overnight.

It was easy to see how the young were drawn to him. He was handsome, charming, charismatic, and adroit at ingratiating himself to anyone who could call more attention to him. I count myself proudly as one of the "anyones."

When I started to promote Tim's interview, a new manager had arrived at the Playboy Club. He was offended by Tim from the start and unfortunately had good reason to be. Tim and I were having dinner before a late night interview. A half hour before we were to leave, Tim asked if he could have some privacy to "get his head together." I called the manager over and asked if Tim might be able to use his private

---

[3] *Playboy*, "Playboy Interview: Timothy Leary: A Candid Conversation with the Controversial Ex-Harvard Professor, Prime Partisan and Prophet of LSD" September, 1966.

office. As time passed and Tim hadn't returned, I asked the manager to please check on Tim for me. A minute later he came running back. "You've got to see this for yourself. Get upstairs fast!" The office door had been left ajar, so I didn't knock. I should have. There sat Tim, buck naked with a huge grin on his face, sitting cross-legged on the manager's desk and gratifying himself. I quickly backed away, the manager almost resigned, and Tim later gave a great interview!

Tim had been given access to a 4,000-acre estate in upstate Millbrook, New York, by a wealthy benefactor. It included a sixty-four room mansion where he invited friends and acolytes to join him in long weekend LSD sessions. He invited me to accompany him to one. I was afraid to dabble with acid, not for lack of curiosity, but because I knew myself too well. I worked hard all my life to keep my defenses under control and couldn't chance their falling apart. I was afraid of the ugly things I might discover. Tim offered to be my personal guide, and I almost succumbed. It was hard to say no to Tim Leary. I'm thankful I did.

If I had ever been tempted by psychedelics before, I never would be again. I agreed to accompany Tim to Millbrook as long as I wouldn't be under pressure to participate. It turned out to be a terrible occasion. Blinding strobe lights and ear-splitting music were part of the scene—I was prepared for that. I wasn't prepared, however, for the vomiting and banging of heads against walls, the screaming and ferocious flailing of arms and legs. I thought LSD was a peaceful experience. The participants I was watching seemed to be fighting for their lives! If this is what was meant by expanding consciousness. . . . Tim said that what had happened that evening was an aberration, but I, for one, was not convinced.

During the period I was promoting Tim and his Playboy Interview, he founded the League for Spiritual Discovery (LSD), a religious movement that sought constitutional protection for the right to take LSD as a sacramental substance. Fundraisers were held all over the country, with the final and most celebrated one at the Village Theater on Second Avenue in the East Village. Tim arranged for me and a friend to have front-row seats. Before the show, he greeted me with his usual affection. Within ten seconds, a line had formed to my side filled with young men and women reaching out for my arm, my shoulder, the cheek where Tim kissed me. They wanted to touch the spots that Tim had touched. I had seen movie stars. I had seen fans. But this was a cult. Tim was enjoying it all too much, and I was afraid where it would take him.

Jim Garrison

Jim Garrison, the District Attorney of New Orleans in 1967, fiercely believed that President John F. Kennedy was killed in November 1963 because he was working for a reconciliation with the USSR and Castro's Cuba. His assassins were a group of anti-Communists and Cuban exiles, a number of whom were former employees of the CIA—and the CIA itself concealed vital evidence from the Warren Commission. His theory, for which he was both vilified and praised, involved complicated interconnections of members of the New Orleans gay community and covert CIA and FBI officials.

When his controversial interview was published in *Playboy Magazine* in October 1967, he was delighted to cooperate with me. But there were ground rules. For his safety, all interviews were to be taped in advance and not broadcast until he was back in New Orleans. At his hotel I was to register him under a false name—he chose Dr. Lester Livingston—but he insisted on staying at the New York Hilton. Jim was a tall and broad-shouldered man who easily stood out in a crowd, and his photo had already been plastered in newspapers and magazines.

I suggested that a smaller hotel in a residential area might better serve his needs for anonymity, but, no, he wanted the New York Hilton. To placate his fear of being followed, the car and driver he hired had to round any block twice before he would get out.

A final rule: I was to give details of his whereabouts to no one. All contact with him had to be made through me. He hoped I wouldn't mind if he gave my home phone number to "confidential informants" he was planning to meet up with.

The interviews went exceedingly well. He was passionate about his subject, Kennedy's assassination, and conspiracy theories were the rage. On his last day in New York a radio station gave my phone number to a man who intimated that he had valuable information for Jim. Some of the people Jim asked to call me sounded a bit lunatic, but they were generally polite and no problem. This person, not known to him, was not. This person, in fact, threatened my life. "I know where you live. If you don't give me Jim Garrison's phone number, I will kill you!" Considering him to be nothing more than a crackpot, I pretended to ignore what he said, asked for his phone number, and promised to pass it on. The caller wouldn't trust me, and his threats grew more vicious. At that point I put down the phone and immediately called Jim. This is how the conversation went:

Me: "Jim, I'm frightened. I just got a call from someone who wants to talk to you, and he threatened to kill me if I didn't give him your number."

Jim: "It's no problem. I carry a gun."

Me: "Jim, it's me he's threatening, not you. I don't carry a gun!"

Jim: "Call the police. They should be able to help you. I've got to catch a flight. Thanks for all your help."

I did call the police, and fortunately the person who threatened my life never called back.

The Playboy Mansion

The Playboy Mansion on Chicago's Near North Side was, as a colleague poetically put it, a horny bachelor's wet dream come true. Engraved on the front door were the words "Si Non Oscillas, Noli Tintinnare!"—a loose Latin translation of "If You Don't Swing, Don't Ring!" The mansion featured game rooms, an underground swimming pool entered by sliding down a fireman's pole, a grotto with an inside waterfall, and room service whenever one desired. It also served as offices and living quarters for head honcho Hugh Hefner and his entourage. There was a nonstop flow of Playboy Playmates, and Bunnies took up residence in many of the mansion's seventy rooms. The mansion served as Party Central for Hefner and his buddies, politicos, famous writers, professional athletes, and celebrities like Frank Sinatra, Sammy Davis, Jr., Tony Bennett, and Bill Cosby, all of whom preferred Hefner's "amenities" to any of the hotels in town.

Anyone who worked for Playboy was familiar with the kinky goings-on at the house. I was probably the only one who didn't believe it—I thought it was hype to feed into the erotic fantasy of the Playboy myth. I was asked so many questions about the Mansion that I finally suggested to the PR Director in Chicago that he arrange for me to see the place for myself. I paid my first visit to the celebrated mansion on 1340 North State Parkway in the spring of 1967. I was as curious as anyone about what went on behind those closed doors. I expected to see Playmates, or at least Bunnies, flitting around the house showing off their wares. Not a one. Their dorm, with its own kitchen and dining area, was in another wing. I didn't see one celebrity. It must have been an off night. Sunday was movie night in the grand living room, and all employees were expected to attend. Enormous crystal chandeliers hung from the twenty-foot ceiling, and the walls were adorned with original art ranging from artists like Pablo Picasso to Playboy contributors Leroy Neiman and Shel Silverstein. Large bottles of Pepsi, Hefner's favorite drink, and homemade popcorn were in place. At 8:00 PM sharp, Hefner, in his signature royal blue silk pajamas and robe, made his regal entrance. To the left of one of the marble fireplaces was a huge leather couch, where Hefner sat with four lovelies on either side, interchangeable young ladies auditioning to be Playmates, who were put up in rooms next to his. I hate to disappoint you and wish I could share some gossip, but that was the most sex I witnessed in the Playboy Mansion. Matinees at the local movie house would have been more exciting. I'm sure things were different on weekends when, I'm told, fun, games, and orgies were nonstop—but I can't personally attest to a thing.

The staff was helpful and accommodating, yet during my first day, my only day, I found myself disoriented. Was it something in the air? That was it! There was no fresh air. The circulation was controlled by machines in the cellar. There were no windows in the living and entertainment quarters in the Playboy Mansion where Hefner presided. One couldn't see outside, and, of course, no one could see in. The quarters were Hefner's inner sanctum. He approved of anyone who entered. Big-name entertainers performed for him personally. One could order lobster and champagne at two o'clock in the morning, sleep all day, or play pool (or swim in one) at any hour; one could do anything one wanted to do, with anyone one wanted to do it with (courtesy of Hefner), at any time at all. At the Playboy Mansion, the world was run by Hefner. He was the one and only master!

I found Hefner's extreme egotism even more off-putting than the sexual lunacy about which, though I had no firsthand knowledge, I was finally convinced by two of the butlers, who confided in me that everything I'd heard about was true.

Hugh Hefner

What was Hugh Hefner really like? I never found him as personable, charming, or sexually exciting as he was portrayed to be. Then again, I didn't aspire to be a Playboy centerfold.

Full credit must be given to Hef, as he liked to be called, for breaking barriers and revolutionizing the way people thought and spoke about sex. Playboy was, as Hef sometimes put it, an antidote to the repressive atmosphere of the 1950s, and if he had to publish photos of naked girls to prove it, that's what he'd do. Playboy fed into the fantasies of millions of male readers, and being in a position to live out his own fantasy with the backing of a brilliant PR team, Hef became known as one of the world's most famous and envied womanizers.

Hef's visits to New York during the mid-1960s were primarily at my behest for appearances on TV shows hosted by Johnny Carson, Dick Cavett, Mike Douglas, and Merv Griffin. The only time we spent one-on-one together was in limos to and from the airport. I met him for first time in 1963 in New York and was taken aback by his remarkable lack of curiosity. Whatever interest I thought he might have in the various projects I was doing on behalf of the magazine or what was going on culturally in New York—it wasn't there. I kept looking for the intellect that came across in his editorials or the sense of humor he was rumored to have, but his conversations with me were much more mundane. I concluded that he was more of a guy's guy, preferring buddies with whom he could share and compare sexual conquests to a PR girl who knew her place and remained there. There were two times however, in the six years I worked for him, that we played an important role in each other's life.

The first involved an award-winning public service series on New York radio station WINS in 1964 called *Trialogue*, which featured a prominent rabbi, minister, and priest discussing religious and social issues of the day. I thought it might stir up some excitement to bring Hefner into the mix. It took some doing and many hours of entertaining the clergymen, at their request, of course, at the Playboy Club, where I finally got them to agree to discuss Playboy and the Sexual Revolution with Hefner over the course of four one-hour shows. Hef was acutely aware of what a coup this was (the transcriptions of each broadcast ended up in the magazine as part of his lengthy and often difficult-to-read series titled "The Playboy Philosophy"), and to his credit he was quick to express his appreciation to me for making it happen.

The second time began with a phone call from a Playboy executive in Chicago. Hef was demanding that I put someone on *The Tonight Show*. The someone was a nineteen-year-old woman he had recently met who refused to sleep with him. She later became Hefner's girlfriend and a television star, but in 1969 she was but one of many young ladies with large breasts as their sole credits. Hef tried everything to change her mind. Expensive jewelry and the promise of a photo layout in the magazine. Meeting Sammy Davis, Jr., and Frank Sinatra in person. He bought airtime on a local television station where she and her family lived and had them replay segments of a TV series he hosted, *Playboy After Dark*, for twenty-four straight hours, hoping it might impress her. None of it worked. There was only one thing she wanted: to be on *The Tonight Show*. It finally became their quid pro quo, thus the phone call to me.

I asked Playboy's PR man if I could pretend that this woman was Hef's fiancée. No. His girlfriend? No. Could she sing or dance? Was she making live appearances anywhere? No, no, and no. To be frank,

I was told, my job was on the line. Hef did not take well to a woman turning him down—after all, he was Hugh Hefner—and it was up to me to make the situation change. I wanted to ask why he didn't call Johnny Carson directly, because by that time they knew each other quite well, but thought better of it. If he had wanted to do it, he would have done it. He probably knew it was a crazy idea to begin with.

I was having an impersonal affair at the time with one of Johnny's producers and knew that I would at least get a hearing before being turned down. He did the best he could. If Hef would propose marriage to the young lady on the show, or even if he would introduce her as the woman who had stolen his heart, the producer would put her on immediately. Hef wasn't about to do either. Though I'd been warned that my association with Playboy might come to an end as a result of this failure, I soon embarked on a Playboy-related adventure that would be one of the highlights of my life.

18

Puerto Vallarta: A Fantasy Come True

Hugh Hefner's fantasy was to bed every woman in the world. Mine was more realistic: I wanted to be a beach bum. At thirty-two, before it was too late, I wanted to step out of my city self and find a place where life didn't revolve around meetings and appointments, where I could shed my defenses, be silly, stop living up to other people's expectations, and rediscover my own. In my Playboy office was a film poster that read SOMETIMES YOU HAVE TO LEAVE THE THINGS YOU KNOW, AND THE ONES YOU LOVE, TO BE YOURSELF. I wanted to be that self.

Turning fantasy into reality was less complicated than I dared think. In extenuating circumstances Playboy would grant executives a leave of absence with pay. Recently my life had been threatened once again—this time by a militant group of anti-Castro Cuban exiles who believed that a *Playboy* interview with Fidel presented him in too complimentary a light. As the magazine's PR representative in New York, I was once again the object of strangers' misplaced furor. I was whisked off by police to a hotel and put under seventy-two-hour protection until things calmed down, but my nightmares as a result of this turmoil persisted. On that basis Playboy accepted my request for paid leave—and I knew just where I would go.

Shortly before I started to work for Playboy, I had accepted an invitation from Xavier de la Torre, a fashion designer I met at a party thrown by my then-boyfriend Steve in New York, to visit him in Puerto Vallarta, where he owned a boutique. In 1963 Vallarta was still a relatively little-known picturesque fishing village, replete with pristine beaches, lingering sunsets, narrow cobblestone streets, and colorful markets on Mexico's Pacific coast. It turned my heart. Through Xavier I met an unusual group of expatriate Americans, hippies, eccentrics, artists, and writers, who had made it their home. I took to their attitude of laissez-faire with unexpected ease. Little did I know that six years later I would be back on a lifelong odyssey to regain those very special feelings of clarity, wholeness, and peace.

The fact that I already knew someone there made a repeat visit even more appealing. For insurance I sent Xavier thirty issues of *Playboy Magazine* before I arrived. If, for any reason, I wasn't able to make a favorable impression, for sure the magazines would!

He made reservations for me at the Oceano—the most sought-after hotel in town. My spacious room on the second floor overlooked the bay, and each night I fell asleep to the sound of waves crashing beneath my window. I was fortunate enough to have a private bathroom and shower (not all of the sixteen rooms did) for my two-month stay. The lobby windows opened directly to the sea. Breakfast at the Oceano was an institution, even for guests at other hotels, and the Oceano bar, where a musical trio entertained each evening, was the place where local expatriates, tourists, power brokers, and hustlers, along with the builders, engineers, architects, and realtors directing the redevelopment of the town met at the end of each day. For the grand sum of twenty-eight dollars a week, I had a new home. The first night I made a vow to myself: The only schedule I would follow would be my own. I would eat when I was hungry, sleep when I was tired, drink when I was thirsty, and screw when I was horny. I was going to indulge the child in me, and do what I wanted to do when I wanted to do it.

It didn't take long to see how different things were since my first visit in 1963. The following year John Houston, the eminent director, had chosen Vallarta as the location for his film *Night of the Iguana* starring Richard Burton. Burton had been very much in the news ever since he and Elizabeth Taylor began their extramarital love affair in Rome. Their torrid relationship transfixed millions, and when she joined him in Vallarta, the publicity was overwhelming. In what seemed like almost overnight, hordes of tourists followed, and the town took on a different hue.

In the spring of 1969 the changes were obvious. There were more cars on the streets and more noise. New restaurants, galleries, and designer boutiques had replaced tiny dwellings, storefront sandalerias, and cantinas. One could even find copies of *Time*, *Newsweek*, and the *Los Angeles Times*. Construction of new hotels and private homes had become a local industry. Six years earlier at Los Muertos beach, if two beach boys showed up for work, one would likely have nothing to do. Now their time was spent playing up to blond lovelies from Southern California, who they hoped, after being shown a good time in Vallarta, would whisk them back to the States, where they might have a better future.

Many local customs still delighted and amused. Onlookers continued to applaud sunsets each evening. Every Sunday at dusk local men and women, dressed in their finery, circled each other flirtatiously on the central plaza fronting the Church of Our Lady of Guadalupe. Street vendors hawked roasted cobs of corn, candy apples, popcorn, and fresh oysters. Mariachis played for their own amusement. When there was a full moon, gardeners climbed to the tops of the trees and hung red flags to ensure that their plants would grow properly. An old man I first met in 1963 still strolled the streets ringing his bell at 6:00 AM to alert home-owners that garbage would be picked up three hours later. Women of Indian descent, convinced that hot water caused arthritis, washed their clothes by pounding them on the rocks of the icy cold Rio Cuale, which bisected the neighborhood where Elizabeth Taylor and Richard Burton now lived. And the service in restaurants hadn't much changed. "If you want it by tomorrow, order it today!"

So this is what happened at the end of my first week: Xavier's bou-tique, the Bazaar Vallarta, was located half a block from the Oceano. Most afternoons Xavier held an open house for friends and customers. Three days after I arrived, he threw a get-together in my honor, where I was able to catch up with people I had met six years earlier and through them make new acquaintances. With one particular exception, a man who tried to engage me in conversation but whose manner I found disturbing, it didn't take me long to feel at home.

I went to sleep relatively early that night, checking to make sure I locked the door behind me as Señora Pura, the manager of the hotel, insisted. Around 2:00 AM, I heard a noise near the foot of my bed. Someone had entered my room. Within seconds the person was rummaging, and not very quietly, through my closet and opening and shutting drawers. There was no phone in the room, no way I could call for help. My first fear was of rape, but the man seemed much more interested in my possessions than me. Next I knew he was hovering over my bed. "Where's the stuff?" he asked. I remained mute and terrified.

"The cocaine!" With great relief, but even more confused, I some-how answered with lucidity. I didn't use cocaine, I didn't have any co-caine, and what made him think I did? I asked how he got into my room, and he didn't answer. He only wanted to know what the drug dealer had told me. What drug dealer? What the hell was going on? I

Not yet ready to take on the world.

Mother and child in Chicago when life was less complicated; my favorite photo of the two of us.

Now you know how to get to Grossinger's!

Grim determination at the skating rink.

Be it ever so humble . . .

Jackie Robinson had nothing to fear.

Tania and Karla at her mother's lobby "office."

Grossinger staff show, 1954. Mel Brooks contributed sketches. I'm second row, seventh person from the left.

My band, Tania y Sus Mamboleros, entertaining the troops at Fort Devens Army Camp, 1953.

Mother with Jackie and Rachel Robinson at Grossinger's.

Va-va-va-boom! Tania returns to Grossinger's after marital breakup, February 1959.

Mr. and Mrs. Neil Jacobs, Detroit, Michigan, October 19, 1958

Showing off my kitchen table where my book *Weekend* was co-authored, 1980.

Publicity photo for 1975 edition of *Growing Up at Grossinger's.*

Tania and Hugh Hefner having an intellectual discussion about sex at New York's Playboy Club, 1964.

Schmoozing with Tim Leary before a radio interview, 1966.

Stepping out of the Lions Head
bar in Greenwich Village where my
literary career began, mid-1980s.

Tania with Anne and Stan Rice at their annual black tie New Orleans
Writers Conference party, 1991.

It may not be Grossinger's, but
it's certainly home.

Surrounded by two most accomplished men: Pete Hamill and Tania's
most important person, Art D'Lugoff.

said I didn't know what he was talking about and certainly didn't know any drug dealer as I had been in Vallarta just a few days. Without another word, he backed out of my room. Five minutes and it was over.

It took until the night before I departed eight weeks later to discover what was behind that experience. At the moment he left, I was too frightened to do much of anything. Sleep was out of the question, and my stomach was in spasms. I repeated to myself in retrospect, "That guy could have killed me!" Over and over I relived the evening. I had come back to the hotel directly after Xavier's party. Señora Pura was still behind the front desk. How did a stranger get a key? There were close to twenty people at the party. I spoke only to the man I was uncomfortable with for a few minutes and didn't even get his name. Why was I singled out? And by whom? More important, could I ever feel safe at the Oceano, or even in Puerto Vallarta, again?

Xavier was already having breakfast when I came downstairs the next morning. His reaction was far from what I expected. He not only didn't seem surprised; he almost made light of it. He assured me, with a smile I found hard to understand, that I was in no danger and urged me to pretend it never happened. He also cautioned me not to mention it to anyone, especially Señora Pura. "I am asking you to trust me," he said. "Strange things happen in Mexico. I promise on my mother's life that nothing bad will happen to you while you are here." I had two choices; turn around and go home, or opt for trust.

I opted for trust.

So much for nirvana!

Much as I gave lip service to avoiding routine, the predictable rhythms of each day offered a sense of security and meaning. Breakfast seemed to last forever. Bloody Mary pours at the Oceano started early in the morning as the expats who lived in town gathered to wait for the nearby post office to open and catch up on the previous evening's gossip.

Those Bloody Marys were followed by more at the beach. Los Muertos, a five-peso (a peso was worth eight cents at the time) cab ride from town, was where most people spent the day. A mat, chair, and table cost another peso. Within ten minutes a veritable procession of Mexican vendors and children paraded from one end of the beach to the other, peddling their wares: castanets, pottery, seashells, jewelry, riding crops, hammocks, shawls, shirts, hats, scarves, rugs, ceramics, beads, tablecloths, wood bark carvings, tapestries, stuffed iguanas, jewelry of onyx and silver, watercolors, ponchos, blankets, puppets, coconut oil, artificial flowers—anything a tourist could possibly want as a souvenir.

There were a number of informal beach shacks that served lunch. La Palapa, one of my two favorites, specialized in fresh shrimp cocktails, with forty of the tiny crustaceans (I counted them) for six pesos; El Dorado featured tasty crepes that sold for eight. I preferred my fish fresh from the sea. Fishermen would return with their catch shortly before noon, build a fire on the beach, rub the fish with salt and lime, and grill the fish over the fire. When finished, young kids would skewer the fish, stride along the beach, and sell them to hungry sun worshippers. For three pesos, I could plant the twig in the sand and pick off the flesh with my fingers. For dessert, there were cones of fresh watermelon, papaya, cucumbers, and pineapples sold by hefty Indian women for another three pesos, a healthy and veritable feast for forty-eight cents. A refreshing Mexican beer brought the entire lunch tab to a most affordable seventy-two cents.

I would laze in the sun, dive through the waves at high tide, chat with friends, read, doze, walk the beach to the less-populated areas, and reflect more often than not on a how lucky I was to be there. Sometimes someone would invite me for a sail; other times I jumped on a sightseeing boat to meet new people and indulge my newfound love of the sea. Toward the end of the day I would head back to the Oceano, catch up on my mail, write in my journal, visit with Xavier, or let whatever was about to happen, happen. It was a most languid lifestyle, sometimes too languid for someone used to the rhythms of New York. But languid never meant I was bored.

I experienced two different lifestyles in Puerto Vallarta. The first month I was an outsider, a tourist who went out with other tourists because I was too new to be accepted in any local's inner circle. By the second, my last, I had met many expat Americans who called Vallarta home. They ranged from retirees to businesspeople, celebrities, artists, and writers.

And what a cast of characters they were:

Xavier: Former Jesuit priest from Mexico City, titular head of the gay community, fashion designer, owner of Bazaar Vallarta, avid reader and raconteur, generous host, confidant of Elizabeth Taylor and Richard Burton, alcoholic, friend, and someone very anxious to have a child.

Florencia: Xavier's twenty-four-year old model, muse, and manager. In loveless marriage to an American builder twice her age. Had loved Xavier since her late teens. Bedded him once, and believed she might have been pregnant (he promised to marry her, if true, and never sleep with another man). She miscarried. He never slept with another woman, but Florencia remained hopeful.

Jorge: Ten-year-old "chico," rascal, caretaker, best buddy, pest, one of the kids who attached themselves to anyone staying for more than a few days, carrying messages (telephones rarely worked) and running errands in return for a few pesos, lunch, or maybe a comic book or pair of shoes. Few things remained secret from an observant "chico."

Sharman the hustler: Mid-thirties. Beach boy who worked his way up to owner of a nightclub, where everything and everyone was for sale. A most unsavory man not above seeking "hush money" from tourists open to blackmail. He had a crush on me.

Elena Cortez: Fifty-nine-year-old, heavy-set, self-proclaimed witch. Owner, Los Quatros Vientos, a quirky outdoor restaurant atop a steep hill with a magnificent view. Best value dinner in town (a prix fixe menu of soup, salad, entrees, three vegetables, pasta, dessert, and coffee, for $4.40). Cocktail hour open only to select invitees. If there was something about you Elena didn't like, she'd ask you to leave. Proclaimed she met me in a previous life. "You have the primitive soul of a Mexican. You embrace death."

Clarence, the helicopter pilot: Claimed he rose from poverty to become a Navy pilot, Volkswagen dealer, insurance salesman in the Far East, marine biologist, and, at the time I met him, a death-defying evangelical flying classified missions he couldn't talk about to dangerous areas of Mexico. I was the first Jew he ever met. He was the craziest guy I'd ever met.

Leah: A woman from Venezuela down on her luck. Met her husband, a construction worker, in Mexico City. Came to Vallarta to become a tour planner for VIPs. Her sights were higher than her expertise, his drinking a serious problem. Lived in a shack on the outskirts of town with outdoor plumbing, no running water, and roosters running wild in the backyard. Books by Gunter Grass, Walt Whitman, Leo Tolstoy, and Norman Mailer made it a home.

—⁓—

Miguelito, my new prepubescent "chico," is at the stage where he tries to emulate his older brother. He tells me stories about all the women who want to go to bed with him (never mind that he's too young to shave!). Why won't I go out with him? No hustle, he promises. I can order anything I want; it doesn't even have to be beer. He promises to wear long pants.

—◇—

I am invited to Leah and her husband's home in the boondocks for lunch. I bring toys for the children and a big chocolate cake. A neighbor with three kids of her own, one of whom delights in crawling all over me, joins us. She tells us that she just put her eight-year-old twins in the local hospital. Typhoid fever. I can't take my eyes off her two-year-old, who has just blown his nose on my blouse. I impolitely excuse myself and run out. When I get back to the hotel, I throw my blouse in the garbage, jump in the shower, and scrub myself so fiercely that I almost bleed.

I take my temperature every hour for the next two days.

—◇—

I'm having cocktails at the Oceano with a young couple from San Francisco. She is eight months pregnant and mentions she has been bleeding for two days. Within seconds, her water breaks. I run to Señora Pura for help. We get her to the bathroom and try to make her comfortable. The ambulance finally arrives.

The next morning, I see her and her husband calmly having breakfast downstairs. "What happened?" I ask. "Why aren't you in the hospital?" "We ran away," she explains. She miscarried shortly after she arrived. The hospital frightened her more than the miscarriage. The hospital had no blankets, no food, no toilet seat covers, no nurse on the floor.

My heart goes out to the twins with typhoid fever.

—◇—

Richard Burton and Elizabeth Taylor have returned to Puerto Vallarta with assorted children, nannies, and household help. Burton drops by the Oceano each morning for his "eye opener" before the post office opens. We are introduced, and he picks up on my last name. I tactfully do not mention having already met Elizabeth Taylor with Eddie Fisher at the Catskill resort where I grew up. "She always talks about Grossinger's," he tells me. "She never knew Jewish food could taste so good!" Two days later I am invited to dinner. Dinner at Chez Elizabeth and Richard has been called for 8:00 PM but guests, a potpourri of locals and tourists with whom the couple have become friendly, come and go at their leisure. Casa Kimberly, located in "Gringo Gulch" where most of the rich foreigners live, is an arresting seven-bedroom, white stucco villa with a breathtaking view of Banderas Bay and the entire city. Elizabeth, in a flowing caftan and even more stunning in person, greets me with the words, "It's not as fancy as Grossinger's, but. . . ." We both laugh. I am impressed by how informal the evening is. Despite rumors of the couple's excessive drinking and fights that often get physical, everyone that evening is on their best behavior. Drinks are served nonstop on two separate balconies, along with guacamole and taco tidbits. Dinner is a simple buffet of cold soups, assorted salads, two kinds of chili, tortillas, and fresh fruit, with ice cream and cookies for dessert. Conversations, much of which are centered on who is sleeping with whom and how the tourist influx is diluting the charm of Puerto Vallarta, flow effortlessly. Elizabeth, predictably, is the center of attention. The highlight of the evening is when she leads a conga line to her private quarters to show off the heart-shaped bathtub Richard has commissioned for her. The mariachis stop serenading at midnight, and those of us still standing take our leave shortly after.

—⁂—

Nights soon became predictable. Rum, the spirit closest to the usual Scotch I drank too much of at home, at Xavier's, followed by more cocktails at the Oceano, dinner at a local restaurant, and then house or beach parties and nightcaps at the Piano Bar near the Oceano. The only things that changed were the players.

The best parties were the deportations. The police turned a blind eye to recreational drugs, except when Americans were caught trying to give or sell them to Mexican children. If an American expat was caught turning on a kid, he was given a three-day notice. He was then "deported," which meant he would have to cross the border back to the States. If he made a generous payoff to the chief of police before he left, he'd be allowed back in two to three weeks. It became such a joke that not only were deportation parties the best fun (with the best marijuana, cocaine, and LSD in town); the chief was always the honored guest, and in fact usually passed the word as to who was being deported and on what day so that two parties wouldn't conflict with each other. I must have attended at least half a dozen.

I didn't sleep with all the men I met in Vallarta, but I shared a bed with enough of them to make me question why it was so easy for me to have one-night stands. How could I handle casual trysts so effortlessly without remorse or guilt? Certain words come to mind. Loose. Easy. Promiscuous. Slut? A character deficiency, perhaps? That's not how I saw myself. I was single, self-supporting, with a job at Playboy that put me in touch with some of the most interesting and exciting men in New York. I was discriminating. I never brought a man home I wouldn't want to be seen with in public, though some of the more famous and married of them might not have felt the same way. I desperately feared commitment. I was no closer to coming to grips with Neil's rejection of me ten years earlier than I was when my marriage came to an end. I still had trouble seeing myself as sexually attractive, even though my associations with men since then would have led a more secure person to believe otherwise. What did I have to lose?

Puerto Vallarta, for all its recent development, was still very much a small town. Beneath every surface of gaiety lies darkness—this I should have remembered from Grossinger's. People who were parochial and prejudiced where they originally came from didn't leave those traits behind just because they had moved to one of the loveliest places on earth. The drama I was privy to involving people I hardly knew often dispirited me. Privacy was virtually impossible. Everyone, many prompted by their "chicos," seemed to know everyone else's business. The gossip was often cutting, from ugly to downright destructive. I can only imagine what people said about me! At a certain point my discomfort with this kind of drama got the better of me, and I began to pull away.

My eight weeks were coming to an end. My fantasy hadn't quite lived up to my reality. It occurred to me that fantasies seldom do. I found myself becoming impatient. The sun was too hot, the humidity overbearing. Los Muertos was too crowded. Every beach was too crowded. The damn mosquitoes got on my nerves. Why didn't the hotel toilets flush properly? I was tired of showers—I wanted to take a bath! It was time. I wanted to go home.

A friend wise in the ways of departures from Vallarta cautioned me, "Once your return reservation is confirmed, it is as if you've already left. You withdraw into yourself. You end up preoccupied with what you have to face when you get back, knowing that, depending on what you left behind, it may not be pleasant. And by the way," he advised, "be prepared on your last night to get the worst case of *turista* imaginable. It happens to the most cautious of us. Something about the body acting out." He was correct on all counts.

Only two things remained to attend to. The first was the party Xavier was throwing for me in conjunction with a mutual friend's deportation. It was an unforgettable evening —music, dancing, laughter, and much sentiment. Almost everyone I knew in Vallarta, including Richard Burton and Elizabeth Taylor, turned up. My frustrations of the last days floated away in the sweet ocean air. I looked around at so many of the friends I made, recalling with great affection their graciousness to me and hospitality. I had set out to meet and experience new people—and meet and experience I did. I established a new lifestyle and managed, if not always to my advantage but certainly with no regrets, to indulge my inner child. And on that last evening a part of that child still wished there was a way I could hold onto those feelings forever.

Xavier's toasts were interrupted by the chief of police, who embraced me as though we had known each other all our lives. "You're a very good girl," he said in his broken English. "You don't get in trouble. You don't do the cocaine." "How do you know?" I asked. "Because we inspected your room," he said. "Remember the first week you arrived?" He didn't have to say another word. I ended up laughing in spite of myself. "Some detective," I told him. "He never even bothered to check my purse!" And Xavier lifted another glass in salute.

When I went to pay my final bill, I realized I was being charged for only seven of my eight weeks. Señora Pura gave a short shrug. "I didn't charge for the first week," she said. "I know what happened to you that night, but I had no choice. The police chief forced me to give his officer the passkey. You didn't register a complaint, even though I would have understood if you had. My reputation could have been ruined if any of our guests found out. This is my way of saying 'thank you.'"

And then the *turista* took over.

With a vengeance!

19

Christy Brown's
Down All the Days
and Malachy McCourt

Shortly after I returned from Puerto Vallarta, Hugh Hefner made good on his threat to have me fired for not putting his girlfriend on *The Tonight Show*, and I was officially unemployed. I didn't have to look far for a new job. My first offer was from Bob Guccione, the publisher of *Penthouse*, a male magazine that had made its mark by printing frontal nudity (something *Playboy* had eschewed) without any pretense of the editorial balance *Playboy* provided. I had met Bob and his staff at various functions, and we had mutual friends in London. He would, as he so sensitively put it, love to hire me, if only to "rub Hefner's face in it!" It occurred to me that there might be better reasons for someone to give me a job, so I turned him down.

The second offer came from the well-known public relations firm of Rogers, Cowan & Brenner. RC&B was the most famous agency on the West Coast; there was hardly a celebrity or movie star that the firm didn't represent. On the East Coast RC&B had added a corporate division, and the year before I was fired, the agency was hired to serve as a PR consultant to Playboy Enterprises.

I did not like Henry Rogers. His agency was charging Playboy an exorbitant amount of money (some of which I would have liked to see go into my own promotion budget), and rarely did I see what they did to earn it. Once every few weeks executives would fly in from Playboy headquarters in Chicago, and we would all meet to go over strategies for the next period of time. There was rarely a meeting when Henry, with great arrogance and aplomb, didn't come up with what he considered to be brilliant ideas which, shyly at first and then more aggressively, I had to shoot down with the explanation that I had already done it, I was currently working on it, or it wasn't feasible for reasons I would then spell out. His hostility toward me was evident, which is why it came as such a surprise when my second job offer came from him.

His call was brusque and to the point. Without even asking the figure, he promised to increase my salary by 50 percent (and I was so dumb that instead of giving him a higher figure, I told him the truth!). I would have the title of Director of Broadcast Promotion, Corporate Division, with a window office and secretary. My first response was, "But you don't even like me, Henry," to which he replied, "I don't have to like you. This is business. I'd rather have you on my side of the table than across from me."

It was the worst job I ever had. It's not that I didn't know how large PR agencies conducted business. It was that I knew I was not a corporate type. Tell me what you want me to do, give me my space, don't second-guess my every move, and it will be done. Stop me if you see me screwing up, but until then back off. This was not the way the corporate division at RC&B worked. Everything was done according to protocol. All communications, with copies to counterparts in the Los Angeles and London offices, were conducted by memoranda, even something as simple as checking interview dates with a colleague. At times I believed I spent half of my time reading memos from people I didn't even know and the other half responding to them. Even thank-you notes to media contacts had to be sent in triplicate. This provoked my first balk. Many of the people I worked with were friends, and my communications with them often included personal asides. That was not the RC&B way, so I would end up typing one kind of letter for office distribution and sending out another message privately. The next stumbling block was my disillusionment at discovering how the firm billed its accounts. Clients usually signed monthly or yearly retainers and were charged additionally for time spent by executives working on the account. In effect, the longer it took the executive to produce results, the more valuable he or she was to the agency. The more hours that could be billed back to the client, the more money the agency made. For example, to place a client's representative on *The Today Show*, or shows hosted by Johnny Carson, David Frost, Mike Douglas, Merv Griffin, or Dick Cavett, was a coup for which many agencies charged a bonus. Putting guests on talk shows is what I specialized in, and over the previous decade I had developed an enviable track record in this regard. It would take someone without my experience hours upon hours of written proposals, meetings, pre-interviews, and back-and-forth discussions before finally making a placement. I could often do it in fifteen minutes.

"How can we only bill them for a quarter of an hour?" my account supervisor would argue. "We have to demonstrate how complicated it was, how much time it took you to accomplish this. We have to charge them for all that!" At other times if two staffers exchanged ideas on a promotion, the client was billed twice. I was instructed how to exaggerate my timesheets, but we billed the client for that time, too. The worst part of my association with Henry Rogers was that I hated the accounts he assigned me. Ex-Lax, the chocolate-flavored laxative account, which meant that I had to sit straight-faced through a meeting as he promised the company's dour CEO that I could set him up with Johnny Carson, was one. Shortly after, having been accused of "not having an Ex-Lax mentality," I was told that I would no longer be able to have the pleasure of working on it. Charmin toilet paper was another account to which I was asked to contribute my expertise. Don't ask! Ditto for Alka-Seltzer. When making proposals to new clients, I would be hauled into board meetings and introduced as "the best broadcast promotion specialist in the city." A number of companies signed up because of that. Because their companies weren't appropriate for the mainstream TV talk shows, I was rarely ever able to deliver on Henry's promises. After a certain point, the clients didn't renew their contracts, but the agency had already netted tens of thousands of dollars, and nobody seemed to complain.

After six months, I didn't have to wait for the firm to fire me. I quit!

My next, and last, full-time job was as publicity director for the publisher Stein and Day, Incorporated. I was able to combine my long-standing love for books and talent for broadcast promotion in a small, informal, supportive setting—a welcome respite from the corporate intricacies of RC&B. Over the next twenty months I would promote books on politics, pop psychology, humor, current events, autobiographies, fiction, and history. None were as challenging or personally rewarding as the novel I am most proud to have been associated with, the international best-seller *Down All the Days* by Christy Brown, which in 1989 was turned into the Academy Award–winning film *My Left Foot*. I can't think of many publishers other than Stein and Day who would have taken the risk in agreeing to publish that book. Novels were difficult to promote in the best of situations. This was probably one of the worst situations. Christy Brown, writer, poet, artist, was born in the slums of Dublin, one of twenty-one children, of whom only thirteen survived. At a young age he was diagnosed with a rare disease called double athetoid cerebral palsy. His body was misshapen, he was partially paralyzed, and he could barely speak. He could not hold a pen. He could express himself in print only by manipulating the toes of his left foot and tapping out letters in code, which one of his sisters then put into a meaningful order. That was how his fictionalized memoir, *Down All the Days*, a playful expansion on his true memoir, came to be written.

Christy Brown, despite his handicap, was utterly charming! Everything about New York excited him, especially the energy of the people he saw on the streets. He loved to laugh and had a wicked sense of humor that became more cutting the more he drank. Christy never shied away from people, never asked for pity. His courage and determination were wondrous, and I became equally committed to do absolutely everything I could, despite the odds, to make his book a success.

That we would get press coverage when the book first came out was a given; Christy was a curiosity, a "freak" as one book reviewer let slip to me. There would be no dearth of newspaper and magazine reporters interested in hearing his story. Setting up interviews on national TV with someone who was palsied, slurred his words, and was almost impossible to understand was another matter. I refused to let it faze me.

The *Today* show, the most important book-selling TV show in the country, was the first I approached. I had a friend, Paul Cunningham, a lover of Irish literature, who was also a segment producer on the show. I arranged for him to meet privately with Christy, Christy's brother, and me in the hotel suite we had taken for the Brown family. Paul had read the book and was dazzled by what Christy had accomplished. Putting him on the air with Barbara Walters we knew would never happen, but after days of going back and forth with various ideas, Paul was able to get the producer of *Today* to agree to have someone off camera read excerpts from the book, as well as show background footage of where Christy grew up, along with interviews with mentors in Dublin and members of his family. We sold thousands of books the first day!

I still liked the idea of someone reading excerpts, but I wanted it to be *on* camera and for the audience to see the real Christy Brown. Only then could they begin to appreciate what an astounding talent the man had and what an almost-impossible task it had been for him to produce such an outstanding piece of literature. I had a friend in Greenwich Village who owned a drinking establishment, a writer, actor, and larger-than-life rollicking Irishman named Malachy McCourt. (He and his older brother, Frank, would both go on to write best-selling memoirs.) I gave Malachy a copy of the book and asked if he'd like to meet the author. The author was delighted to meet an authentic Irish barkeep. The first meeting at Malachy's bar began around 9:00 PM and continued long after last call. The affection between the two was palpable; they had an uncanny ability to make each other laugh. I had made a match.

Stein and Day was slated to soon publish a book titled *The Americans*, an Englishman's take on America, by TV host David Frost. I had placed a number of writers on his show through the years and was well-known to him and his staff. David also knew that I would be responsible for promoting his own book. I made an appointment with him and his producer and made the following pitch: Why not have Malachy McCourt (who was familiar to many viewers from his many appearances on *Ryan's Hope*, *Search for Tomorrow*, and *One Life to Live*) appear on the show with Christy? Malachy would read a few segments on camera, and if they were both tanked enough before they went on, Christy would be able to respond in a semi-understandable way.

It would be a different kind of live television, to be sure, but it would certainly get attention.

After much negotiation, that is:

David: Maybe they shouldn't drink before the show.

Me: If they don't, there's no show.

David: What if Christy falls off his chair?

Me: We'll strap him in. If the strap breaks, we'll take a commercial break, focus on the Irish musicians we hired for the spot, pick him up, and proceed from there.

We all knew by then that we could count on Malachy to improvise and make it work. And work it did! After the show, which was taped at the Little Theater next door to Sardi's, where Betty Friedan first appeared on *Girl Talk* in 1964, Stein and Day publishers Sol Stein and his wife Patricia Day hosted a dinner for the publishing staff, Christy, Malachy, and David Frost and his production team. Word of the show's success had obviously spread. When we made our entrance, the entire dining room stood up to applaud. It was the first time I had seen Christy cry.

I imagine I could have stayed with Stein and Day as long as I wished, but as I am sure you know by now, Natasha, there are certain things in life one cannot plan.

20

Mother's Last Decade: Montecatini, Italy

My mother left Grossinger's in 1962. The thought of starting a new life as she began her sixth decade must have been terrifying, though I never took it into account, and she never took me into her confidence. The previous year she had taken accumulated vacation time to find a place to live, and on one visit to Florence discovered, less than a half-hour away, the charming Tuscan village of Montecatini Terme. Montecatini was well known to society's elite—royalty, sophisticates, and socialites gathered there to "take the waters" at thermal spas reputed to cure conditions of the liver and add years to one's life. Jacqueline Kennedy Onassis, the Shah of Iran, Princess Grace of Monaco, Winston Churchill, Cary Grant, and King Hassan of Morocco were among the many noted visitors who graced Montecatini's cobblestone streets and stayed at the Grand Hotel La Pace.

My mother returned to Montecatini later that year, took a room in an inexpensive *pensione* nearby, and ingratiated herself to La Pace's managing director, Mr. Gino. By the time she departed three weeks later, she had been invited to become La Pace's and, by extension, Montecatini's unofficial ambassador to visiting Americans. Gino knew that Grossinger's catered to the wealthy American clientele he wanted to attract, and the fact that my mother was multilingual, was elegant, and had a European soul convinced him that he had made an admirable choice. That she also maintained contacts with former Grossinger guests and had a daughter in public relations in New York who could bring Montecatini to the attention of many potential guests added to her résumé. Gino offered her a home at La Pace. She would have no expenses. She would be treated as his personal guest.

I was equally enthralled with Montecatini the first time I visited. There were no buses, no streetcars; everything one might need was within walking distance. La Pace was only a short walk through lush gardens and verdant greenery to Tettucio Terme, the town's most famous spa. As early as seven o'clock each morning, tuxedo-attired violinists played Strauss waltzes as visitors walked counterclockwise around the designated paths, often in three-quarter time, sipping their sulfurous waters as they wished their liver spots away. Immediately thereafter they would repair to their respective hotels and gorge themselves on high-fat breakfasts.

My mother thrived in Montecatini. Quite a few Grossinger guests visited on her recommendation, and she knew exactly how to entertain them, which fashion designers they might want to meet, and the most interesting places in Florence to visit. She received medals and honors from city officials for the money she raised among guests for local charities, and her happiness, as she expressed it in her letters, was intoxicating.

My darling Tania, I sit writing this to you as I take my coffee in the lovely gardens of the spa. Montecatini is so beautiful early in the morning. The tranquility that exists here is unlike any I have ever known. I thank God for giving me this gift in my later years, the gift of nature and beauty and peace.

How fortunate I am to be able to be consciously alive every moment of the day, to have ears and eyes and a warm soul sensitive and responsive to beauty which surrounds me everywhere. I think my feeling of elation, of happiness, is transmitted to many people I come in contact with, so I make friends here easily.

The gala at the Museum where I was honored as *Donna* [an honorific connoting respect] Karla, Montecatini's best friend, was extremely successful. I looked very chic in a white caftan embroidered with gold piping given to me by the Queen Mother of Morocco. (Darling, if anything ever happens to me, be sure that you keep this lovely dress. It is worth a fortune!) The other day at the local market, most of the vendors greeted me with the usual "Buon Giorno, Donna Karla." They give me discounts without even being asked, saying it is a way to thank me for all that I do for them.

The Governor's wife invited me personally to the party given on June 2, the Independence Day of Italy. A Cardinal came from Rome along with my friend who is the Minister of State. Gino escorted me to a gala affair with all the Dignitaries. God is so good to me!

I wish God had been as good to her during the winter months when la Pace was closed and she returned to America.

It wasn't easy to tell my mother I was working for Playboy. Karla Grossinger had very puritanical ideas about sex, and here was her daughter working for a magazine that celebrated photos of quasi-naked women and a hedonistic lifestyle that was famous all over the world. I even considered the possibility she might disown me. Not for the last time, I underestimated her.

At first the only person to whom she mentioned my association with the magazine and Club was Gino (she wanted to make sure it wouldn't jeopardize her job). Au contraire! He recognized the buzz it would create at La Pace and immediately announced it to the entire staff. Their reactions took her by surprise. When could I send some copies? How many different centerfolds did I have? (She had to ask one of the guests what a centerfold was!) The word spread to shopkeepers and cafe owners, who requested that when I came to visit, I bring copies of *Playboy* for them. Her pride in me increased exponentially when she learned that I could entertain freely at the Club. Many of the doctors associated with the spas in Montecatini came to New York for medical seminars, and my mother reveled in extending invitations on my behalf for them to spend an evening with the Playboy Bunnies. As long as people in Montecatini were impressed that I worked for Playboy, I got the feeling that my mother wouldn't have cared if the magazine showed pictures of actual fornication. My association with Playboy made her important; that was what counted.

The first winter La Pace was closed, my mother came back to New York and shuttled between my apartment (my roommate had moved out the year before) and Grossinger relatives who lived in Jersey City. She asked me, as she had promised Gino, to place her on talk shows so that she could promote Montecatini and La Pace, and I was only too happy to comply. Virginia Graham at *Girl Talk*, whom my mother had also known at Grossinger's and who, by now, had forgiven me for the Betty Friedan incident, was happy to have my mother on her syndicated TV show, as were all the other broadcasters whom I asked for a favor. My mother was a natural on air—gracious, charming, and possessed with an enviable facility for tactful but titillating name dropping. The Countess this, the Prime Minister that—she was a walking chronicler of the European high and mighty, which audiences seemed to find fascinating. She also wanted to visit the Playboy Club, where even among the semi-clad Bunnies she felt surprisingly comfortable. She knew it would make for entertaining conversation when she returned to La Pace.

The problem was that she had few friends in New York. When she stayed in my Greenwich Village apartment, she was no longer a star, and there was little either of us could do about it. The woman who moved into my apartment had left the charming Donna Karla a continent behind. In her place was a control freak with a desperate need to be the center of attention.

Everything I did was wrong. The way I decorated my apartment. The clothes I wore. "You still have no taste!" She made my friends uncomfortable, belittled my accomplishments, monopolized conversations, and spoke only about herself. Scenarios changed unpredictably. One day she was dependent on me. She wanted me to love her unconditionally and overlook, if not condone, her faults. I couldn't do it. To ask for unconditional love when my childhood was so full of conditions was unfair. As a child I would have given my life for a mother who loved me even when I was ten pounds overweight, someone I could depend on and count on to protect me from the people she knew tried to take sexual advantage of me and who would stand up for me when I was treated shabbily by the Grossinger family. Then the relationship would change. She wanted to be a mother. What she wanted then was that I confide in her, ask her advice, and open my heart to her. I couldn't do that, either, and for damn good reason. I was aware for years that whatever lip service she gave to loving me didn't make up for the shattering truth that she never liked me. She didn't like my lifestyle, my friends, the way I looked, the men I chose to go out with. She didn't like that I had begun to turn to alcohol to help me through the nights when she was living with me. There was nothing about me that she liked, unless for some reason it made her look good. Then, yet another transition. One winter, the day before she arrived in New York, I was hospitalized once again for my Tietze syndrome, the inflammation of cartilages between the rib cage and diaphragm. Her first words to my friend Barbara were, "How could she do this to me?"

She visited twice during the twenty-one days I was there.

When I was finally released, she was forever at my side. Not for companionship, but so that I would pick up the tab when we went out. She held my hand as if we were lovers. I had been assigned yet another role: the partner. It was desperation. It was loneliness. It was also confusing and so very, very sad. I probably could have been kinder and more understanding, and could have tried harder to be more like the daughter she always wished I had turned out to be. But she didn't make it easy for me, and I failed each time I made the attempt.

In the spring of 1971, the last time she was in New York, after eleven seasons at La Pace, it was increasingly complicated to find a level on which we could communicate. Her jealousy of any success I had was horrible. A friend came by to congratulate me on being listed in *Who's Who of American Women*, an accomplishment I was smart enough not to have mentioned. Her reaction was predictable: "The only reason I wasn't chosen was because I wasn't born in America."

When she left at the end of that March to return to Montecatini, we were not on good terms. It was the last time I saw my mother.

21

Death Takes Its Toll

I was still asleep when the phone rang. "It's a good thing you're not still married to Neil," the voice on the other end said. "He's dead." I could barely make out the words. Something about a head-on collision, drunk, not the first time. "You don't know how lucky you are!" It was my aunt and uncle in Detroit, the relatives who had introduced us in 1958 and in whose home we had been married four months later.

Lucky? My fingers lost all feeling, and the rest of me soon followed. It had been eleven years since Neil and I were in touch, but my feelings of guilt were still palpable. He died before we could ask for each other's forgiveness.

I still had his letters. Every October 19, the date of our anniversary, I slipped on my wedding band before I went to sleep and tried to remember the good times. We had parted as friends, but the sentiment, as most women who've lived through broken marriages will attest, didn't last long. Letters I sent the first year were returned unopened, calls when I was a patient at the City of Hope in 1960 went unanswered, and after that I gave up. That my marriage to Neil damaged me was a fact of my life. He never apologized to me. That was his choice. But there were two of us in the relationship, and I'd hurt him, too. I believed that without acknowledging where I was at fault I could never fully relate to another man. I needed to apologize in person. Now it would never come to pass.

Late that Sunday I placed a call to his brother, Ray. I'd known through a mutual friend that Neil had gone off the deep end in the years since I'd left, turning to liquor and drugs. His family knew that I was the one who walked away from the marriage, and Ray blamed me for everything that happened thereafter. "You killed him," were his exact words. "I hope you're happy now."

Two people almost died that day.

When my mother returned to Italy, she reassumed the rhythm of her beloved European life. I abided by her request and wrote two or three times each week, never quite sure whether she actually wanted to hear from me, or whether when the *charge d'affaires* who sorted the mail strolled through the lobby to deliver the letters, it made her feel important. "See how much my daughter loves me? She writes almost every day!"

Her letters overflowed with repetitions of compliments paid her by society people she met in Montecatini, quotes from articles mentioning her, and more honors she had been selected to receive. She was still gloriously happy at La Pace. If only, she repeated letter after letter, she had a daughter who loved her.

The cable from Italy was under my door when I returned from work. "Dear Tania," it read. "Am near you. Our beloved Donna Karla left us this afternoon in Roma, Hotel Flora. Call for me anytime. I shall be there for you. Tuo, Gino." The cable made no sense. La Pace had closed for the season that day, and my mother had planned to spend a week in Rome before visiting guests she had met at La Pace in Johannesburg. After that she would return to New York. So why was Gino sending me a telegram confirming what I already knew, that she left that morning for Rome? I obviously hadn't read it very carefully.

The message on my answering machine was more specific. The U.S. State Department confirmed a cable it was about to send stating that Karla Seifer Grossinger was found dead at the Flora Hotel, Rome, Italy, November 1, 1971, 15:15. Her passport number and other details followed. "Body identified by Gino Mariottini, Director General, Grand Hotel La Pace, Montecatini, Italy. Please advise what arrangements to make." My cousin Paul at Grossinger's was also notified and had spoken to Gino by the time I was able to reach him. He explained that my mother had joined friends for lunch when she reached Rome early that afternoon. Toward the end of the meal she mentioned feeling uncomfortable, and they drove her back to the hotel. According to the hotel's manager, thirty minutes later she called for a doctor and said she was having difficulty breathing. By the time the doctor arrived, no more than ten minutes after her call, her heart had given out. Gino, her emergency contact, immediately drove down from Montecatini to make the identification and notify the American Consulate.

My mother, Donna Karla, the woman who had given birth to me, had died alone, a continent away, the one thing in life she dreaded. Just like that. Over and out. Frightened. Alone. Nothing.

I can't recall my emotions the moment I heard she had died. All I remember was a black hole. Anger? Sadness? Relief? Regret? These would all manifest in due time. At the moment I had decisions to make and a myriad of details to attend to. I didn't shed a tear.

The Special Consular Services duty officer at the State Department was most helpful. I was told to wire $1,300 to the embassy in Rome so that it could release and send the body to its final destination. Getting the money together was not the problem. The problem was the final destination. It was a subject my mother and I had never discussed.

Where did she want to be buried? I had no idea. Her brother Fabian in Detroit didn't know, either. My father had been buried in Chicago shortly after I was born, but there had never been mention of a family plot. Cremation? Gino had a suggestion that might have pleased her, but I was hesitant to accept. There was a convent, The Little Nuns of Montecatini Alto, for which she often raised funds from guests at La Pace. The Mother Superior held my mother in such esteem that as soon as she heard of my mother's death (a headline in the major newspaper in Florence read DONNA KARLA DI MONTECANTI ESTE MORTE; my mother would have been proud of that), she called Gino and graciously offered to bury my mother on the convent's hallowed grounds. I was most touched by her offer, noting, I'm almost ashamed to add, that it would exempt me from the responsibility of having to make arrangements in America. At the same time I recognized that the nuns most likely didn't know that my mother was Jewish, which could make things very complicated. Gino assured me that he and the convent could work things out, as long as I didn't mention it to anyone at La Pace and the burial took place immediately. I was so tempted to say yes. My mother loved Montecatini more than any place in the world, but because of a promise I had made to her years earlier, there was no possible way I could leave New York in time for a burial in Italy.

Before my mother left Grossinger's in 1962, she told me that she had bought $20,000 worth of U.S. savings bonds in both of our names. If something happened to her (the only time in her life we discussed her death), I had to promise that my first act, before notifying anyone, was to remove them from the safety deposit box she had rented in a bank near my apartment, for which she then gave me a key. She knew that as long as she lived, no matter how badly I was in need, I would never touch them without permission. "Even before you cry," she added, explaining that it had to do with my not having to pay an inheritance tax if I cashed them before anyone discovered she was no longer alive. Then and only then was I to send an obituary to the *New York Times*. "Make sure it is long, my darling, and very complimentary.

And promise not to tell them my age." I followed her instructions and was the first person at the bank the next morning. I would need money to pay burial expenses.

Paul Grossinger had already notified members of the Grossinger family in Chicago, and my cousin Rose, whose father was my father's brother, benevolently took it upon herself to make the necessary arrangements at a cemetery not far from where both of our fathers were buried. I couldn't have been more grateful. Gino was able to tell the nuns in Montecatini with more than a slight exaggeration that my mother wished to be buried next to her husband, and I was able to direct the State Department to send my mother's body to a funeral home in Chicago, satisfied that the right decision had been made.

I was still waiting to cry.

I sent her obituary to the *New York Times*. I had included her age as seventy, unknowingly subtracting three years (she was seventy-three when she died, which I didn't know until I later saw her passport's date of birth). I hoped she understood that even in death I tried to do exactly as she asked.

I took three days off from work, welcomed friends who came by to extend condolences, and waited for calls or visits from relatives, hotel guests, or staff who had known her for years. In that regard it was a shockingly lonely *shiva*!

I flew to Chicago with my cousin Paul three days before the funeral. The funeral home had waited until my arrival to identify the body. I couldn't bring myself to do it. Karla, the mother I remembered, even though we had our differences, was vibrant, beautiful, alive—I couldn't bear to see her lying all alone in an unadorned wooden coffin. I asked a cousin to do the honors. It was a cowardly thing to do. One more action that would come back to haunt me.

I still hadn't shed a tear.

That Saturday evening, my cousin Rose and her husband hosted a family dinner at their private club, followed by brunch the following day, which my Detroit relatives attended. I went through both at my robotic best. My mother was buried in the Austro-Galician section of the Waldheim cemetery in Forest Park that Monday. Prayers were uttered by an Orthodox rabbi I had never met, and then it was over. I stood back in complete silence. I didn't belong there. I didn't belong in a cemetery surrounded by dead people. I ached to run away.

22

After My Mother Died

My Aunt Regina, a first cousin to my father, and my Uncle Meyer opened their home to my mother during the Montecatini off-seasons when her staying with me became unbearable for us both. Meyer was a well-known lawyer and Jewish activist in Jersey City, and he and Regina were the only Grossinger relatives not financially or emotionally dependent on the hotel. My mother trusted them implicitly.

In February 1965, she had asked Meyer to draw up her will and be its executor. It is important that you understand how I felt about anything I might inherit from my mother. I never coveted her money, I never believed I was entitled to it, and I never depended on it.

Bequests in that will were made in varying degrees to Gino and specific charities in Montecatini for which she had raised money. The "rest, residue, and remainder of my estate, whether real or personal, and wherever situate" was left to me.

It was written five years before I made an off-the-cuff remark to my mother that if I ever had $1,000, I would consider investing it in a show being put together by friends who already had a series of hits on Broadway. The idea that if by some miracle I ever ended up with that kind of money I'd put it in a Broadway show was simply ludicrous. Anybody who knew me would have known that! At the time the words came tumbling out I was just trying to make conversation with her, to fill a void across a dinner table. Because of my comment, she determined that I didn't know the value of money (the fact that I had been self-supporting since I was nineteen obviously stood for nothing), which caused her to ask Uncle Meyer to draw up a second will—one that, I was to discover, made it only too clear that it wasn't only money she was withholding; it was also her confidence in me, her respect, and, as always, her love.

In late 1970, on receipt of new instructions that a lawyer guest at La Pace had written out for my mother, and distressed by its content, Uncle Meyer wrote my mother a letter, which he also sent to me without her knowledge. It was the first time I was aware of the details. It read in part:

> Your stated provisions leave Tania your estate as follows: 10% when she reaches age 35, 10% more at age 40, 20% more at age 50, and the balance of 60% at age 60. It is my personal feeling that this could possibly work an injustice to her should she ever be in need. Karla, dear, Tania is now 33. She has the maturity of judgment, in my opinion, of those older and wiser than we. Often we truly fail to see the trees because of the forest. Therefore, please do not be offended if I suggest to you that you do not extend your motherly love and concern beyond the age of thirty-five. The psalmist said long ago, "Ah, if man were but mindful of his latter end." As God-fearing people we are mindful that our lives are in His hands. Thus we act as beings with a moral sense of values and good conscience. I beg you to reconsider and write to me what you would have me do with your new will. May God be with you and give you long life, health and happiness.

> He never heard back.

When I called with news of my mother's death, after offering condolences and support, Uncle Meyer asked if I had a copy of my mother's second will. I told him that I had only a copy of the letter he had sent her. The following day he told me that after going through all of his files, he was unable to locate his copy of that will, and he asked if the American Consul in Rome mentioned finding it among her possessions. I said no. "Since we are the only two people who knew of the second testament," he then said, "and no copy of it seems to exist, it appears I have no choice but to offer the first will, which I do have and has been duly witnessed, for probate." And that is exactly what my beloved Uncle Meyer did for me. After the bequests, I would inherit everything outright.

Considering her estate was so uncomplicated—no debts, no real estate holdings, a few blue chip stocks (AT&T, General Electric, and Chase Manhattan Bank), two minimal savings accounts in Manhattan banks, and a safe deposit box in Montecatini, I thought settling it would take place in a matter of months. But, thanks to idiotic Italian bureaucracy, it took close to two years and endless trips to Montecatini to settle everything.

My first visit to Italy started out on a high note and quickly ended in disaster. Most impressive was the memorial service for my mother the day I arrived, which was attended by every dignitary in Montecatini, including the governor of the state, the mayor, and the chief of police. Also in the audience were newspaper editors from surrounding towns, nuns from the convent, directors of the many cultural institutions she raised money for, all of the neighboring hotel and café owners, the entire staff of La Pace, and as many of the local residents as could fit into the church. The highlight of the celebration took place when I was asked to unveil a stunning bust of my mother sculpted by a local artist that was so incredibly lifelike that I almost lost my balance.

It was later placed in a position of honor at the entrance of the Accademia Dell'Arte, the town's most prominent museum.

I had with me a letter from the American Consulate in Rome listing all the effects my mother had on her person and in her room (including their monetary value) at the Hotel Flora the day she died. What they considered "a fair and just appraisal" of her belongings, I will never understand. They listed, among other things, six fancy cotton dresses, which they evaluated at $12; twelve pairs of gloves, mostly cloth, $6; brown coat with fur collar, $15; gold-colored knit stole, $2; red silk scarf, $1; mink stole, $50 (this was missing when I was finally able to reclaim her property); and assorted hats and boots, nil (worth less than nothing). Among "articles of sentimental value" were a gold charm bracelet and a ring with small diamonds, both valued at $50, both of which were not returned. Even after numerous certificates were duly signed, stamped, and notarized by authorities in both Italy and America, getting those "effects" released to Gino took close to six weeks.

My mother's other possessions were stored in her former room, #642, in the Grand Hotel La Pace. La Pace was closed for the winter, which meant there was no heat or electricity. It was a cold, damp, and dreary January. Gino had made arrangements for me to stay at the nearby Hotel Centrale, to which, as one of only three guests, I repaired each evening for a tasteless meal washed down with a half-liter of red wine, which helped take the edge off my loneliness and keep me warm, and unfortunately led me into restless, nightmare-ridden sleep. Each morning Gino, his head housekeeper, and I huddled on the floor of #642, emptying out overstuffed boxes, old suitcases, and more boxes. Candles provided our only light and heat, and we all caught ferocious colds. My mother always joked about living like a gypsy. It was an exaggeration, to be sure, but looking at the mess on the floor, I was beginning to think she was right.

I was embarrassed, in front of Gino and the housekeeper, to unpack what she had left there. Cheap hats and purses, many from the straw market in Florence, gaudy costume jewelry nobody had ever seen her wear, corsets and girdles I thought went out of style in the 1950s, and nondescript sweaters, skirts, and short jackets. What had happened to the beautiful suits and elegant evening wear she had accumulated through the years? The satin handbags, silk blouses, and Hermès scarves, many of them gifts from visiting guests that she wore at diplomatic events? Where was the white caftan with gold piping given to her by the Queen Mother of Morocco, which she admonished me to be sure to keep? Had someone broken into her room after the hotel had closed? Had she pawned some of her possessions? What had happened to Karla? Who was the woman whose remains I was scrambling through in Room 642? I still can't make sense of it. After two or three days pawing through boxes I couldn't bear to look at anymore, I realized I didn't care. What was gone was gone. She made it quite clear with the writing of her second will that she never wanted me to enjoy anything of hers; I had lived well enough for thirty-four years without her possessions, and I'd live another thirty-four the same way. I told Gino to first clean and then put everything back in the boxes. For all we knew, there were valuables underneath many of the things we hadn't yet unpacked. It made no difference. I suggested that we send everything to the nuns in the convent. Let them auction whatever she left behind to raise money for the poor. At least it would do someone some good. All I took for myself were the oversized envelopes of unfamiliar notebooks, papers, and photographs she had carried with her, but never shared, everywhere she traveled. Her secrets.

The year 1972 remains a blur. Uncle Meyer took over the role of executor with great alacrity, and I assisted whenever asked, searching out lawyers with ties to the Italian Consulate to coordinate with lawyers in Montecatini, closing out my mother's bank accounts, transferring stocks to my name, and keeping Uncle Meyer apprised of everything going on at Gino's end. The sticking point was a safe deposit box my mother had taken out in both of our names at a bank in Montecatini. Even with certified copies of the death certificate, proof of my identity, and my having given Gino my power of attorney, the bank would not let us open the box. The papers were never sufficient. I wanted to give up. Gino, however, expecting that I might find at least some of the jewelry we knew my mother once owned and perhaps some additional money, insisted that we follow through. The director of the bank came up with one intricate excuse after the other. We asked advice, we cajoled, we showed anger. Nothing worked until Gino threatened to pull La Pace's very major account out of the bank if the safety deposit box wasn't turned over immediately. That did it. No more procrastination. On July 6, 1973, back in New York, I received his cable: "Finally everything cleared!"

This is what we found in the box: $1,339 in cash, less than what I had already spent on air transport to and from Italy. Jewelry? I had her various rings, necklaces, and bracelets appraised for insurance purposes shortly after I returned home. Their total worth? $1,600. Either someone stole valuables in her absence, or they remained hidden in boxes I left behind. I can't help thinking it was the nuns in Montecatini Alto who came off best.

The unveiling of my mother's headstone in Chicago was on September 3, 1972. I still hadn't made peace with her death . . . or life. My Uncle Meyer and Aunt Regina flew to Chicago, as did my relatives from Detroit, to join me and our family there. It was a short and simple ceremony, tastefully done. At the very end, Uncle Meyer asked to say a few words. He took out a letter, which he explained was given to him by my mother on October 7, 1949, when I was twelve years old and she was about to take her first vacation away from Grossinger's. He was the only person who had ever seen it.

My dearest, darling Baby,

Just a few lines before I am leaving on my trip to Europe. I am not going to stay long but if something should happen to me, I want you to know that you are my greatest blessing and that I thank God every day for giving you to me. You are a wonderful girl with a good heart and good character and I hope and pray you should grow up well and be a fine woman. I know you will. You have a wonderful clear mind and a good heart; you will always use good judgment. Be always honest, have courage and know that life is good as God is good. God is good to me and believe me I always counted my blessings. I pray he should give me enough years and health to bring you up right. You had a wonderful father; he was loved and respected by everybody. He was a wonderful husband and we were so very happy together. I do hope that you will meet a fine, wonderful man and that you will have fine, wonderful children, full of love like you are. Be always full of love, give love to people, you will get more love from them. Be happy, don't cry and if something should happen to me, please don't mourn. Life at its best is so short and I would not want to see you unhappy. I will always watch over you and be always near you. You are my Baby and I love you oh so very, very much. Forgive me please if I scolded you. I am so proud of you and wanted you to be perfect. Every child needs guidance. I am only sorry that I had to work, was always tired and had not much patience. You are smart and understanding and I do know that you understand and forgive. Keep up your reading, listen to good music; books and music are wonderful friends. Be a good friend and an upright woman. You will have the respect of everybody. As to boys, please Darling, please don't just go out with anybody. Wait until you will fall in love, as love is the most beautiful thing in this world. Remember all our little talks we had; when you will meet the right man you will be so much happier as you will have so much more to give him. Well, darling, the music is on. They are playing a wonderful Viennese waltz. My heart is so full of love for God and you and I pray I shall come back to you in good health and we shall enjoy many good hours together. Amen.

All my love to you, Darling. Bless you, Mama

And then, holding on to the headstone for support, for the first time since my mother died, I cried.

23

Running Away from It All

After half of the $20,000 savings bonds was dispersed for bequests, expenses including flying my mother's body to Chicago from Italy, the funeral, my multiple travels to Montecatini, taxes, and legal fees, I retained close to $15,000, including her stocks and money left in her New York bank accounts (minus the contents of her safety deposit box in Italy, which wouldn't be mine until the next year). It was less than I expected but probably more than I deserved, and I felt guilty even thinking of touching it. Her inheritance was not a gift—her second will hadn't even intended for me to have it—it was not left with love, so I pledged to turn to it only in an extreme emergency. I was confident I'd always find a way to support myself and that my life was not going to change financially with the end of hers.

In the year 1972 I spent more than six months away from home in the Village. The airlines had a curious fee structure in those days. It was cheaper to fly to Italy for a stay of three weeks than it was to return within a week. Gino pointed this out to me after my first visit, along with the suggestion that because he was in a position to arrange complimentary hotel accommodations in places I had never been, I should take advantage of staying in Italy. And that's exactly what I did, not having the vaguest idea I was laying the groundwork for a future career.

I was not exactly a novice traveler. I had, during my Playboy years, made trips to London and Paris, the Caribbean and Mexico, and, of course, when my mother was alive, Montecatini, Florence, and Rome. But this time it was different. Because I couldn't juggle both my position at Stein and Day and my travel back and forth to Italy to sort out my mother's estate, I had been forced to resign. I now had no job, no mother with whom I was obligated to keep in touch, and no boyfriend. I had only myself.

The stamps in my passport began to resemble the colorful stickers on steamer trunks wealthy travelers brought aboard grand ocean liners. I flew to Rome, of course, Milan, Madrid, Lisbon, the charming towns of Santa Margherita and Portofino on the Italian Riviera, Torremolinos and Marbella on Spain's Costa del Sol, the intriguing cities of Marrakesh, Casablanca, and Fez, the breathtaking Atlas mountains in Morocco, and, finally, Guatemala, at the invitation of an American family I had met through my mother in Montecatini.

—⁜—

Spring, 1972. Santa Margherita, Italy. Still mourning the loss of my mother, I am staying at a hotel she once frequented. It is low season, few guests, and I am too much alone. I wander aimlessly up a hidden path, mesmerized by the lure of a flute and distant drum. I find myself on a secluded terrace where there are no diners, only the two musicians and a bartender who pours champagne. He points me to a chair. The instrumentalists continue to play. No one speaks. The four of us sip drinks, each in our own separate world. Sadness floats away.

The next day I attempt to retrace my steps. I never hear the music again.

—⁜—

Palm Sunday, 1972. Lake Atitlan, Guatemala. The night before I leave, the manager of the hotel invites me to join him the next morning for a 5:00 AM boat trip around the lake. The sky is black as we depart, the stillness pervasive, awesome, almost mystical, as if the world has disappeared and we remain. We cruise slowly around the lake's perimeter, periodically joined by small families of Indians in canoes carrying palm fronds in honor of the pre-Easter holiday, our hushed escorts as we sail from one native village to another. Two hours later the sun begins to rise as we make our way silently across the water back to the hotel, once again feeling alone in the world, once again alone with God.

To this day, whenever I have trouble falling asleep—or my dentist suggests I meditate on something beautiful—I think back to Palm Sunday, Lake Atitlan, and peace.

—⁂—

It was a remarkable series of adventures, but after all the traveling, I still had to come to grips with the question, "What now?" Beyond my inheritance I had put aside enough money to support myself for almost a year. I wanted to explore new opportunities and be on my own, even if it meant giving up professional status, a paycheck I could depend on, and expense accounts. I couldn't possibly have predicted how my life was going to change, but for certain I knew the time to find out was then.

My mother haunted my dreams, crying that I didn't mourn her sufficiently, threatening to destroy me if I dared to spend her money, and badgering me for not continuing to write. I would wake up petrified. She wasn't watching over me, as she promised in the letter Uncle Meyer read at her graveside. If she was, she would know I finally did cry over her death and that I had no intention of spending her money. Perhaps then she would also forgive me for not writing to her—and I'd be able to sleep through the nights.

24

Karla's Letters Discovered

It took more than a decade; I was close to forty-five before I could open the folder marked PERSONAL that I had brought back from Montecatini. I knew there were aspects of my mother's life that she never wanted me to know about. Had she not died so suddenly, and had I been a better person, I might have honored what was likely one of her last wishes, that her privacy be preserved, but at the time it was more important that I seek the truth about the enigma who gave birth to me.

My mother was three years older than I knew (born in 1898, thirty-nine years old when she gave birth to me, and seventy-three when she died). Many women lie about their age, so I can't pretend to be shocked. What did stun me, however, was discovering that her academic credentials, of which I was always so proud, were a fraud. For years, at her instigation and following her lead, I bragged how my mother not only spoke thirteen languages and had graduated the University of Vienna with a bachelor's and master's degree but was just one year shy of her Ph.D. in philosophy at Northwestern, which she pursued as soon as she came to Chicago. Transcripts from the University of Vienna show not only that she didn't receive a master's but also that it took from 1919 to 1925, six years, to earn her first degree. According to her marriage certificate, she married my father, whom she met in Vienna, in 1921. Passenger records confirmed by the Ellis Island Foundation list his arrival in America aboard the *S.S. Cleveland* on May 1, 1923, two years later. Alone. There is no record of her traveling with him, and her transcripts verify that she continued as a full-time student at the University of Vienna for the next two years.

She joined my father in Chicago at some point in 1925. A Transcript of Record issued by the Graduate School of Northwestern University attests to her attendance (under her maiden name) for six years between then and 1930. During that period she accumulated only nineteen semester hours, not even enough to qualify for the master's degree she pretended to have. Her supposed lifelong desire to become professor of philosophy, which she sacrificed in order to give me such a *wonderful* life at Grossinger's (not to mention render me guilty for decades) was nothing more than a self-serving chimera.

There was also something strange about the year 1927. According to the registrar at Northwestern, she was excused from taking classes both semesters "by order of a licensed physician." A different letter from the school's dean to the director of the Immigration Bureau in Washington requested permission for her to be able to return on her student visa after a visit to Vienna to see her family (who lived in Poland, not Vienna). A third communication was written that year by a politically connected businessman beseeching the recipient to expedite the process whereby she could become an American citizen, pointing out that she was currently on staff of one of the leading real estate developers in Chicago. Which variation of her life in 1927 was true, I have no idea. What I found significant was that she had already learned, as a comparatively young newcomer to this country, how to somehow befriend important people and fudge the truth when it was to her advantage.

My mother fell in love with Paolo on a Mediterranean cruise in 1934, three years before I was born. I was familiar with his name even before I read his letters. I accidentally found a photo of him in her

dresser at Grossinger's, which uncharacteristically moved her to confess that he was a man she was once very much in love with. That my
mother loved a man who was not my father was terrible for me to hear.
I remember blurting out, "How could you do that to my father?" Her
response, which probably says more about her than she would ever
want anyone to know: "I paid my own way!"

Paolo was Australia's trade representative to Italy. He was dignified, cultured, my mother's intellectual equal (unlike my father), and,
like my mother, also married, although his family supposedly stayed
behind when he was posted to Rome. His letters, dating from 1935
until the late 1950s, were filled with references to requited love and
memories of moonlit nights in Venice, Assisi, and Rome. They also
included lighthearted scolds for my mother's not writing more often.
While my father was still alive, she arranged for Paolo to send his letters
in care of a confidante in the suburbs. After my father died, Paolo sent
a tender cable of condolence from Italy asking if my mother needed
him by her side. In 1941, when we lived in California, she sent him a
photo, which he accepted as "a beautiful precious talisman" he would
forever keep close to his heart. I was often mentioned in his missives.
"Please let me kiss, through you, darling, your sweet, beautiful baby,"
or "that little treasure of yours, that lovely daughter that I will meet
someday, sooner than you think, perhaps." Referring to a trip he was
about to make back to Australia, he wrote, "I hope not to appear too
pretentious, but I am *sure* everything will be over by spring." If by that
he meant he was leaving his wife, it was not to happen.

One of the last letters my mother received was at Grossinger's in
1951, when Paolo was in New York bemoaning the fact that so many
years had passed since they were together. If their attachment had been
as passionate as his correspondence led me to believe (how I wish I
could have read her letters!), I wondered why she hadn't arranged to

see him then or on one of the many other visits he seems to have made to America. I thought of the journal she started in Montecatini: "I was always very romantic and dreamt a lot about a wonderful man whom I would meet someday and love forever. I never wanted to compromise. I did always the most and best I could in my work but I would not compromise with my soul. I never gave up my ideals. I wanted to be an ideal woman and I was that to many wonderful men who loved and idolized me and have never forgotten me." Maybe she suspected that her epistolary romance with Paolo was preferable to what real life could provide?

We moved to Los Angeles twenty months after my father died. After my father's estate was settled in 1938, my mother was left with $1,000 ($15,000 in today's currency) from a trust fund—enough for someone of her courage and cunning to start a new life. It was only after she died that I discovered she never cashed the check.

There was no reason my mother, a single, most attractive woman, shouldn't have had an active social life; I simply wish that she hadn't felt it important to hold on to some of the more graphic correspondence. She was, shall we say, full of surprises. Among her many suitors was the "horse doctor." He was a physician wealthy enough to own a ranch in the San Fernando Valley, where he kept horses that he let me feed whenever we stayed over. My mother told me that I was so fond of him that I once crawled onto his lap and whispered, "I really hope you are going to marry my mommy, 'cause then she can stop working and spend all her time with me." Shortly after that he broke off the relationship, and I was told it was my fault.

The man she and I grew to love most was Jack Gunnerson, my soon to be "Uncle Jack." I believe they met not long after we arrived from Chicago, and they were together on and off for at least four years. He was from a well-known society family in Los Angeles and was involved with a newspaper conglomerate called the Associated Filipino Press. Uncle Jack and my mother were deeply involved (I didn't realize how much until I found those letters), even though she stopped seeing him periodically because she said he drank too much. I suspect Uncle Jack asked my mother to marry him, but suddenly he, too, disappeared from our lives. One morning a story appeared in the society pages of the *Los Angeles Times* announcing his elopement to a woman half his age. My mother cried a lot that day. His name was never mentioned again.

At least my mother had a job to keep her occupied. As you know, in the early 1940s Mr. John was the most celebrated designer of millinery in America. Well-known doyennes of society, stage, and screen for whom he created unusual headwear included the Duchess of Windsor, Vivian Leigh, Gloria Swanson, Greta Garbo, and Marlene Dietrich. I often wonder how, with no experience in fashion, my mother talked herself into becoming manager of John-Frederics, his elegant Rodeo Drive salon in Beverly Hills. She must have had the backing of some very influential people to be offered such a glamorous position.

Among her treasures I discovered issues of *Photoplay, Silver Screen,* and other movie magazines belonging to her new French identity, Mme. Savonier, with images of Gloria Vanderbilt, Zsa Zsa Gabor, and Joan Crawford. I now believe at least one of the reasons I was sent to the Christian Science Sunday School two blocks from where we lived was because Joan Crawford's two daughters attended there. Column items described my mother as being squired by Prince Michael Romanoff, owner of the celebrity-studded eatery Romanoff's (often accused of a shadowy past, he was even more a creature of self-reinvention than she was), along with other distinguished members of the Hollywood community. I recall tagging along with my mother to an extravagant Christmas party (I was warned beforehand not to tell anyone my last name) hosted by Elsie de Wolfe, the legendary interior designer known internationally as Lady Mendl. A photo of little Tania curtseying in front of the Lady even made the cover of a local newspaper. I'm sorry my mother didn't preserve it.

In the beginning of 1944, the life my mother so carefully crafted for herself came to an end. Flowers for Mme. Savonier no longer graced the front of our door. Invitations to glamorous parties were no longer tendered. She was distracted and acted in ways I didn't understand. Sometimes she couldn't pick me up at boarding school, and I would have to stay there for the weekend. When I did come home, she made me go to the kitchen when she spoke on the phone. She even seemed to be afraid to go out at night. It was a terrible time, and it broke my heart to see her that way.

Many years later, when I was living in New York, I ran into Mr. John, the famous milliner for whom my mother worked, on West 57th St. We exchanged hugs and pleasantries, and I finally managed to ask what had been disturbing me for all the many years—why he had fired my mother. His answer was as mysterious as the situation. "It caught up with her." He refused to explain.

I understand much better now why Jennie's offer to relocate the two of us to Grossinger's in 1945 when I was eight years old was so inviting. I was under the impression that my mother's decision was based on Jennie's promise that I would finally have a family. Perhaps she also knew it was in her own best interests to get away from Los Angeles. Once we were ensconced at Grossinger's, I was even forbidden to write the friends I left behind at school. When asked about her past, she always changed the subject, and I was told to politely answer, "I don't know," when anyone questioned me. That was easy enough for me to do.

Perhaps as a consequence of having a secretive mother and an overactive imagination, the loose strings she left behind continue to frustrate me. Do I believe she had ties to organized crime or that she was involved in something illegal? No. I think it's possible she had an association with a security agency headquartered either here or in Europe. There are so many holes in my mother's biography, beginning with her first visit to America. What to make of the influential figures in Chicago in 1927 who ensured that she could travel to Europe and back in spite of the immigration quota in place? What to make of her staying behind in Vienna for two years after she married my father? Or her ability, considering her limited background, to insinuate herself into relationships with people who would alter her life in unexplainable ways? How did she meet so many of the men she befriended in California? Why were they so often "on the road"? How could she afford her fashionable outfits, her solo vacations, and my expensive schooling, especially after she lost her job at John-Frederics? Certainly her salary didn't cover those expenditures. And yet it was possible that men showered her with gifts because she was charming and good company—but my instinct tells me it was more than that. Rumors abounded that Prince Mike Romanoff was an agent for the FBI. Did that have anything to do with his relationship with my mother? And what did "it caught up to her" mean? Had she really at some point in California outlived her usefulness, and, if so, what was the usefulness she outlived? What exactly was the Associated Filipino Press, and why was Jack Gunnerson traipsing all over the country on its behalf? I asked a friend who was an FBI agent to see if he could track it down. "As a news operation it never existed," he told me. "It was either a shell corporation, a company that serves as a vehicle for business transactions without itself having significant assets or operations or a cover, not uncommonly set up by the FBI."

Maybe I didn't do the right thing in reading what wasn't mine to read, after all. One of my mother's favorite maxims comes to mind: "Don't ask the question if you're not prepared for the answer." Perhaps this time I should have listened to my mother.

25

Seeking Professional Help

"**A**nd I hate myself for being alive!" After a few drinks, having these words come from my mouth scared the hell out of me. It would be absurd to think, knowing the unique pressures I experienced growing up, that I wouldn't have psychological problems as an adult—especially just a year after my mother died. But still.

I did once ask my mother for financial assistance, even offering to return it with interest, but was promptly turned down. "I should loan you money so you can tell a psychiatrist what a terrible mother you have?"

I thought I could handle life's crises, self-imposed and otherwise, on my own, but after my drunken outburst, I knew I had to reach out.

Finding a psychiatrist wasn't easy. My physician gave me a referral who, even before getting to the standard opener, "Why are you here?" told me that he could never get a reservation at Grossinger's for Passover. The fact that I wasn't in a position to help his case agitated him even more. Fortunately, someone else directed me to the Postgraduate Center for Mental Health, a well-regarded clinic that accepted patients at a fee I could afford. It was not easy. I was reluctant to trust and expert at masking feelings and detouring conversations away from the personal. When necessary to protect myself from hurt, I lied. Ed Stephens, the psychiatrist assigned to me, would have none of it. Finally, with enviable patience, coupled with my realization that if I didn't open up soon, I was wasting both time and money, he managed to help me. I saw him twice weekly, and our time was largely spent dissecting the many layers of conflict between my mother and me. I became aware of my self-destructive patterns, including the belief that I could never have what everyone else had and would always have to settle for second best. I realized I would "rehearse" in excruciating detail an array of doomsday scenarios relating to infidelities, death, and disasters involving myself and people I loved.

Two years after our first conference, Dr. Stephens, reflecting on the progress we had made, suggested it was time for our sessions to end.

I was confident I would never again loathe myself for being on this earth. At least I hoped not. I pray that during your lifetime you will never have to deal with such a damaged self-image.

26

Growing Up at Grossinger's

I was always being advised to keep a diary. "You might want to write about Grossinger's some day!" Fat chance. I'd had about as much of the hotel and my family as I could stand. In youthful certainty, writing about them was the last thing in the world I would ever think of doing.

The first time I considered the possibility was when I started at Playboy, and the noted social/political satirist for *The Village Voice*, Jules Feiffer, said that if I ever wrote the book, he might be interested in doing illustrations. Both of us, however, were so busy with other things that it never got past a conversation. *Growing Up at Grossinger's* came up once again in 1972, the year after my mother died. I met a literary agent named Dan O'Shea, who expressed the possibility of representing me if I ever decided to write it. I accepted his offer.

There was one drawback—I wasn't a professional writer. Not a problem, said Dan. He would find a ghostwriter, or an "as told to" collaborator. To prove his interest was sincere, he immediately set me up with another of his clients, and everything was fine until I saw the collaboration agreement his client drew up. A 60 to 40 percent share of the publisher's advance in his favor was fair; the 85 to 15 split he offered on royalties was not. The hours I would spend being interviewed and the story of my life had to be worth more than 15 percent. My coauthor wouldn't compromise, which brought our partnership to an end.

"Try it yourself," Dan proposed. "Worse writers than you have had books published!" I would have preferred a more reassuring vote of confidence, but he had a point.

In January 1973, over one of our weekly cocktail sessions, Dan told me he had an announcement to make. I expected it to be that he could no longer represent me because I wasn't financially viable.

"I've just agreed in principle that you are going to do a book that will pay you $5,000, and you have six months to get it done!"

It was the first time booze ever sobered me up.

"I can't possibly write *Growing Up at Grossinger's* in six months. I haven't even written the first paragraph."

"I forgot to tell you," he added. "The name of the book is *The Book of Gadgets*."

I had never seen Dan drunk, but how else to explain what I'd just heard? What I know about gadgets? I was a card-carrying klutz! I grew up in a hotel, where I never had to fix anything. I lived in a rental apartment, where my best friend in the building was the super. A stud was someone I might want to date, not something to do with nails and a wall. Had O'Shea lost his mind?

This is how he explained it: He was confident I would write *Growing Up at Grossinger's*. But did I want to be known as a one-book author? If I wrote *The Book of Gadgets,* a subject about which I knew nothing, maybe I could convince myself and others that I could write almost anything! Plus an advance of $5,000 was a figure not to be taken lightly, because I was unemployed. What had transpired, he explained, was that he had just met with a book packager, a person who develops a concept and then puts together all the elements needed to produce it, that is, author, illustrator, editor, photographer, indexer. The packager then sells the finished product to a publisher, who takes responsibility for printing and distribution. Bernie G., the packager in this case, had a publisher named Drake interested in *The Book of Gadgets*. Bernie asked Dan if he had an author who could take it on, and I was volunteered. Two drinks later I agreed to give it a try. My life at that point was all about change; what did I have to lose?

I entered a whole new world of specialty stores (Hammacher Schlemmer, Hoffritz, Abercrombie & Fitch), catalogues (Sears Roebuck), inventors, hobbyists, and science fiction writers, a most fascinating gamut. Fortunately this was pre-cyberspace, so I didn't have to be technologically proficient.

First I set up my table of contents, which included such titles as "The Great Gadgetsby," "The Gadgeting Gourmet," "I Get High with a Little Help from My Friends [bar]," "Getting There Is Half the Fun [travel], and "Mother, Please, I'd Rather Do It Myself." My favorite section was the last, "Gadgets of Fantasy and the Future." Woody Allen, a friend from my Playboy days, gave me some ideas for this one. Once I had my titles, filling each segment with narrative, interviews with experts, and illustrations turned out to be easier than I had imagined.

I completed it two months ahead of schedule. Not long after, at one of our cocktail sessions, Dan had another announcement. The book packager had gone bankrupt, and Drake Publishers folded. I could keep the advance, and all rights to *The Book of Gadgets* now belonged to me. In other words, I was stuck with a 360-page manuscript that, unless he could sell it to another publisher, I could use to wallpaper my apartment.

Much of my time after that was spent at a bar on Christopher Street called the Lion's Head. The Head, as it was affectionately known, was located next door to the *Village Voice* offices at the time and served as a second home to many writers, reporters, politicos, performers, off-duty cops, club owners, and Village characters. It was primarily a male watering hole, but periodically a lady, if she could accept the coarse vocabulary and knew when to keep her mouth shut (never interrupt, never correct), was admitted into the holy circle. It was the Head's proximity to my apartment a half-block away that I found most appealing. The people who hung out there knew I had worked for Playboy and were familiar with Grossinger's, which meant that every now and then someone would by me a drink or even ask what I was up to. I considered myself so out of their league that I never even spoke about writing. Until one slow afternoon not long after the publisher of *The Book of Gadgets* went out of business.

Shlenk, the bartender, started a friendly banter with me. "I'm tired of seeing your face around here. Why don't you get a life?" So I related the sad saga of my mini-publishing experience, adding something I had never told anyone else, that I'd like to be a travel writer. He threw a dime across the bar, pointed to the pay phone, and said, "Here, call Bill Honan, the travel editor of the *New York Times*," and gave me the number. "I can't do that," I said, taken aback. "If you ever want to drink here again, you'll call him now! Give him your name, tell him you're at the Head and that 'Shlenk' told you to call." For sure, I wanted to drink there again, so I called. "What do you want to write about?" Mr. Honan asked politely but brusquely. I mentioned the subject of women traveling on their own, something I had become quite familiar with during the previous years. "Someone's already written that!" he said. I then suggested a follow-up about women dining out alone. "Not interested. Let's not waste each other's time. Tell me what you can write about that nobody else can." "Well," I said rather sheepishly, "I grew up at Grossinger's and. . . ." He abruptly hung up.

"How the hell do I know if she can write?" I heard Shlenk say as he answered the phone behind the bar. "She can drink, that I can tell you. Only kidding. We love her here. No, she doesn't own the hotel. Her father was a cousin or something, but she grew up there and knows a lot of famous people." He gave me a huge smile. "OK, kid, make an investment in yourself. Use your own dime and call him back." Five minutes later I had an assignment. The first writing assignment of my life with the most prestigious newspaper in America. Even now I find it hard to believe.

On Sunday, January 13, 1974, the front page headline of the *Times* travel section read GROWING UP AT GROSSINGER'S, OR RAISED WITHOUT RESERVATIONS. Beneath it on the left-hand side were the words BY TANIA GROSSINGER. The article, along with photos, continued with almost two full pages inside. Letters to the editor about my article were so numerous that they ran for seven weeks, each with a different sub-headline, such as THE CATSKILLS, THE MOUNTAINS, THE BORSCHT BELT, and, finally, MORE TANIA. More Tania. The *New York Times*!

And on the Friday after the article was published, Dan O'Shea and I had offers to expand it into a book from eight different publishers.

I was finally going to write *Growing Up at Grossinger's*.

All by myself.

But not before Hollywood came calling.

Ten days after my article appeared, I received a call from RSO Films, a production company in Hollywood founded by an Australian entrepreneur named Robert Stigwood, who at the time also represented the hot musical group called the Bee Gees. Howard Rosenman, one of his producers, wanted to expand the article into a series or film on television. I was familiar enough with the business to know that the odds weren't on my side, but I wanted to hear him out.

My first call was to an entertainment lawyer I knew from Grossinger's, who agreed to represent and not charge me unless a deal went through.

I put together a presentation for what I hoped would become *The Goldens*. I pictured it as a dramatic TV series that starred a precocious thirteen-year-old, her thirty-five-year-old, recently widowed mother, who had just inherited a hotel in New York's Catskill mountains, and a revolving cast of characters who visited and worked there. Two weeks later, during which I wrote almost nonstop, I boarded TWA, first class of course, as a guest of RSO films for my first whirlwind encounter with the wheelers and dealers of Hollywood. And what a ride it was!

The last time I had been in Los Angeles, I had just graduated Brandeis and taken a job with the City of Hope. This time it was different. This time I was treated like a VIP. I repressed all the horror stories I had heard about doing business there. I was on a high! The first article I ever wrote had been published in the *New York Times*. Eight book publishers in New York were vying for my signature on their contracts. Hollywood had come to me. How disappointing could it be?

Everything started out as promised. I was ensconced in an elegant suite at the celebrated Sunset Marquis. My first evening, RSO held a cocktail party to introduce me to the agents and network representatives with whom we would meet more formally during the week. RSO's publicity team bombarded trade publications like *Variety* and the *Hollywood Reporter* with press releases, and soon enough I was reading articles that said, "Tania Grossinger has signed with RSO films of California to develop a ninety-minute television film based loosely on her experiences growing up at Grossinger's in the Catskills. NBC is reportedly talking with RSO about a deal." We scouted potential locations in Lake Tahoe. Never mind that no papers had been signed and we had never even met with NBC. Hollywood was the land of hype.

But then, NBC came calling.

Our first obligation was to put together an outline for a sixty-minute introductory episode of *The Goldens*, which we did. If NBC liked it, the network would pay for the show's production and broadcast it as a tryout. Based on the response of the public and the press, the network would decide whether to continue it as a series. NBC submitted to RSO a list of experienced comedy writers it would like to see involved, the playwright Neil Simon among them—however, RSO had approval on the writer. My lawyer reviewed the contracts and was concerned that while producers had agreed that I'd be credited as the creator of the show and receive a royalty for each episode, I was to have no involvement in the writing, casting, or production of the pilot. *The Goldens* was my baby—nobody understood the characters or background the way I did. But on this they would not budge.

The writer RSO chose for the pilot was from the Midwest, was not Jewish, and had never been to the Catskills.

The script she finally submitted featured a rundown Jewish hotel at the end of World War II—rabbis in Orthodox garb, old men in undershirts smoking cigars and playing pinochle in the card room, and the widowed Mrs. Golden sitting on the rickety porch looking up at the sky and lamenting to her late husband, "Isaac, vot should I do?" The thirteen-year-old daughter? She was foul-mouthed, oversexed, and bore no resemblance whatsoever to the youngster in my original outline. I shuddered at the thought that someone might think she had anything to do with me. It did not come as a surprise when NBC's director of program development finally sent a letter stating, "The appeal of *The Goldens* is too limited to reach the broad audience we aim for in our primetime programming." It was one of the wisest decisions NBC ever made.

Was I disappointed? Of course. But the experience came with its own reward. New York publishers had increased their offers when they learned of Hollywood's interest, because it gave them hope that the book *Growing Up at Grossinger's* might eventually become a movie.

Out of bad sometimes comes good!

27

Publication

The morning my article appeared, I got an early call from a woman named Sandi, who introduced herself as a representative of David Mc-Kay Publishers and asked that I not sign with anyone until her publishing house had a chance to make an offer. Did she have the authority to make me an offer? She did not. She was a recent hire, an assistant editor, but had big plans for herself. Her initiative impressed me, and I sleepily went on to explain the two-book requirement Dan had conceived—if a publisher wanted *Growing Up at Grossinger's,* it had to publish *The Book of Gadgets* first. I also gave Sandi Dan's contact information and permission to present both the *Gadget* and *Grossinger* titles at her editorial meeting the next day. When the choice came down to similar offers from McKay and one other house, I asked Dan to go with McKay. I liked Sandi's spunk and admired her determination—she reminded me of myself ten years earlier, when I was twenty-six. In five years she would become one of the industry's top acquiring editors and return my confidence many times over.

The Book of Gadgets required minimal editing, and its publication was set for November 1974. I had nine months to get *Growing Up at Grossinger's* in David McKay's hands. The challenge of writing the book was much more complex than putting together the *Times* piece. With the newspaper I had been concerned about the word count. With the book I had to worry about revealing personal information about the Grossinger family—including information about my mother.

After the *Times* article came out, Paul and Elaine, Jennie's son and daughter, who inherited the hotel after her death in 1972, came down to New York to wine and dine me and treat me to some Broadway shows. There was nothing they wouldn't do for me. My article was thoroughly complimentary and well received. I had no illusions that their show of affection was anything personal. I had created a media storm and attracted new business for a hotel whose owners were giving me something in return.

I had two options. I could continue to write about Grossinger's in the same admiring tradition of the *Times* piece. If I *just* wrote about celebrities like Jackie Robinson, Eddie Fisher, Jerry Lewis, Rocky Marciano, Harry Belafonte, Debbie Reynolds, Elizabeth Taylor, and all the many others I had been privileged to know—I could have a best-seller. I would also, by saying only laudatory things about the family, have access to their mailing list of more than 250,000 current and former guests.

The other option was to write a true story about what it was like for a young, impressionable kid to grow up at a famous resort run by the renowned Jennie Grossinger, who in person was so very different from the admiring image her PR people had crafted. I could also disclose what I knew about how certain celebrities behaved out of the public eye—stories their press agents prayed would never see light of day. That could be a best-seller, too! So what did I do? I didn't write the book-length press release the family would have loved—that hypocritical I couldn't allow myself to be. I didn't write a tell-all, either—better I should keep my disillusionments to myself. So I straddled the fence and paid the price on both sides.

In person, by mail, and by phone I interviewed more than 100 former guests and staffers. Some of their recollections embarrassed me.

"You were a little kissing bug. All you wanted to do was kiss, kiss, kiss." "Whenever a man said nice things to you about your mother, you would plaintively ask, 'Will you be my daddy?'" One I enjoyed hearing came from the reservations manager who shared the bathroom with us in Pop's Cottage. "Your mind was a steel trap. For someone your age you had the greatest perception of human frailties. You also never failed to express them." I drove my cousin Mary Ann and childhood friend Patsy crazy with questions about the silly things we did as kids, our teenage crushes, and confidences we shared. It was fascinating to discover how differently we remembered those days, and as a result I had to end up beginning many sentences with, "As I remember . . ." "If memory serves . . .," or "It is my recollection that . . ." Paul and Elaine, hoping that if they cooperated with me I wouldn't publish anything to embarrass the family, issued an open invitation to revisit the hotel and meet with anyone I wished. I willingly took them up on it. I hadn't been back for five years, and there were many new faces and department heads. My mother had passed away only three years earlier, and I was stunned to find so few executives who had even heard of her. It was all very strange.

Once I began to write, the words flowed comfortably. So many people in the course of my life had asked the question "What was it like growing up at Grossinger's?" This time, instead of responding with a few short sentences before changing the subject, I answered by writing a book. I finished ahead of the deadline and expected my new editor (Sandi had been promoted to another division) to be as pleased with what I had written as I was. We were both disappointed. I thought I had name-dropped almost to the point of embarrassment. She wanted more. Her explanation was stunningly direct: "No one cares about you, Tania. They only want to know about the famous people." This did not do wonders for my ego. I tried to make the case that the title of the book was not *Celebrities I Have Known* by Tania Grossinger. It made no difference. She returned the manuscript with a one word instruction: Rewrite!

My agent told me that I had no choice unless I wanted to return the $10,000 advance McKay had paid, so I compromised by excising some (but not all) of the more personal episodes and expanding the celebrity anecdotes. I also provided them with photos of Eddie Fisher being "discovered" on the Grossinger Playhouse stage by Eddie Cantor, the PR staged event that kicked off his career; Eddie Fisher marrying Debbie Reynolds (against his better judgment) at the home of Jennie's daughter, Elaine; Paul Newman and Rocky Graziano wearing Grossinger T-shirts; and Kim Novak posing on the "G" ski slope (she was sleeping with our "skimeister" at the time). The book, to my horror, was beginning to read like one gigantic gossip column. My editor was thrilled!

Growing Up at Grossinger's came off press in October 1975, and the next month I threw a cocktail party in my apartment to honor its publication. Busboys who were now doctors, lawyers, and entrepreneurs attended, as did former telephone operators and reservation clerks, members of the athletic staff, dance teachers, musicians, guests I had kept in touch with through the years, and my childhood friends Patsy and Mary Ann. My publisher arranged multiple newspaper, radio and TV interviews in New York and sent me on a book tour to Boston, Philadelphia, Hartford, Pittsburgh, and Cleveland—all cities with large Jewish populations. I addressed the annual meeting of the American Bookseller Association, the industry's premier gathering of book buyers. I spoke at Brandeis women's committees, Jewish community centers, and synagogue groups—any forum that would have me. When the budget didn't permit airfare to the West Coast, I did interviews by phone. There was no opportunity I let pass. But with media exposure came complications.

I had gone out of my way when writing the book to present the hotel in the best possible light. I gave readers a sense of how much work it took to make sure every guest's experience lived up to expectations. I showed how the game "Simon Sez" was played to bring singles together, and how dining room seating was arranged in advance with colored pegs on a specially designed board so that there would be a balance of men and women. For the first time readers learned about Playhouse ratings charts that determined which Saturday night headliners were invited back, and about Sunday afternoon staff meetings where each complaint reported the previous week was examined and apologized for. I reproduced nine-course gourmet dinner menus and offered up tasty tidbits, including how many eggs were cracked each week (27,000) and miniature pastries baked each day (4,700).

Now, I'll be the first to acknowledge that the picture I painted of Jennie Grossinger was not emotionally flattering, but as far as I was concerned, it was well deserved. I hoped that the Grossinger family would realize, after reading the book, how much private information I was privy to, how many hurtful tales I *could* have divulged had I not been as sensitive as I was. Not for the first time, I overestimated them. Not only did they withhold the 250,000-name mailing list from me and refuse to sell the book in the hotel gift shop; they badmouthed the book and its author. What right did I have to write about the hotel? My mother was a member of the staff, a hostess, who had been married to a cousin in Chicago who had no connection to the hotel. Neither of us was a real Grossinger. The family resented the book's very publication.

The *Times* editor had heard from a number of advertisers who were also Catskill resort owners complaining that Grossinger's had received special treatment from the paper. His answer to them was that no one else who grew up at a resort hotel ever contacted the *Times* to write a story. I would add that no one from the Grossinger family ever sat down to write a book. The opportunity had been open to anyone!

Even with all the family's machinations, sales got off to an enviable start. Each time I did an interview, they rose. And then, with no notice and to the shock of both myself and my agent, a conglomerate in England bought out David McKay. Out the door and in quick succession in the Manhattan office went the president, the publisher, the treasurer, the paperback and film rights director, my editor, the public relations director, and sales and advertising managers. Every professional vital to the publishing success of my book, gone! And with them any hopes I might have had for even a moderate, if not best, seller.

28

The Literary Years

One morning I awoke with an idea. *The Great American Sex Book*. It was the 1970s. The sexual revolution. Creative genital explorations, cutting-edge experimentations, little was off limits. Was it just talk? As much fun as participants made it out to be? How did it affect relationships, and what was the price we paid for this freedom? It occurred to me that I might be able to turn this curiosity into a book. I began by interviewing more than fifty men and women of various ages, backgrounds, and lifestyles about their most exciting, unusual, and intimate sexual experiences. Fantasies, fetishes, taboos, all were grist for this auditeur's mill. Looking back I can't believe I was cheeky enough to think that friends or perfect strangers would actually confide in me about things that were none of my business, but not only did they cooperate; a few insisted on contacting me with updates for weeks after I canceled the project.

It didn't take long to realize that sex was much more fun to participate in than write about. Listening to strangers' sexual exploits, probably more wishful thinking than reality, first became repetitious, then boring, and finally a burden. The highlight of this ludicrous experience was an interview that Al Goldstein, the editor of *Screw* magazine, who had a teenage crush on me when his father was a part-time photographer at Grossinger's, set up in 1977 with Larry "Hustler" Flynt, who had just been convicted of pandering obscenity and engaging in organized crime. We met at the Park Lane Hotel on Central Park South. Flynt said that he was uncomfortable talking about sex with "such a lovely lady" but volunteered to share with me a surprisingly tender reflection on love.

I'm probably one of few people of my age [fifty-five] that's ever experienced, witnessed, or really knows what love is. Most people have a total misconception. If I had to define love, the only thing I think about is a little sort of story out of my life. When I got out of the service, my mother told me I should go down to Kentucky and see my grandparents because they probably wouldn't be around too much longer. They lived in the same county for fifty years. They'd been married for sixty. They were both pushing ninety. The first morning I was awakened at 7:00 AM by a rooster setting on a fence post crowing. The first thing I saw out of the window was my grandfather shuffling his feet through the garden. Soon he walked back in the hallway to my grandmother's bedroom, where she was in bed not able to get up, hair white as snow. He eased in beside her bed, sat down, and tapped her on the cheek. She turned over to look at him, and he had a flower in his hand. And he handed her the flower and told her how her face looked like a beautiful spring morning. And it hit me like a bolt of lightning. And I thought to myself, "That's love! That's love!"

Out of the mouth of America's most famous pornographer.

It soon dawned on me that I didn't have the credentials or "platform" to give this kind of book credibility. With no regrets and a few laughs under my belt, I quickly brought this experiment to an end. The loss was not total, however, because one discovery I made led to my next undertaking.

Is Women's Lib Failing Women?

From many of my successful career-women friends came professions of sadness and disappointment that the new feminism created pressures and frustrations they hadn't anticipated. A letter written at the time to "Dear Abby" clarified much of what I was hearing.

It went something like this:

I am tired of being a lonely, self-reliant adult. I am bored with liberation. I'm fed up with sexual freedom and sick to death of life without commitment. I'm no longer able to live by the old rules, but I can't find any new rules that work. I'm a lonely, self-reliant, liberated adult, and, quite frankly, I despise it.

Abby did not follow up. I decided to try.

Liberation offered women options, choices, alternatives, and new identities. But there were still those, like the woman who wrote to Dear Abby, who found its contradictions and complications difficult to live with. For them, emancipation promised more than it could deliver, and not a single book published during this period honed in on their disillusionment.

To reach middle- and working-class housewives who may have felt that books like Helen Gurley Brown's *Sex and the Single Girl* didn't address their personal concerns, I approached Sally Jessy Raphael, a popular radio personality who would subsequently host her own TV show, with an idea to give my research a start. I asked if she would let me appear on her WMCA radio show, not to promote a book, as was usually the case when she interviewed authors, but to enlist her listeners' help in writing one. The question to them would be, "Is Women's Lib failing women?" The answers they called in would be anonymously incorporated into my book. The emotionality of the feedback, pro and con, amazed us all. There was no question that there was much that feminism had not yet explored. I recognized facets of myself in several of the listeners' responses. Searching for freedom, relishing the freedom, not knowing how to deal with so much freedom. I imagined readers, if they were honest with themselves, would as well.

Like the sex books, the project didn't get past this initial stage, much to my disappointment. Reaching out to experts, setting up interviews across the country, and transcribing tapes even before setting out to write a manuscript would require more resources than I could afford without a publisher's commitment. Dan O'Shea, the agent on my first two books, had disappeared months earlier. Without notice he closed his office, moved out of his apartment, and cut contact with everyone he knew. Despite many efforts to find him, he hasn't been heard from since. Because there was still hope he might return, and I was still under contract to him, no other agents would represent me. Without an agent, I couldn't get the attention of a publisher. So there I was, left with what might have been a good idea but unable to follow through.

The Great Gadget Catalogue

In 1977, through no effort of my own, I finally had a third book published. The editor I worked with on *The Book of Gadgets* had moved to another publishing house and approached me about writing a follow-up. It would be called *The Great Gadget Catalogue* and include clever descriptions and more than 200 illustrations and photographs.

I explained the problem I had with my missing agent, and she took it upon herself to introduce me to Anita Diamant, a well-known literary agent who agreed, as a special favor, to take me on without a formal agreement. I had enough contacts and research material left from the first book to make *The Great Gadget Catalogue* easy to write and easier to promote. The press release lauded it as "a useful and amusing compendium that explains, describes, and tells you where to buy hundreds of innovative, often incredible, devices that tickle your fancy." Then the reviewers chimed in. "Guaranteed to evoke giggles and sighs of envy." "Lively collection of zany, ingenious contraptions and contrivances." *Good Morning America* promoted it. The *New York Times* gave it a commendable write-up. And when one of the most important travel publications wrote, "Gadget freaks of the world unite. Your book has arrived!" I knew that my income was guaranteed for at least the coming year.

29

Psychics, Seers, and the Supernatural

Have you ever believed and not believed in something at the same time?

This is not a trick question. For years I have been fascinated by the paranormal. Parapsychology, the supernatural, Ouija boards, fortune tellers, Tarot cards, palm readers, telepathy, clairvoyance, ESP, past life regressions, voodoo, mediums, mystics, psychics, the occult, anything to broaden the confines of daily routine. With enthusiasm, with reservations, with cynicism, joy, and disappointments, but always with an open mind, I've, to some degree, dabbled and delved in them all. As a child I never felt bound by the traditional five senses—I believed even then that there were additional ways to communicate. If our psyche is driven by the unconscious, which we can't see, hear, taste, touch, or smell, what's to prevent a parallel situation in other aspects of life?

As in many other lines of work, there are charlatans. We make it so easy for them. "Do you know someone with the initial M? T? P? Of course we do. "You've been feeling tired lately. You must be stressed." "You are going to come into a large sum of money." "Do you have a problem with your health? If not someone very close to you does." "Do you have a daughter?" No. "You did in a previous life and she made you very happy." "You will soon get a phone call with good news." "You have an admirer who loves you from afar." By the time our tellers-of-fortune have fed back to us what we've expressed through body language or verbal reactions, we believe they are geniuses and grease their palms in gratitude.

I'm no less vulnerable and admit I've been suckered by the best, including John Lennon and Yoko Ono's personal psychic, who asked me to leave mid-reading because everything he had divined about me was incorrect. When I challenged his "insights," he accused me of being hostile. That was the first time he was on target. That said, no disappointments could possibly outweigh the extraordinary experiences I've had.

Reverend Mildred Stranno

I had never met a less imposing psychic. Sparrow-like, frail, legally blind, and so unassuming she seemed to meld into the furniture. Her name was Revered Mildred Stranno, a woman in her early sixties who appeared much older, a Baptist minister, widow, and retired nurse who had inherited a rent-controlled apartment on East 85th Street.

Our first meeting took place at noon on July 3, 1974. After a few pleasantries, she asked if there was something specific I wanted to know. "Tell me about my father," I said. That was my test. The minute I was told that he had just taken ill but would recover or that he now regrets divorcing my mother and would soon come back into my life, I knew the psychic was full of wet tea leaves. Reverend Stranno closed her eyes and took so long to speak that I feared she had fallen asleep. "Your father died shortly after you were born," she finally said. "He might have been in his late thirties. I see an image of him leaning on a cane." I didn't know which to react to first—that she knew my father died when I was very young, or her mention of a cane, about which I had never heard. I don't recall much else about that first meeting, other than her saying I needed to have more faith in people, that I should eat more leafy vegetables, and that in my mail I would find an envelope enclosing something resembling cardboard with large green print. In my mailbox that afternoon was the first copy I had seen, in large green print, of the cover of *The Book of Gadgets*. But back to the man with the cane.

The only living person who might have known something about him was my now elderly Aunt Regina, my father's first cousin, who lived in Jersey City with my Uncle Meyer, the lawyer who was so helpful after my mother died. My father and mother lived with Regina and her parents in Chicago when they first came to America. After three days, she finally returned my call. This is what she said:

Darling, this is so peculiar that you're asking about that. Just last week, I'll tell you when . . . it was the day before July 4, and I was waiting for Uncle Meyer to pick me up so that we could drive up to Grossinger's for the holiday. He was late, as usual, and I didn't know whether to make lunch or what I should do. I started to dust in the living room and came across an old photo album I hadn't looked at in years. I opened it up, and there was a picture of your father leaning on a cane in front of the nursing home in Chicago. He'd been transferred there after his second heart attack, and you were just a baby. I don't know if your mother ever told you about that—you know how she hated to talk about the past—so I made a promise to myself to show it to you the next time you came over. And then you called and asked about it. Isn't that something?

It certainly was something. My Aunt Regina was looking at the photo in Jersey City at the exact moment, shortly after noon on July

3, that Rev. Stranno "saw" it in her mind on East 85th Street. I was stunned. The Reverend obviously had a gift that, sensing my interest, she volunteered to share with me. I was only too willing to comply.

New phrases entered my day-to-day vocabulary: auric healing, astral visitation, chakras, magnetic energy, psychometric reading, astral projection, spirit guides. The Reverend gave me books, which we discussed twice a month. I accompanied her to Sunday afternoon meetings of the Spiritual Science Frontier Fellowship and went to lectures by noted psychics and mediums. Most accepted as certainty that the subconscious mind contains all that happens in life and that its direction is already planned according to the karmic law of cause and effect. (This law, I cynically noted, also offers practitioners an automatic fallback position. When their predictions don't come true, they can always explain, "In theosophy and metaphysics there is no concept of time. If not now, in another life. Karma works in mysterious ways.") Some considered God or archetypes of their individual faiths to be their divine inspiration. Others singled out guardian angels or spirit guides. After six months of heavy immersion, however, the dichotomy became too intense. I was living in two worlds, one fueled by intellect, the other by anything but. I was expecting too much and looking for answers which either didn't exist or were beyond my comprehension. With apologies to Rev. Stranno, with whom I remained in contact for years, I directed my energy elsewhere—but not for a moment do I regret the time invested. My curiosity about everything I learned turned out to add a most interesting dimension to my future travel experiences, writing, and life.

In 1978 I traveled to Rio de Janeiro, where I was introduced to the practice of Macumba, a faith akin to voodoo centered around the worship of spirits. My chronic condition, the Tietze syndrome, had flared up due to extreme humidity in the air. My medications weren't taking effect, and I was open to any possible relief. A guide I befriended offered to escort me to a service, making sure I understood that outsiders were welcome to observe but not participate. My inner self told me otherwise.

Let me set the stage: The *Terreiro,* or house of worship, located in a semi-affluent suburb, was spread over three floors. To the left of the entrance was a small store selling religious ornaments, Colgate toothpaste, and, incongruously, Portuguese translations of Norman Vincent Peale's *The Power of Positive Thinking.* Above the altar on the main floor were signs reading DAI DEGRACA O QUE DE CRACARE CEBESTOS [GIVE FREE WHAT YOU RECEIVE FREE] and AMAIVOS UNS AOS OUTROS [LOVE ONE ANOTHER]. A dozen men dressed in white pants and loose tunics adorned with multicolored necklaces drummed and danced feverishly to keep evil spirits at bay and attract those that were pure. The pure spirits would then be sent to the *maos do santo* (female priests) on the second floor, who were responsible for giving advice, counsel, and healing. The third floor was reserved for psychic surgery. I headed for the second.

Women in long white dresses were assembled in groups of five waiting for the Macumba mother priest to start the ceremony. In a few minutes a bejeweled, heavy-set woman took center stage in the middle of the room, blowing thick smoke from three cigars she smoked simultaneously—three because it is considered a lucky number and cigars because the spirits are attracted to them and their smoke is said to cure viruses. To everyone's surprise but my own, she bolted through the audience, grabbed my arm, brought me back to the center, asked my name, pointed to my chest, and grimaced in pain. Immediately I was surrounded by one of the groups of five. As the mother priest began her incantations, one young woman blew smoke from her trio of cigarettes (only the mother was allowed cigars) in my face, another rubbed my back, two ran their arms up and down my body, and a fifth stared unblinking into my eyes.

Suddenly the "mother" arched her back and, shaking in trance, began to laugh. My immediate reaction was to giggle back. As her shaking became uncontrollable, so did her laughter. Suddenly I heard another kind of laugh, almost a cackle, harsh and frightening. What shocked me seconds later was that the bone-chilling sound had, without my willing it, emanated from me. At the same time I felt a great energy surround my body, especially my chest, what occultists refer to as the "aura." The next few minutes I can reconstruct only from what I was told; I have absolutely no memory of them.

I gather that the women in my surrounding group continued to massage my back, arms, and legs, one more frantically than the other. Our so-called laughter, by then more like screams, even frightened the onlookers. The mother priest ripped from her neck the chunky silver chain that held both a cross and Jewish star with the number thirteen in the middle, pushed it into my hand, and screamed my name, Tania, three times.

The first thing I recall was what felt like a twenty-pound weight departing my chest. Immediately everything became calm. I took a deep breath, opened my eyes, and pressed down on my ribcage. No pain. For the first time in months, not even an inkling. Through her prayers and intercession, the guide later explained, the evil spirit that caused my problem had been set free. It would never trouble me again.

Had I truly been possessed and an exorcism performed on me? Much as I would like to think so, almost a year later, though I was grateful for even that long a reprieve, I once again felt the same pain. But the story is not over.

At the airport the next evening I heard my name paged. Approaching the appropriate desk I was surprised to find Rhea, the guide who had accompanied me the night before. She handed me a small purse and said, "This is a gift from the mother priest. She seems to like you and asked for your name. Inside is a vial of red liquid. She said not to open it until you are faced with the biggest problem you think you've ever had. Then you must empty it into a warm bath, and the problem will disappear." Before I could even thank her, she disappeared in the crowd.

At home I dutifully placed the vial on a bathroom shelf. Every time I found myself in a situation where I thought it might help, it occurred to me that something worse would likely come along. This went on for two years. Then came a serious situation. I missed my period. I missed a second period. This was, without question, the worst problem I had ever had. One sleepy two o'clock in the morning, I went into my bathroom, removed the vial from its perch, drew a bath, made up a little prayer, emptied it into the water, and immersed myself. I imagine you know what happened next. My problem was no longer my problem. Coincidence? More than likely. I obviously wasn't pregnant, and had I waited another day. . . . But my connection with the mother priest was not over.

A few days later I received a call from a heavily accented lady, who introduced herself as a Colombian who lived in Queens and had just returned from Rio. She said that she had been at a friend's home, where she was introduced to a woman said to be a Macumba priest. The woman asked a favor of her. When she got back to New York, would she look in the phone book and call someone named Tania Grossinger and tell her the following? On such and such date, at such and such time, "I was praying for her." I checked time differences between the two cities. She had been praying for me at the exact time on the exact night that I emptied the vial of red liquid in my bath. My caller was told that it might not make sense to her but that it would to me. "Does it make any sense to you?" she asked.

—∞—

Los Angeles: As a child in Beverly Hills I lived with my mother at 121 South Elm Drive on the corner of Wilshire Boulevard. The three-story, white stucco building was owned by a wealthy Mexican woman, Sra. Mildred Villasenor, whom I remember as very kind. She always gave my mother gifts to put in my Christmas stocking. I have many happy memories of 121 South Elm. It was, until I moved to Greenwich Village, the only real *home* that I ever had. I had always yearned to see it one last time, but each time I returned to Los Angeles, the building had been sold to a new owner, and there was no one to whom I could speak.

—ɷ—

It is now 1989, and I'm invited to visit a friend in Beverly Hills. Once again I make the visit to South Elm Drive. Once again I ring the landlord's buzzer, and once again no one answers. This time, however, a young woman brushes past the entrance and, assuming I am a fellow tenant, beckons me to follow. Follow her I do, directly to apartment 2C, her apartment, my apartment. I hope the expression on my face doesn't frighten her. I try to regain control, introduce myself, and explain my emotion. To my delight she nonchalantly opens her door and invites me in. Despite the obvious redecorations, I recognize it immediately. The Murphy bed jutting from the wall adjacent to the dressing area, the tiny kitchen to the left, and on the far side of the living room the corner bathroom where I once locked myself in and had to be rescued by the fire department. I stand transfixed.

The young woman begins to speak. "Now I understand why I had to leave work early," she says. "I've never done anything like this before, but a voice in my head kept saying, 'Go home. Go immediately. Leave now, or it will be too late.' I always trust my inner voice," she said. "And here you are."

And here I am. After forty-two years. A wish fulfilled, thanks to the sixth sense of a stranger.

—◊—

Guatemala: It is the spring of 1972, and I am spending two weeks with a family I met when my mother lived in Montecatini. As a parting gift they hire an English-speaking guide, Manuel, to tour me through Antigua, Chichicastanengo, and Lake Atitlan. I share with him my desire to meet a *bruja* (witch doctor). His aunt happens to be one, and the day before I leave, he takes me to her home. She tells me, among other things, that in a previous life I lived in South America and was once a witch, which is why I am so drawn to *brujas* in this life. Interesting, but not as much as her last eight words: "It will take four days to get home."

This is the same year a number of planes have been hijacked by D. B. Cooper copycats, the Black Panthers, and escaped cons. The flight to New York is five hours. It does not require a great leap of faith to imagine that (1) my plane will be hijacked and (2) even if it is, I don't have to worry, because I will eventually return home. I take the possibility seriously enough to put extra snacks and personal essentials in my carry-on bag. For a moment I even consider disclosing my secret to the agent at the check-in counter, but common sense prevails. I board, fasten my seat belt, have a cocktail, read my book, and five hours later land as scheduled at JFK. I swallow my disappointment; at least I arrived home on time.

I check my phone messages as soon as I'm back in my apartment. I am currently dating a man whose mother lives in Savannah. While I'm away he has decided to visit her and leaves a message suggesting that I go back to the airport and catch the next flight there. We will spend some time in Savannah, he tells me, and then rent a car for a leisurely drive back to New York. "It will take four days to get home."

—∞—

Vancouver: I am visiting that beautiful Canadian city for the first time. I'm hosted by the Westin Bayshore hotel and ensconced in a penthouse fit for a potentate. During the night I feel a painful squeeze on my right arm.

The next morning I am joined at breakfast by the hotel's public relations woman. "How are things going?" she wants to know. The suite is incredible, I tell her, almost like its own little empire. Did I have a good sleep? Finding her question perhaps a bit curious, I mention the squeezed arm. To my surprise she starts to laugh. "The ghost of Howard Hughes," she says. The famous Hollywood producer had, in his last years, turned into an eccentric recluse and had spent a number of months at the Bayshore before his antics became so outrageous that the management forced him to leave. He gets his revenge, my host tells me with a straight face, by wreaking havoc on every guest who checks in to "his" penthouse.

I have the bruise to prove it.

—∞—

In Hong Kong many fortune tellers work out of stalls surrounding the Wong Tai Sin Temple in residential Kowloon. In 1984 I am facing a professional dilemma: to continue as a freelance writer, start my own business, or return to the corporate world. My Chinese guide, who will serve as translator and write down what I'm told, directs me to Mr. Kon Tin Man, an ageless wisp of a man with crystal-clear skin, horn-rimmed glasses, and a few strands of white beard. He asks to see my right hand. "Your first finger is shorter than the third," he explains. "You are in a state of confusion." He then asks for a question. "Do I have a future as a writer?" He tells God my name, birth date, and question. Methodically he shakes and then throws from a tortoise shell a handful of Chinese coins dating from the reign of the Chang dynasty, which he proceeds to examine. Next he lights a joss (incense) stick, mutters an incantation, and consults an ancient almanac. Finally he speaks. "If you can make a living as a writer, you should continue; however, if you start your own business, you will have great financial rewards. As a writer you will not be as successful, although when you die your writing will be famous."

I did not go back to the corporate world or start my own business.

30

Life as a Travel Writer

—⚬—

Santa Fe, New Mexico. June 1991. So here I am, seated sideways on a fat donkey named "Help!" and being pushed (literally) by two guides up the Sangre de Cristo Mountains outside of the main city. I am not a naturalist, I am not a donkey rider, and the air is so thin that I can hardly breathe. I am also the target of friendly yet barbed comments from the lively and much more agile group I am traveling with. I'm having the time of my life!

This is the way our trip is described:

Depart Santa Fe for tour of the Pecos National Monument, home of the ancient Pueblo culture on Glorieta Pass [so far so good]. From there we proceed to the high country of the Sangre de Cristo Mountains to meet wranglers for an easy, one-hour horseback riding trip. [They really meant "donkey," and easy it definitely is not.] Ride will end at a Base Camp where the chef from the Inn of the Anasazi where we are staying will provide a fabulous End of The Trail dinner, along with fine spirits to cure the Cowboy Legs. [Yes!] Transportation back will be provided by van. [Thank God!]

It is only the promised tequila bar that keeps me going. Finally (I am the last, of course) we arrive at an isolated campsite whose base on a cliff overlooking the most scenic part of the Pecos National Forest somehow convinces our entire group we're on top of the world. Then again, I doubt the top of the world would include a three-star chef and open barbecue pit prepared to grill steaks, burgers, and chili-glazed baby back ribs. As the sun begins to set and stars take command of the universe, a cowboy appears on a horse from the other side of the mountain. Guitar in hand, he invites us to join him in choruses of "This Land Is Your Land" and so many other folk songs that for a moment I think we are back at a hootenanny in Washington Square Park. We drink, we dance, we sing, we share secrets, we give thanks for the giant trees behind which we can answer nature's call, and we gluttonize beyond belief. If only Help didn't have to still carry me down part of the mountain.

As all good things must, the evening comes to an end. Help, it turns out, does not live up to his name; he has wandered off to greener pastures. The only way to get me back to the van is for Mr. Cowboy and Mr. Chef to personally carry me down the incline so that I can write about it.

What an incredible way to make a living!

—⁂—

Spring, 1989. Sosúa, Dominican Republic. During World War II, the Dominican Republic opened its doors to a number of Jews fleeing Eastern Europe. One of those Jews was my mother's first cousin, Dora Schmitt. The reason for President Rafael Trujillo's beneficence, I was told, was that when one of his daughters attended a Swiss boarding school, the only two girls to befriend her were Jewish. I've also been told that this story is nonsense. It doesn't matter. Part of my family was saved from the Holocaust and made new lives for themselves in the small town of Sosúa on the island's North Shore. Only a handful remain, but I am told that one rabbi still lives there part-time.

The bus from Puerto Plata, where I am staying, takes me to the center of town. I am pointed to a rundown wooden shack, where an old man in jacket and tie (in ninety-five-degree weather) naps on the porch. A boy who fortunately speaks English nudges him awake. I explain my family's relationship to Sosúa and show him the large piece of paper on which I have printed in block letters DORA SCHMITT; HORO-DENKA, POLAND. Tears come to the rabbi's eyes. He remembers Dora well. "She was very intelligent and loved to dance," he tells the boy, who translates. "She was a big flirt, and her husband didn't like that." He falls back asleep. I ask the young boy to tell him when he awakes that Dora and her family have settled with relatives in Detroit and are all doing well. I make a contribution to the synagogue on their behalf and thank the boy for his time.

Stodgy, humorless Dora a flirt?

I can't wait to tell my family.

—⁂—

St. Thomas, U.S. Virgin Islands, 2004. I hate when resorts, especially those known for high standards, are chintzy. I am here to write a cover story for a bridal magazine and am staying at the most opulent hotel on the island, the Ritz Carlton. The suite I am assigned would cost upward of $600 a night. The first thing I notice as I enter is a small table holding a bottle of drinking water. The necklace around the bottle says $1.00. A guest at the famous Ritz Carlton is paying more than $600 a night and is charged $1.00 for water? This is class?

The first evening the general manager hosts a cocktail party and asks if everything is to my satisfaction. I get right to the point. "Isn't it a bit tacky to nickel-and-dime guests for water when they're already paying so much for the room?" He looks at me in phony disbelief. "Of course we don't charge for water. That is ridiculous." He blames it on the housekeeper who, he says, must have misunderstood. He assures me that the notice will be removed and asks that I please don't mention it in whatever I plan to write.

Experience has taught me to not take every manager at his word. I share the story with a colleague who is flying there the following week. His suite is in the same cottage as mine. When he returns, he brings me the "Water, $1.00" collar from his room as a souvenir.

—⁂—

March 1994, New Orleans, home of Anne Rice, best-selling author of *Interview with the Vampire*. I have been invited to speak about travel writing at a Writer's Conference hosted by the New Orleans convention and visitors bureau. Ms. Rice has volunteered to host an outdoor black tie party for us at her Garden District mansion. It is a gala event featuring Dixieland music, jazz bands, and food stations manned by the most famous restaurateurs in town. Champagne flows freely. Only one of the downstairs bathrooms has been allocated for guests. The line to use the facilities continues to grow; nothing seems to move. At long last a frustrated editor checks to see if the person inside is ill. The door is unlocked. She screams, then bursts out in laughter. What she discovers is a larger-than-life papier-mâché mannequin of a vampire sitting on the "throne."

Anne Rice at her creative best!

—⁂—

Santa Marta, Colombia, 1976. The package tour to Colombia includes a stay at the seaside town of Santa Marta, where Simón Bolívar, the liberator of much of Latin America, died in 1830. I join a group of guests gathered on the beach, cocktails in hand, as the sun begins to set. A strange noise from the sky startles us. A small plane, heading directly toward us, crashes into the water only a few yards away. There is no lifeguard. We beg the bartenders to call for help, but they have other things in mind. Almost in unison, they strip to their skivvies and rush to retrieve bales of what has fallen from the downed craft. The plane was too heavily weighted, loaded down with marijuana being smuggled out of the country. They know they can resell it and make a fortune. It is a weekly occurrence.

Working the beach bars in Santa Marta, I discover, is the best job in town!

—⚬—

My last time in the Caribbean, 2006. I have finally given up the ghost!

I no longer stare at the heavens and talk to a star, the one where, when I was a child, my mother told me my father lives. Through the years I've poured my heart out to that special star, confessing sins, sharing dreams, pleading for understanding and forgiveness. This week, on a press trip to Martinique, it has come to an end.

For four nights now I have sat on my hotel balcony, unable to locate the one that belonged to me and me alone, the one that always twinkled back when I stared at it so that I'd know my father was listening. I need to tell him about you, Natasha—how much I enjoy confiding in you and how important this one-sided relationship has become. I search the sky endlessly; not for the first time I feel anger at my father for abandoning me, just like his star is doing now, only to be overcome by a more profound realization. I am trading one fantasy, a star in the sky who I think is my father, for another, a daughter I don't even have.

—⚬—

I never went on vacation with my mother. A worldwide traveler, her journeys took her to such far-off locations as Ceylon, Istanbul, Alexandria, Tahiti, and Vietnam, not to mention almost every continent in the world. I couldn't get her to take me on a day trip to Manhattan. She once said that being away was the only time she felt alive. It wouldn't have been like that with us, Natasha. I can't imagine not wanting to introduce you to worlds that might one day clarify your life as they once did mine.

After my *Times* article was published, I began to get calls from publicity people in the hospitality industry inviting me to visit hotels, resorts, and destinations they represented. They assumed, having been published in the *New York Times*, that I was an experienced travel writer. Why not? I was a seasoned traveler. My background provided me with insight into hotels and the tourism industry. My last name was well enough known in the industry to open doors, and I had no responsibilities at home.

I had a lot to learn. "You get paid to go on vacation? How lucky can you get?" So many conversations started that way when I added the words "travel writer" to my business cards. Yes, it was fun, and, yes, I was fortunate, but still it was work, more complicated than one imagined, and not always as exciting as one presumed. I think you might get a kick out of what a travel writer's—at least this travel writer's—life was like, especially when I started out.

In pre-Internet days, travelers got their information from articles they read in newspapers and magazines. To attract potential visitors, public relations people put together press trips on which writers were invited to sample, at the host's expense, the attractions of the clients' hotels, resorts, cities, or countries. As you can imagine, conflict of interest is inherent. A property representative gives us writers free airline tickets, wines and dines us with alacrity, takes us on tours of nearby points of interest, and makes our stay as memorable as she possibly can. But what if the destination doesn't live up to its reputation or its colorful brochures? Maybe the beach that "overlooks the ocean" overlooks it from five blocks away. Perhaps the service is sloppy, or the food not up to par. When that occurs, those who invited us hope the disappointments can be overlooked. Because they are paying for my trip, the tendency is to expect that, in return, what I write will be flattering. In certain instances writers are only too willing to comply. They don't want to disappoint their host; they also don't want to offend the PR person, who might represent other locales the writers want to visit without having to pay.

Each writer has her own style and sense of integrity. Mine is very basic: I respect my readers. I may be paid by my editors, but my allegiance belongs to those who trust what I write. I've caused bruised feelings, and I've been put on a more than a few PR executives' do-not-invite list because I reported on what I saw, even if it didn't jive with what my host wanted me to present. There have been times when editors instructed me to write only complimentary words because the destination I would be traveling to advertised in their publications. I turned down that kind of assignment, too.

"Write what you know" served me well. What I learned after my mother died was how to travel by myself, so I sold my first two articles to *Working Woman* magazine, one about making traveling solo a memorable experience, and the other about what hotels can do to make women travelers feel at ease. When they were published, I used my contacts to appear on talk shows and share my advice with listeners. Having both print and broadcast outlets made me more valuable to the travel public relations people and endeared me to magazine editors whose publications I would mention on air. They thanked me by considering me for additional assignments.

I was off to an excellent start!

Serendipity has always played an important role in my life. When I was living out my fantasy in Puerto Vallarta, I befriended a man who represented Westin Hotels and introduced him to people who helped resolve a labor dispute involving the resort they were about to open. A decade later he invited me to join a group of writers he was sending to the Shangri-La, Westin's premier hotel in Hong Kong. On that trip I met a young man from Philadelphia, a freelancer like myself. A handful of years later he called from Des Moines, Iowa. He had just been appointed travel editor of *Better Homes and Gardens* (one of the best-paying women's magazines in America, with a circulation of 8 million readers). Would I like to write for him? Assignments for articles about "Hidden Bargains in the Caribbean," "The Lure of All-Inclusive Vacations," "Package Tours to Russia and China," and "New York's Best Free Attractions" quickly followed.

Another time a woman from my Playboy days recognized me at a social gathering and mentioned that she was a contributing editor to *Good Housekeeping*. Not long after, "Dining Alone and Liking It," "Eating Out With Kids Celebrity Style" (where famous people like Robert Redford and John and Yoko took their families in New York City), and additional food-related pieces increased my inventory and also led to a side career as restaurant consultant. Another meeting brought me to the attention of an editor at *Ladies Home Journal,* and I began to write about charming hotels and restaurants in San Antonio, New Orleans, San Francisco, and Chicago—including Oprah Winfrey's Eccentric, her first (and last) venture as a restaurateur. I became the travel editor of *Long Island Jewish World* and two other Jewish American weeklies with a readership of 240,000. Stints on the Travel Channel in the early 1990s as travel correspondent-at-large for Arthur Frommer's *World Almanac of Travel* and for Sally Jessy Raphael's *TalkNet* a decade later followed. By then I had the luxury of choosing where I wanted to travel, an enviable opportunity that ultimately involved a heartbreaking incident.

When asked about the worst thing that ever happened on a press trip, the last thing I ever thought I'd have to say was that a colleague, with whom I was traveling, disappeared.

31

Travel Writer Disappears in Jamaica

In early 2000 I asked the owner of the popular, all-inclusive Sandals resorts in the Caribbean, about which I frequently wrote, if he could arrange for me to visit his new property in Varadero, Cuba. I had been to Cuba once in the mid 1970s and wanted to return, but politics made travel from America complicated. The owner, whom I also considered a friend, was in a position to facilitate it if I flew there via Jamaica, his headquarters. Soon enough I was notified of a small press trip including me and Claudia Kirschhoch, an editor at *Frommer's Travel Guides*. I met Claudia briefly for the first time on a Wednesday on the way to Montego Bay, where we would overnight before flying to Havana the next day. We were placed in different hotels and shortly before dinner received a message. The trip to Cuba was canceled. The reason given had something to do with a political episode in Varadero, which no one would fully explain. We were also told that flights back to New York were booked for at least four days, but Sandals would host us at its Beaches resort in Negril during that time. I'd been to Jamaica at least a dozen times, but I'd never been to Negril and was curious, though not curious enough for a four-day stay, to see it. I asked the hotel manager if he could possibly use his influence to secure a ticket back to New York earlier, and luckily he was able to get me a seat for that Saturday.

Thursday morning Claudia and I were driven to Negril. She was a lively, attractive twenty-nine-year-old who had just started at *Frommer's* and couldn't quite believe her good luck. She was close to her parents, she told me, had recently moved into an apartment in Queens, had an on-and-off boyfriend, loved reggae music, and was determined to make the most of her four-day stay. The hotel PR person introduced himself to us when we first arrived, and suggested that we contact him if we needed anything. Contrary to policy, that was the last we saw of him. After dinner our first night we went to the bar overlooking the beach. Business was slow, and the bartenders were conversational, as they had been trained to be. The bartender serving us asked if we wanted to go to a club when his shift was over. I had been to more than my share of Jamaican reggae clubs and begged off. Claudia jumped at the opportunity to have someone escort her to local spots she could maybe write about. At breakfast the next morning she told me she had a great time and was glad she had stayed in Jamaica, and also mentioned that she tried ganja for the first time and didn't like it. I asked again if she wanted to fly back to New York with me on Saturday, but she was happy to have the extra days. Friday evening was a replay of the night before. Drinks, dinner, nightcap at the bar; I went to sleep early; she went into town with the bartender. We had an early breakfast the next morning before I left for the airport. She was clear-eyed, full of energy, excited about what she was doing, sorry I wasn't staying longer, and said that she would call once she got back to the city. Normally this would be the end of a not particularly interesting story. In fact, the story had just begun.

I didn't hear from Claudia but didn't give it much thought—which is why the fax I received from the PR man four days after she was supposed to have left Jamaica came as such a surprise. He wanted to know if I had heard from Claudia and asked that I call him. I immediately tried her apartment and left a message. It was a weekend, so her office was closed. I called Negril and was shocked to learn that she had not been seen at the hotel all week, nor had she checked out.

These are the facts as they were laid out to me. Claudia had gone missing. No one had any idea where or why. Because the last time anyone remembered seeing her was the Saturday morning she had breakfast with me, I was shortly drawn into a maelstrom of incompetence, distortions, lies, legal entanglements, depositions, and worse. I was interrogated repeatedly by the Jamaican police, the FBI, the American Embassy people, the management at Sandals, and Jamaican media. I told anyone who would listen that Claudia and the bartender had gone out at least the first two nights I was there, which the bartender implicitly denied. Of course he did. His job was at stake. It also turned out that he had a girlfriend who would not be happy to learn he had gone out with another woman. Everyone had a different theory. Claudia had wandered off the beach and drowned (no body was ever recovered). She had disrespected a known drug dealer on the beach, and his henchman got back at her. She ran away with a Rasta man to have his babies up in the hills; someone spiked her drink with a date rape drug and something terrible happened; she was kidnapped and sold as a sex slave; she wanted to get away from her parents; she planned it all along; she hired a boat man to take her to Cuba (quite a feat considering that her passport, wallet, cell phone, and camera were still in her room, though I was told that by the time the police were called in, the film had been exposed and the phone calls deleted). The day after I spoke to the PR man at Beaches I sent a fax I thought might be helpful. Had I known the price I would pay, I never would have done it.

Remembering Claudia's passing reference to ganja, and trying to be of assistance, I mentioned that he might want to check the local hospital to see if she had tried it again and suffered a bad reaction. The fax became the centerpiece of the press conference convened at the hotel a few days later. Holding it high above his head so that photos could be taken, a spokesperson announced that it had been sent by Claudia's good friend Tania Grossinger, who had traveled with her from New York, and said that Claudia was into drugs, drank heavily, and was sexually loose. Of course Tania Grossinger had said no such thing, because Claudia was no such person, but the damage was done. Claudia had been successfully set up as a slut. Whatever happened to her she had brought on herself. When a reporter from New York asked to see the fax, he was not allowed. That set off a sea of suspicion, which energized the journalists to dig deeper. The media blitz was about to begin.

I met Claudia's parents, who lived in New Jersey, a few days after they returned from Jamaica, where they had flown directly after their daughter's disappearance. They were still in a state of shock. They wanted to know everything she talked about, no matter how inconsequential it might seem. One thing they told me as they took meticulous notes was that she was acutely anti-drugs. They also asked what they should do about the numerous calls they were receiving from television and print reporters. I was getting the calls as well but directed everyone to Claudia's parents. I wasn't family, I hardly knew Claudia, and I wasn't there when she went missing. The parents, very private people, hated the idea of displaying their emotions in public, and, knowing I had experience with the media, asked if I would do at least some of the interviews. I begrudgingly said yes.

Tourism plays a vital role in Jamaica's economy. What became very clear was that Claudia's disappearance could cause extreme damage to its reputation, something government officials and everyone connected to the tourism industry was not about to let happen. It seemed obvious that whatever happened to Claudia was secondary to protecting the island's reputation. For legal reasons and my own safety, I must be very careful here not to disclose certain discussions, insights, and realities I was privy to. The most I can say is that they were not pretty.

The lie about what I supposedly wrote in the fax that painted such a sordid picture of Claudia's character infuriated me. I wasn't going to let that be the last impression people had of her. The first thing I did was make blowups of the last photo her parents had. In warm weather for two straight weeks I walked through Washington Square Park every afternoon and brazenly approached every drug dealer on duty with the question, "Are you from Jamaica?" If they were, I showed them Claudia's photo with the headline MISSING IN JAMAICA! and made my plea. I begged them to tell me if they had heard anything about her disappearance from their friends or family back home. By now almost everyone had seen her photo on television and in the newspapers. "She's my cousin," I would tell them. (I was advised by a friend of Jamaican descent that a family connection would gain sympathy.) "The parents have promised a reward. If you've heard something that hasn't gotten into the papers, even if it's just a rumor, let me know. I promise it will be worth your while." I was amazed at how warmly I was received. More amazing was the number of leads that came from them, which I immediately reported to the family and the FBI. Some of my informers up here knew more about what was going on down there than the police and the private detectives the family had hired in Negril did.

I threw myself into the investigation more than was probably healthy. Behind the scenes I served as a conduit—passing along confidential information from various people to the few authorities I knew could be trusted. I served as "information central" to the many journalists assigned to the story. I was interviewed on all of the TV networks, appeared on Fox News, *20/20*, and *Inside Edition*, was quoted in the *New York Times, Washington Post, New York Daily News,* and many other publications, including *People* and *Cosmopolitan* magazines. I must admit to a certain amount of ego satisfaction and was professionally grateful for the new contacts I was making but conflicted at the same time. I didn't, with due respect to Andy Warhol, want my "15 minutes" to come on the back of a colleague who by that time most everyone but the parents believed was dead.

The parents were finally forced to accept the likely reality and declare Claudia legally dead. This led to a confidential settlement in 2007 between them and the Sandals resorts. To my knowledge, no one ever suspected the bartender or anyone employed by the hotel to be directly involved in Claudia's death, though I understand it is believed that certain people associated with the hotel could have been more cooperative.

How did Claudia die? This is the first time I've offered my opinion for attribution. Keep in mind that I can't be sure and might also be wrong. From everything I learned I don't believe anyone set out to murder Claudia specifically. I do believe a date rape drug was involved. I believe she had a violent reaction. I believe others know who was responsible and what happened. I believe her body was stuffed into the trunk of a car, and I believe it was subsequently disposed of. I believe that to preserve the reputation of the island, a concerted and coordinated cover-up took place. I believe powerful people had their priorities skewed. Had Claudia been their daughter, I'm sure the outcome would have been different.

This press venture did not have a happy ending. I've always been aware that no journey comes without risks. The experience with Claudia did not diminish my desire to travel, though it did make me more cautious. I continue to consider myself blessed.

32

Israel

In 1937 my mother's younger brother, Jehoshua, immigrated from Horodenka, Poland, to what was then known as Palestine. He immediately joined the Irgun, a right-wing paramilitary group fighting for Israel's independence. An engineer by training, he was wounded so severely on a secret mission that when Israel was recognized in 1948, the government awarded him a rent-free apartment for life on Mt. Carmel in Haifa. I grew up with a sense that he was a real hero and proudly wrote him on Jewish holidays, telling him of my progress at school and other incidentals of my life, and every year he would write back to say how much he wished he could one day meet his sister's only daughter. In 1967 I decided to use part of my three-week vacation from Playboy to make that wish come true. My plans were to spend a few days in Athens and from there fly directly to Israel.

What I didn't know when I started out in mid-May was that there was talk of a possible revolution in Greece. I heard conflicting reports as my arrival date grew closer, but none seemed to involve tourist areas. Imagine my surprise the first morning, as I sat in Syntagma Square, at picking up the *International Herald Tribune* and reading about the riots and soldiers with guns overtaking the very square where I had just ordered breakfast. I looked around me. Men and women strolled nonchalantly around. There was no commotion and no soldiers. I immediately returned to my hotel, where I was assured that in Greece one could never trust what one read in the papers. But this was the *International Herald Tribune*! You can't trust that one, either, I was told. Three peaceful days later I boarded my flight to Tel Aviv.

I checked into the Astor, where I had reserved an oceanfront room for the princely sum of $25 a day and immediately contacted my uncle, who said we would get together by the end of the week. That evening I joined Zvi, a senior intelligence officer in the Israel Defense Forces, and his wife, Adina, whom I had earlier met in New York, for dinner. Together they made Israel come alive! Dinner overlooking the sea in Old Jaffa, a touristic drive through Tel Aviv at night, a drop-by at the home of some friends, and nonstop conversation about the social, political, and religious protocols that divided and united the country. Zvi and Adina also alerted me to the possibility of a war. "If Egypt illegally blockades the Straits of Tiran, the international waterway that leads into the port of Eilat, where most of the oil imported to Israel comes through," Zvi explained, "there could be serious repercussions. Fighting between Israel, Egypt, and its allies Syria and Jordan is a tragic possibility." At 3:00 AM my phone rang. It was Zvi. "They have closed the Straits of Tiran," he said. "I'm reporting to my unit immediately. Go to the airport tomorrow morning and take the first flight out. I may not be able to speak to you again before you leave. Good luck!" I knew Zvi had my best interests at heart. He wanted me to be safe.

Uncharacteristically, I surprised myself. "Hell no!" I said, thinking back to the so-called revolution in Syntagma Square. Maybe this was a false alarm, too. I wasn't going to leave. Everything was so calm earlier in the evening. Wars don't spring up overnight. My uncle was getting older, and I knew in my heart this would probably be the only chance I would ever have to meet him. At dinner Zvi had told me that U.S. Sixth Fleet was stationed outside of Haifa. I laughingly replied that I had never been rescued by the Navy before. Maybe this would be a first!

The next morning the hotel's manager advised me to go to the American Embassy and register my contact and passport information. Two days later, after half the military reservists were recalled to service, I went back to inform the embassy of my next day's visit to Jehoshua in Haifa. What I saw was a crowd of more than 200 American students and tourists gathered in front of the embassy, ready to support Israel and volunteer their services, and frustrated they couldn't get an official to meet with them. They knew they weren't allowed to fight alongside the Israeli Army but were willing to do whatever they could on land: fold bandages, deliver mail, handle traffic, perform any of the day-to-day services that were interrupted by the mobilization. No one at the Embassy would speak to them. There was something about this group's heartfelt need to be of service that moved me. I couldn't get past the Marine Guards securing the entrance but was close enough to grab a megaphone from a youngster in the front row and scream out the following question: "How many of you know the words to 'This Land Is Mine?'" It was the anthem of the 1960 film *Exodus*. The group burst out in song. "This land is mine. God gave this land to me." Our voices grew so loud as we sung about the brave and ancient land that finally the American Ambassador, Richard Jones, was forced to exit his office, face his American constituents, and agree to meet with representatives of those gathered. I was proud of myself.

I met with my uncle the next day, which, I'm sad to say, turned out to be a grave disappointment. The woman who answered the door, my aunt Leah, briefly introduced herself and repaired to another room, not to be seen again. Jehoshua tearfully took me in his arms and suggested I might want to take a nap because it had been a long ride in the shared cab from Tel Aviv (ninety minutes). I quickly recognized it was he who needed the nap and sat silently in the living room until he awoke. Though I knew he spoke fluent English, our conversation was stilted. He did tell me we had distant relatives in Haifa I hadn't known about who were originally from Hungary and who would be taking me to dinner that evening. It soon became obvious he wasn't going to talk about himself, his family, or what it was that brought him to Israel three decades earlier. I knew he and Leah had no children, so we couldn't talk about them, and whenever I asked questions about what it was like growing up in Poland, what my mother was like as a child, even if my uncle had ever met my father, he would shrug and quickly change the subject to, "Are you feeling all right?" Over and over he repeated how much he loved me, and each time I reiterated the same feelings about him. It was extremely uncomfortable, at least for me. When I met my Hungarian cousins later in the day, they explained that my uncle rarely left his apartment, which was why he wasn't joining us, and that he still suffered periodically from injuries relating to his time with the Irgun. It was hard for me to reconcile the uncle I had just met with the man whose letters to me had been so chatty and so curious about America and about me. He had even sent Neil and me a small wedding gift. I felt cheated. I was surprised that my mother, who knew I was planning to visit, hadn't alerted me to his condition. Then again, she might not have known—she saw him perhaps only once in the thirty years he lived there.

I had hoped Jehoshua could shed some light on the family dynamics when he and my mother were young. His insights might give me some perspective on why I was so often held at arm's length where my mother's maternal instincts were concerned. Unfortunately, it was not to be. Through no fault of his own, he remained a stranger. I felt sorry for him. I felt sorry for myself. At least he was able to tell me that he loved me. He held me. That, I told myself, is what I needed to hold on to and remember. And that is what I finally did.

The rest of my stay was very low-key. Parties where I had hoped to meet people were largely canceled. Most of the young men and women were already with their units, and traffic was almost nonexistent. There was an influx of journalists, however. Most congregated at the Dan hotel, which was located next door to mine. They were as fascinated by my association with Playboy as I was by their war stories, so evenings were rarely spent alone.

I remember small things. The cab driver who uttered the words *tsa vunda* over and over as he looked at me through his rear view mirror. *Tsa vunda!* I finally broke my silence. "Excuse me, do you speak English?" "I am speaking English! Tsa vunda! Tsa vunda! You're the only person I've had in my cab all day!" After repeating his words out loud, I realized he was saying, "It's a wonder!" It was indeed a wonder. I was the only fare he had all day.

With the uncertainty of war, I expected a rush on supermarkets for basic supplies. In Tel Aviv women who hadn't been drafted made beelines to beauty parlors. "When our men come home, whenever that may be," Adina explained, "we will look our best."

A few days before my departure, I dropped in to a jewelry store to revisit a gemstone that had caught my eye when I arrived. Maybe I could find something less expensive as a souvenir. The woman remembered me and immediately took out the piece I admired. I'm sorry, I told her, but unfortunately it's still more than I can afford. Of course you can, she said, quoting a figure less than half the price she had mentioned. "You stayed," she said. "Now maybe you'll come back, too!"

Just before I left, I was asked by the manager of the Astor if I could volunteer for roof duty. Because so many staffers were called up, the few remaining guests at oceanfront hotels were being asked to pitch in.

All I had to do was sit on a tall chair, make sure I didn't fall asleep, and, with the high-powered night binoculars they would give me, report if I saw anything "suspicious." I was honored. I was finally able to do something for "my" country. When I ultimately heeded the advice of the American Embassy and checked out two nights before the Six-Day War broke out in full fury (from which Israel emerged victorious), I noticed there were four nights for which I was not charged. When I asked the manager to correct the bill, she shook her finger at me. "We do not charge guests who do roof duty. I'll charge you twice as much the next time!" We both laughed.

"This land is mine!"

It was twenty years before I returned.

For the past decade I have been travel editor of *Long Island Jewish World*, *Manhattan Jewish Sentinel*, and *Rockland Jewish Tribune*. I consider myself a proud and secular Jew who celebrates the High Holidays and wishes she could believe in God as profoundly as she did when she was a child but finds it intensely complicated, especially after the Holocaust, to do so. I'm not affiliated with a particular synagogue, but I've been professionally associated with both Yeshiva University and Hebrew Union College, the education arms of the Orthodox and Reform branches of Judaism. In 1980 Yeshiva University underwent an extreme financial crisis. A relatively small group of industrial titans, through personal contributions, came to its rescue. To honor them, I was asked to create what turned out to be an elegantly illustrated ninety-page book, which I titled *Wisdom of the Heart*. It consisted of interviews with each of the donors, who were asked to share what their acts of generosity meant to them personally. At first some balked at participating, but the responses I was finally able to elicit were warm and tender, very unlike the personas many of the donors exhibited in public. Dr. Alfred Gottschalk, the president of HUC, hired me in 1985 to peruse progressive publications like the *Village Voice* and *Mother Jones* for articles pro- and anti-Israel and advise him whether to respond, and, if so, how. It was unlike anything I'd been asked to do, and I found it fascinating to discover what people from so many different perspectives had to say about Israel.

When, in 1987, *Better Homes and Gardens* asked if I wanted to write a travel article about Israel, I immediately said yes. Although my uncle and his wife were no longer alive, the country was at relative peace, and the thought of sharing my impressions with its millions of readers was irresistible. Unlike my 1967 visit, my itinerary was planned by the Israel Government Tourist Office, and I had a personal guide with access to a car and driver. In less than a week I visited for the first time the Western Wall, the Dome of the Rock, the Church of the Holy Sepulcher, the Old City of Jerusalem that was now in Israel's hands, Galilee, Jericho, the Dead Sea, Golan Heights, Tiberias, Ashdod, Ashkelon, Bethlehem, Masada, Nazareth, and the Mount of Beatitudes. It was almost too much to absorb.

I came armed, as I always do when traveling solo, with names of people to connect with in my free time. I spent a delightful evening with my cousins from Hungary. Ephraim worked for the government and offered to give me a personal tour of Yad Vashem, the National Memorial of the Holocaust. I stood looking at the photographs in the Children's Wing—photographs representing the hundreds of thousands of six- and seven-year-old girls who had been murdered. They looked like me at that age. Same round face, same cheek-length hair style with bangs, probably the same hopes and dreams. Members of my family had died in the camps, and if my parents hadn't immigrated to America, I likely would have joined them as well.

My friend Zvi and his wife still lived in Tel Aviv and hosted a party my first evening. The second night I attended a wedding at a kibbutz. Over the next few days I met the consumer editor of the *Jerusalem Post*, *Jerusalem Report*'s restaurant critic, and the cocktail pianist at the famous King David Hotel in Jerusalem, who introduced me to the underground nightlife scene. A highlight, which I'm sure you will appreciate, was my return to the Astor Hotel, my home base before the Six-Day War. It looked exactly as I remembered: the small lobby, efficient reservation desk, and newspaper stand to its left. An elderly woman standing in a corner came over to see if she could help. Our eyes met at the exact moment our arms reached out to embrace. "You came back!" the hotel manager from 1967 whispered. "I told you I would," I said just as quietly. "I wanted to make sure you didn't need me for roof duty!"

I was home!

I never worked as hard or put as much love into writing an article as I did that one. It was pulled from publication the month before it was scheduled to run, due to the political instability that had just begun to rock the nation in that February of 1998. The editor believed it would deter Americans from visiting Israel, and his instincts, unfortunately, were correct.

In 1990 I was contacted by two friends to join them in handling public relations for the Israel Government Tourist Office. We would, in effect, be working for Israel just as the Intifada (the Palestinian uprising in opposition to Israel's occupation of Gaza and parts of the West Bank) was in full swing. Not exactly a propitious time to promote the country's historic, religious, and tourist attractions. I jumped at the opportunity.

We worked closely with travel writers, airlines like El Al, tour operators, travel agents, evangelical leaders with ties to the Holy Land,

and anyone who had even a tangential relationship to Israel. The political situation was hurting tourism—that we could do nothing about—but we were told by the Ministry of Tourism that our efforts to ensure that Israel continued to be seen in a positive light were much appreciated: "We have been very well served by your journalistic backgrounds, integrity, commitment, and utmost professionalism. In my ten years of service for the Israel Ministry of Tourism, I have never seen so much media placements achieved by any of our PR agencies."

My uncle Jehoshua would have been proud!

33

Love with a Married Man

I LOVE YOU BECAUSE

You make me laugh.

You accept me as I am; no one in my life ever did that before.

Your love has taught me how to trust.

You are romantic, you wear your heart on your sleeve, and you're not afraid to show emotion.

You care about life, about the world, about people, about me.

If there is one drop in your glass, you know for a fact it will overflow! You believe, as your mother promised, that out of bad comes good. That anything, everything, is possible!

You do good.

You share.

You never give up hope!

You are goofy and make funny faces and bring out the silliness in me.

I never felt whole until I met you.

My heart still skips beats when I look at you.

I can't imagine life without you

I love you, my Arthur, with all my heart!

Art D'Lugoff was well known in New York circles for founding the Village Gate, a popular jazz and comedy club and off-Broadway theater in the heart of Greenwich Village. His obituaries in the *New York Times* and elsewhere noted additional accomplishments: theatrical impresario, entrepreneur, human rights advocate, political gadfly (he hired as many blacklisted performers as he could lay his hands on, including Pete Seeger and Josh White), union organizer, reporter, talk show host, adjunct professor at NYU's School for Continuing and Professional Studies, and even a busboy stint at Grossinger's.

That was the public persona, but, darling, there was so much more to the man who would mean the world to me.

On a very special birthday in 2008, twenty months before he died, Art and I exchanged vows, and I read aloud the words that begin this letter in front of close friends at my cousin Mary Ann's Manhattan apartment. We had been together for the best part of thirty-five years. I never wanted to remarry and I never did. Art was already married.

I had series of involvements, as you know, Natasha, some more appropriate than others. I was not without companionship, but by the time I reached thirty-five, love was not part of those relationships. Insecurity, fear, hurt, inability to trust, yes. Love, never. By that time I had come, not without sorrow, but with a curious sense of equanimity, to accept it.

I did not fall in love with Art because he was married and therefore safe. I didn't fall in love so that I wouldn't have to commit to a "real" relationship or because I was still hounded by the belief that I wasn't entitled to what everyone else had. I fell in love with Art because he was the most exciting man I had ever met.

Our paths first crossed in January 1966, when I asked him to bestow a Playboy Jazz Poll Award to the Modern Jazz Quartet, a group then appearing at the Gate. We had a drink, we spoke of his summers at the "G" when he went to NYU, and he invited me to call whenever I wanted to come to his club. I left, delighted to have made a new contact.

Everything changed in 1972, the year after my mother died. I had begun the life of a freelancer, I had kicked the bipolar alcoholic I'd been dating out of my life, and the Lion's Head had become a second home. One evening, seven years after we first met, I saw Art at the far end of the bar, and a very uncharacteristic sense of certainty swept over me. "He doesn't stand a snowball's chance in hell. I'm going to crawl into his heart." It didn't happen overnight, in fact it took a number of years, and there were times when I wasn't sure I'd get there, but I never gave up, and, despite what others might think, I am better for having had the patience to wait.

He was thirteen years older at the time, with three daughters and a son, ranging in age from eight to fourteen.

It was partially because of Art's club that our relationship could develop as it did. A nightclub and entertainment complex is demanding yet flexible where hours are concerned. He rarely had dinners at home. On weekends and evenings the Gate demanded even more of his time. Because I lived close by and worked from home, arranging to be together was easy. Passion, the likes of which I had never experienced, was at the heart of everything we did; making love, sharing meals, laughing at life's idiocies, challenging each other's ideas, and thoroughly delighting in each other's company. I had finally met a man with whom sex could be fun, a man with whom I could be spontaneous and be myself. All he asked was that I accept and return his love.

He taught me, by example, how to trust. I didn't have to tread on eggshells or think twice before I spoke. He accepted my scrambled past, as I accepted his scrambled present. It helped that he was familiar with Grossinger's and could understand the unusual way I grew up. He knew my family and even remembered conversations, usually about classical music, with my mother. I was familiar with the entertainment world that was such a big part of his life, and he'd been a journalist and knew many people in the publishing world, so he was familiar with the ins and outs of my career as well.

From the moment he told me he was married on our first date in Chinatown, I made sure he understood, and I couldn't have been more explicit, that I had no interest in breaking up his marriage. There was no reason for me to walk away from a relationship with Art, however. I had no intention of ever asking him to leave his wife. I was thirty-five years old. My decision not to have children, for reasons with which you are familiar, was firm. I had been married once. I had hurt someone badly and had been hurt even worse. I had no desire under any circumstances to go down that path again.

Knowing up front that there were unspoken rules to an extramarital affair didn't make it easier to live with. After the first few months our interactions became more lopsided than I was willing to accept. We spoke every morning and almost every night, but he was the one who initiated the calls and get-togethers. Because he didn't have a private office at the Gate, he didn't want me to call there. I wouldn't phone him at home. There was no place for spontaneity on my part. The following letter I kept reminds me how upset I was:

> We both acknowledge that our relationship has its share of built-in restrictions and I try as best I can to live with them and not involve you. But what happens when I really need to talk to you and you've cut off communication on my part is that you take absolutely everything out of my control. I am reduced to playing a totally passive role; my sole contribution is to sit back and wait. It's unfair, unnecessary, and it makes me unhappy.

It was the first time he was confronted with the relationship from my perspective and made to realize I was not the only one who would have to make concessions.

We separated for the first and only time after ten months. Art was falling in love with me. We needed to take stock and think about the kind of future, if any, we had to look forward to. He had to consider his marriage and family. I had to be honest with myself as to how I felt about being with a married man. Despite the success a decade earlier of Helen Gurley Brown's *Sex and the Single Girl*, public couplings of this nature in 1972 were still highly taboo. Not that they didn't take place, but certainly not as they do in today's culture, where in many instances they're accepted as a female rite of passage. The question for me went to the core of who I was, who I pretended to be, and who I would have liked to think I was. It went to the heart of standards I had set for myself ever since I was old enough to understand the value of having them. I rationalized that I was a decent human being, and as long as I wasn't personally hurting anyone, I had no reason to think I was doing anything wrong. I wasn't the one committing adultery. And I knew Art didn't take it lightly. He struggled over every decision he made regarding the two of us. No decision was reached without his awareness of the consequences and how others would be affected. Whatever tensions existed in his household didn't begin with me. Was I immoral? That's not for me to judge. Art was a married man. Did that make me love him less? No. I loved him because he was good to me and kind to me and loved me for who I was, which came as such a surprise that it once caused me to challenge his feelings. "You don't really love me," I said. "You never try to change me. Everyone else who professed to love me, my mother and ex-husband especially, had a qualifier. 'I love you, *but*. . . .' 'I love you *if only*. . . .' You never said that to me." The look of incredulity on his face was priceless.

This is not to say it all was sweetness and light. Much of our first two years played out within the confines of my apartment on Christopher Street. Art would come by three to four times a week, in the late morning, early afternoon, cocktail time, late at night. It was cozy, warm, and loving, but in time the confines became too confining. I wanted to share the other parts of my life, not report on them. The number of people aware of our relationship was limited. Secrets, which my mother taught me so well to keep, were one of the penalties of loving a married man. One evening he spontaneously, or so it seemed, suggested that we drop by the Lion's Head. Immediately our private life was public. It was obvious that his situation at home had changed. I noticed it on an more subtle level when he requested leftovers from a restaurant, and he began saying, "*We're* going to take this home," instead of *she's*.

Before long we were openly affectionate at many goings-on around town. We both had a minor obsession with food, and because I was doing restaurant PR at the time, we ate out at least four to five times a week. We went to parties; we gave them. Those Art hosted at my apartment when *Growing Up at Grossinger's* was published and when I turned fifty are still talked about whenever friends reminisce. At various times our professional lives intersected. He was always on the lookout for restaurants or clubs for me to represent, and when the Village Gate on 52nd opened up in midtown in 1997, I handled part of the publicity for him. In turn I helped him put together a series of panel discussions about Greenwich Village for NYU's School of Continuing and Professional Studies and served on the Boards of the Folk Music and National Jazz Museums he was trying to put together. In later years, combining various aspects of our work, his on the lookout for new talent at the Gate and mine as a travel writer, we managed to take many fascinating trips together. I was surprised that he could get away as often as he did, but he assured me, without getting into specifics, that he was able to work it out.

We lived what I came to consider a quasi-conventional life in an unconventional situation. We bickered; we made up. We were there for each other in sickness—he spent as many hours in waiting rooms while I underwent what's called Mohs surgeries to remove basal and squamous cell skin cancers as I did after his back and hip replacement operations—and in every other way. The only difference between us and a married couple was that at the end of the day or night, we repaired to our separate apartments.

Why, as our relationship grew more serious, didn't Art consider leaving his wife? I am going to be candid with you about his family situation. I should note that Art was alive when I began to write these letters. He edited them, reading each one aloud when we were alone to make sure the words sounded like me speaking. From the very first he gave me unqualified permission to disclose anything I chose to about our relationship, including his name.

Art had an overriding reason to keep his marriage intact. Two of his daughters, one as a teenager, and the other after graduating college, were addicted to drugs. Art gave them both unconditional love and emotional and financial support as they shuttled back and forth between rehab centers. There were no circumstances under which he would break up his home any more than it was already broken. The older daughter married someone with a similar problem and gave birth to two boys. Neither parent was able to care for the children, and as a result the boys were raised their first ten years by Art and his wife in their Upper West Side apartment. The two of them took on the responsibility with all its complications unreservedly, and though it didn't bring them closer as husband and wife, it provided a family for those who needed it most. That is the major reason he didn't leave his wife, and if he had, I never would have taken him in. Those daughters were the first of his children to learn of me as they grew up. By the time Art began to bring them into our lives, they were already familiar with the volatility in their parents' relationship and, without being asked to choose sides, accepted me warmly. Most women involved in extramarital liaisons aren't as fortunate in this regard.

I imagine that by now you must be curious as to how I negotiated other aspects of our affair. I can best address this by answering questions friends often asked: "Did the two of you ever talk about his relationship with his wife?" I never lost sight of my mother's admonition: "Don't ask the question if you're not prepared for the answer." Curiosities as to the "what" and "how" of his marriage I kept in check. In fact, when I was in a position to earn a sizable amount of money by writing Art's biography, I turned the offer down. As appealing as it was, I knew I couldn't do an honest job without interviewing his wife, and intuitively sensed that the less I knew about her or their relationship, the easier it would be. Am I implying that if I knew more I might have felt guilt about being with her husband? Possibly. I was not willing to find out. Cowardly? We all select, consciously or unconsciously, our personal mechanisms for survival. This one worked for me.

Was I ever uncomfortable being seen on the arm of a married man? No. I had long since given up the pretense of having to answer to other people, that everyone had to like me, or that I had to live up to others' expectations. When we met someone for the first time, Art always introduced me as "my lady." I was never made to feel any other way.

How was I able to deal with knowing that I would never be first in Art's life? This, I think, is the most difficult thing to accept by women in an affair such as mine. It was easier for me because of the way I was brought up. I was never first in anybody's life, so it came rather naturally.

How can you be sure his wife didn't know? The few times I asked, he assured me that she didn't. I heard from other sources that she did but didn't care. Maybe yes, maybe no.

It was only a matter of time before people who worked at the Gate and knew us both wanted to share their impressions of Art's wife with me. I asked them not to. That I wanted to know as little about her as possible didn't mean I felt animosity toward her. Art would never have married a terrible person. I never considered us to be rivals, nor did I ever feel that we were "sharing" Art. There was one awkward situation, however, that I can only look back on and laugh at.

In the 1990s I was working on a novel titled *Magda's Daughter*. I had given Art a partial manuscript, which he was planning to read at home. One morning I picked up the phone to hear a woman with an Israeli accent say, "This is Art D'Lugoff's wife." The moment I had feared. Before I could catch my breath, she started to speak. "I have just read *Magda's Daughter*, and I love every word of it." What does it say about me that the first thing I did was pick up a pen and write down everything she had to say? It was the first compliment about the book, which had already been turned down by three agents, I had received. She went on to explain how the daughter's relationship with her mother in many ways echoed her own, and how I must find a publisher, and how she would buy the first copy. I was ready to kill Art. How could he, of all people, have given her my copy to read? Was he out of his mind? It was difficult to get her off the phone. As she ran out of positive things to say, I sensed what was coming next. No, not that she wanted me to stop seeing her husband, but that she wanted to invite me to dinner. I quickly explained that in addition to working for Art, I also traveled for business and was about to go out of town for a few weeks. She asked me to let her know when I returned. Seconds later the phone rang again. My sweetheart. "You're a dead man," I said.

He was apologetic. His wife had looked for a newspaper in his office, saw the manuscript on the desk, and took it upon herself to read it. He had no idea what had happened until he saw her on the phone with my pages in front of her. "She thinks you're very lovely."

"I am," I reminded him.

Did Art ever support me financially? No. He was thoughtful with personal gifts and sometimes bought things for the apartment, but I made it very clear that I would not accept anything more. I could cope with being emotionally and sexually dependent, but having to count on a man to support me was anathema. If I ever wanted to leave, I didn't want that hanging over my head.

Wasn't it difficult spending holidays alone? In the beginning, sometimes. There were certain compromises, as I mentioned earlier, that I knew I would have to make. Being alone when he was with his family on certain holidays was one of them. At Thanksgiving, the friends I celebrated with invited him to join us for early cocktails, after which he returned to his family at home. I got used to it. We early on established a tradition of our own for New Year's Eve. Because it was the Village Gate's busiest night, our celebration started and ended early. I set a lovely table for a late lunch of special selections from our favorites restaurants: crab salpicon from El Charro, Salad niçoise from Bar Pitti, and tiramisu from the Grand Ticino, my once-a-year treat, accompanied by Art's champagne of choice. With Michel Legrand's *Umbrellas of Cherbourg* and *Jacques Brel Is Alive and Well and Living in Paris*, a show that played for three years at the Gate, in the background, we would toast each other with love for a new year as rewarding as the last. That his wife, in the earlier years, would likely meet him later in the evening was something I learned to live with. By the time she did, I was sound asleep with a smile on my face.

It was Art's idea after thirty-five years that we have a party to honor and celebrate our commitment to each other, the first time he publicly acknowledged that "it hasn't always been easy." His brother, Burt, three years his junior, a physician with Johns Hopkins in Baltimore and his closest friend (they spoke on the phone at least once a day), officiated. Burt, who was privy to both sides of Art's marital relationship through the years, was always supportive of us. He donned a yarmulke and sang Hebrew blessings in front of twenty of our closest friends, and together Art and I broke the traditional glass. It was the happiest day of my life. Together the two of us had created and made work our very own family. I asked for nothing more.

And then came the call that upended my world.

34

Art's Death and Aftermath

November 4, 2009, had been a good day. Art and I made plans for a late supper, after which he would probably stay over at my place, which he was now occasionally doing. He had been interviewed that morning for a TV documentary about his life and was pleased with the care his wife was getting at the nursing home treating her dementia. At a rehab facility following a second hip replacement seven months earlier, he had picked up a bastardly bacteria called C. difficile made worse by antibiotics that caused him to function like a ten piston engine running on three. In the last few days, however, things had turned around. It was as if his old self had reentered his body and come to stay. Laughter! Vitality! Joy! So nothing could have come more out of the blue than that late-afternoon phone call . When I called to check on how things were going, his son-in-law picked up his cell phone. They were in a hospital emergency room at Columbia Presbyterian. He and Art's daughter had dropped by the apartment a half-hour earlier, and in the middle of a conversation Art collapsed. I immediately called Burt, who was already in contact with the doctors and promised to let me know as soon as he heard anything. He called twenty minutes later. Art had died—though it took six months after the autopsy to discover the reason—a rare aortic hemorrhage.

The enormity of what had happened had yet to hit me. The next days were a blur. I knew the *New York Times* had pre-interviewed Art for the obituary page, which was common for notable public figures, and directed Burt to the appropriate reporter to fill in the details. Art's two younger daughters, now healthy (one in California, and the other the mother of his two grandsons in the Bronx, who was with Art when he collapsed), called every few hours to make sure I was OK. To thank me for loving their father. To remind me they loved me as well. I scrambled into crisis mode repeating, "Don't fall apart. I will not fall apart. Do not fall apart. Art's not there to catch me. Get me through the day. Get me through the night!"

Art's wife could no longer recognize anyone, but nevertheless Burt came up from Baltimore to be with their children that night. The next morning Burt and I had breakfast. "You were Art's life force, his spirit, his élan. You enriched and brought laughter, love, spice, and zest to his life. He was richer, a better person, because of you." Many tears were shed.

The media gave Art's passing the tribute he deserved. I spent almost every waking hour online or on the phone informing friends all over the country and accepting condolences. Everyone who reached out heard me repeat, "What has been seeing me through is that between us there was nothing left unsaid. No guilt. No regrets."

Not that long ago, Art's doctor had told him, "The trouble with you, D'Lugoff, is that you have a twenty-five-year-old's passion in an eighty-five-year-old's body!' As much as I didn't want to face it, eighty-five years were eighty-five years. At least I can hold on to memories of the twenty-five-year-old's passion.

That Art, thirteen years my senior, would likely predecease me was not a subject we spoke of. That doesn't mean I didn't rehearse how I might react. I knew Art wanted to be cremated, which would at least preclude my having to bear the thought of him in a coffin, a lifeless blob on a piece of wood. For sure, there would be a memorial. Perhaps I would have an observance of my own with "our" friends. Maybe I would even sit *shiva*. Most likely I would grieve alone. As for the emotional ramifications—they were too frightening to consider.

The son, who had been close to his mother, and Art's oldest daughter both knew of me, had met me, and probably wished they hadn't. Knowing what I did about their reliability where their father was concerned, I never considered this a loss. What they and Burt decided after Art died was to have an invitation-only memorial for family and friends to be held at Le Poisson Rouge, the club that had taken over the space of Art's Village Gate. A mutual friend of mine and Art's was drafted to help put it together. A first list of guests was drawn up. He pointed out that one name was missing: Tania. Our friend said he thought that might be a problem. His father would have wanted me there. Until that moment I had never felt the full consequence of loving a married man. Reality hit me. I was an outsider. "I don't want to be anywhere I'm not wanted," I cried to Burt. To Burt's credit, he didn't tell me I was overreacting. He knew I was on emotional tenterhooks. "Don't do this to yourself," he said. "This is about their own screwed-up relationships with Art. It has nothing to do with you. You were the curator of my brother's heart. You were as much his family as he was yours. That's what you should hold on to, not their craziness. And if you don't go to the memorial, I don't, either." I still hurt, and Art wasn't there to make it better.

The moment Burt assured me I was welcome I had second thoughts. Was it really necessary for me to see blown-up family photos mounted on a collage or flashed across a screen? I didn't trust Art's son and his sister not to make a scene. I wished I had not made a point of wanting to attend.

The memorial, considering family infighting and how quickly it was put together, was almost perfect. Burt recited, with great emotion, the poem "Ithaka" by C. V. Cavafy, whose outlook on life reflected Art's: The journey is always more significant than the destination. More than 350 people attended; it was standing room only. I was standing at the bar near the exit, in case I felt the need to make a quick escape, and turned my back whenever they showed family videos. Wine was a good escort. The son was unexpectedly polite and thanked me for coming.

I got through it pride intact.

One of Art's younger daughters, who was helping clean out his apartment, asked if there was anything of his that I wanted. I immediately thought of the matching black onyx ring bands he had spontaneously bought from a street jeweler on MacDougal Street twenty years ago. The smaller one fit my ring finger perfectly; I have never taken it off. He kept the matching ring in a special box in the top desk drawer in his office. The box also held some pewter mementos we used to exchange with the words "kiss" and "love" embossed on them. I didn't want this daughter's older sister or brother to see them. There was also a T-shirt Art loved that I asked her to claim in my stead. On his eightieth birthday I had it made up for him, with the troubadour logo from his business card on top. Underneath were printed three words: In This Lifetime! It was a reference to the zany projects he constantly juggled. The journey, not the destination, indeed! "Whenever you put it on," I told her, "you will know you have your father and even a piece of me close to your heart!"

Art's wife died four months later. I was surprised at the sadness I experienced. She had been part of my life for thirty-five years. I was grateful to her. If she and Art had a more fulfilling relationship, he never would have been open to me.

Phase One began with Art's death. Phase Two ended with the memorial. And then Phase Three kicked in. I didn't want to talk about Art anymore. I didn't need to let go; I needed to hold him even closer. I was having troubling thoughts. "My heart is about to break. 'All the king's horses, and all the king's men. . . .' I am too much alone. Emotionally disengaged. Detached. Disconnected. Why does the feeling of emptiness take up so much space? Drinking too much. Puts me to sleep. Why bother to stay awake? No one will ever love me again. The passion has gone out of my life." And then one morning I awoke, months later, and Art was not the first person I thought about. Maybe one day—not today but some day in the future—I would be OK?

Art enjoyed hearing Jonathan Schwartz on National Public Radio. One Sunday he had called to make sure I was listening; Tony Bennett was singing about us. It was "I Do Not Know a Day I Did Not Love You," by Richard Rodgers and Martin Charnin. The minute he finished I went online and printed out the lyrics. For Art's eighty-fifth birthday I had them, along with a copy for myself, laminated and framed. Six weeks after Art died, I tuned in NPR for the first time. At that very moment (some may call it coincidence, not I!) Jonathan was doing a live interview with Tony Bennett, who was telling listeners that "I Do Not Know a Day I Did Not Love You" had always been his favorite song. He proceeded to recite the last two lines aloud:

You will not know a day I do not love you
The way that I have loved you all our lives.

35

Post-Art

I put on a good face the half-year after Art died, but it was all a facade. My cousin Mary Ann sent an email during that shadowy period complimenting me, because "in your mourning you are doing things to connect, share, and not shut down." How off-base she was. I had never been as forlorn. I lost track of the real me, even doubted at times there was one. You don't stop loving someone just because he isn't there. The romantic snippets on my answering machine, the private jokes, the moments that made me delight in being alive—I didn't have them anymore. I remember being gifted one morning as part of a travel promotion with a fifteen-minute massage. It was the first time a person had touched my body since Art passed away. It wasn't sensual. It wasn't warm. It was all business. A frightening reminder that no man would ever touch me again with love.

Perhaps I should have turned to friends, but everyone I knew bore their own sorrows; I could no more alleviate theirs than they could alleviate mine. Had I been Art's widow, would anything have been different? I don't think so. I was particularly fortunate—and aware that women in similar situations might not be so lucky—in that his daughter in Los Angeles and brother were in frequent touch, and I never doubted their love. By then, however, the person I needed to reach out to was myself. My self. I didn't know where to find it. I had nothing to give.

The level on which I was adrift was not only internal. Restaurants for which I consulted changed management and brought in their own people. The travel outlets for which I wrote died out as the Internet flourished. Hotels and destinations no longer took ads in print publications. For information, tourists turned to websites whose creators told curiosity seekers what they wanted them to know instead of what they needed to. Sunday newspaper travel sections all but disappeared. The few press invites that came my way focused on adventure travel and were interested in younger, more active writers. My presence was no longer desired.

The past three years I had served as travel-correspondent-at-large for Sally Jessy Raphael, who, after being fired two weeks shy of twenty years as host of her eponymous TV show, created an Internet show called *TalkNet*, which she asked me to join. Whenever I returned from wherever I'd been, I'd do two fifteen-minute interviews with her that were broadcast all over the world. I would be doing them to this day if she hadn't recently gone on hiatus. Permanently. In other words, my days as a travel talk show guest or writer, unless a miracle were to occur, had come to an end.

In 2007, through Dermot McEvoy, author, friend, and Lion's Head drinking buddy, I was introduced to Tony Lyons, the president and publisher of Skyhorse Publishing, who was interested in reissuing *Growing Up at Grossinger's*. Considering the fact that the book was first published thirty-two years earlier and had since fallen out of print, it came as a total surprise.

Grossinger's had closed its doors in 1986. Many were surprised that the hotel had lasted that long. It brought to mind a "beware of what you wish for" moment I had as a young adolescent watching a magnificent sunset atop the Grossinger Hill above Route 17. A thought had occurred to me then: "This is so overwhelmingly beautiful. If they could just get rid of the people!" The Catskills as a resort destination had started a mini-decline around the time my mother left in the early 1960s. It grew even worse as time went on. Jet travel and packaged tours that made travel to other parts of the world more convenient and affordable were the most prominent, but the not only, reasons. Women celebrating their independence no longer traipsed to the mountains with their parents to meet appropriate husbands-to-be. Rumors that gambling was coming to the Catskills were forever being floated. Hotel owners hesitated to make structural improvements because of a secondary rumor that they'd have to invest another $10 million to qualify for a casino license. Americans became more health-conscious, and eight-course, calorie-laden repasts became less of a draw. TV paid entertainers more than most hotels could afford. Catering to conventions was no solution; the seasonal guests who thrived on personal attention stopped coming. Efficiency experts were brought in. "Make the meal portions smaller." "Install a cover charge for entertainment." "Cut the staff." "Fire the head of the housekeeping department." How could you fire Aunt Rose? Most of the successful Catskill establishments—Grossinger's, the Concord, Brown's, and Kutsher's—were run by families whom guests felt a part of. It didn't take long for the younger generations to move on. They no longer wanted to be part of them, and a once-thriving resort area became history.

So why republish my book in 2008? *Dirty Dancing* had already introduced the culture of the Catskills to an entire new generation. And we knew we could always count on the lure of nostalgia, especially that of the Jewish community.

I came to Skyhorse with an enviable background in publicity and a list of contacts on which we could build. The Skyhorse staff contributed their promotion and sales expertise way beyond what an author usually received, and as a team we set up more than forty speaking engagements, many of which I was even paid for, and almost twice as many media interviews. It was the best publishing experience I'd ever had. Art was invaluable. His contacts with Jewish organizations and media outlets provided me with coverage in places we never anticipated, and his encouragement and pride in me never wavered. But even those promotions eventually came to an end.

I was hoping that these letters to you, Natasha, might be the next step in my career.

36

Trying to Reconcile with Mother

I t is hard to reconcile with someone who is dead. I spent a great deal of time after I lost Art thinking about my mother. Without her there would have been no me; because of her there is no you, Natasha. I needed to make a semblance of peace, if not with her, at least with myself. I'm not sure my attempt was successful, but I know I made the best effort I could.

Seeking clues about her mysterious past I might have missed first time around, I once again pored through the journals and papers I brought back from Montecatini, wondering if she ever reread them with the same scrutiny and if the woman she became would even recognize her younger self. Considering all the compromises she ended up having to make, I hope, for her sake, she wouldn't have.

I was mesmerized, as always, by the elegant and sensitive way she expressed herself in print:

I shall never forget one drive from Malaga to Granada in the late afternoon. The fading of the glaring sun made the winding road in this arid, rusty, mountainous country look like a silver stream. Here and there were scattered little white villages amongst olive groves which were of the most beautiful silvery green, over it a thin veil of golden shadows and above it all silence, an unspeakable silence. It was as if the world there guarded a great secret, a secret of past glory and beauty, or past storms and who knows of what future. In those two hours I have lived through centuries and felt very strangely a part of the great earth that moves in its orbit, seemingly untouched by the destiny of its inhabitants. Races, nations, individuals may go, the world still goes on.

Who was that woman masquerading as my mother, and why did I never get to know her? Most of her journal entries pre-Montecatini are undated.

I used to be a lot alone as I was always sent to my grandparents because I was too wild [this I have difficulty imagining!] and made too much noise playing with my younger brothers and sisters.

If I would have been a Catholic, I would have become a nun; at 16 I became very much interested in philosophy and as I was always an extremist, I wanted to live a secluded life in a Cloister with beautiful gardens and lead a contemplative life. Or I would have liked to be a famous courtesan, a beautiful, brilliant woman having around her the most brilliant men of the time. Well, I became neither, but my life certainly was not mediocre.

I used to go on long walks with my mother, we would talk about everything. We were good friends. I thought my mother knew everything best, I hoped that I would someday have a daughter who would be my best friend; alas, fate wanted it otherwise, and this is the greatest tragedy of my life.

Not a word is mentioned about going to the University in Vienna, meeting my father, or losing family in the concentration camps. Rereading her younger fantasies of a life surrounded by stimulating people, I continue to find it hard to understand what it was that attracted her to my father, a relatively uneducated businessman with few cultural interests. In the letter my Uncle Meyer read at my mother's headstone unveiling in 1972, she wrote that my father was "a wonderful husband and we were so very happy together." He died in 1937. She fell in love with Paolo on a cruise in 1934. I wish she could have explained that to me, too.

We know there is a great deal of mystery surrounding my mother's early life in Chicago and later in California. Nothing I read cleared that up. I wished she had written more about being the oldest of five children and the relationship she had had with her mother. Was she forced to "mother" her siblings, and did that affect how she felt about children? I certainly didn't detect any fondness between her and her brother, Fabian, in Detroit when I married, and she made only one effort in thirty years to see her brother, Jehoshua, in Israel. She waited sixteen years to become pregnant after getting married, which in the late 1920s to mid-1930s was most unusual. That I was unwanted or at best an accidental baby does not do wonders for my ego, but the possibility deserves consideration. Perhaps her reasons for not wanting to have a child lie, as do mine, with the way she was brought up. It is also conceivable that the mysterious lifestyle she chose stood in the way of her becoming a mother. For all I know it was my father who didn't want a family. It is futile to grapple with this longer or more painfully than I already have. I am here, Karla was my mother, and life goes on. I stand as a testament to her and am my own reward!

My mother raised me to be an affectionate and decent human being. She shielded me from any personal problems, disappointments, or depressions she might have had. Many found her warm, charming, and sympathetic—many made a point of telling me how proud she was of me. She never raised a hand to me and rarely her voice. She wasn't mean. Hearsay, scuttlebutt, and scandal never passed her lips. I never heard her express bitterness or speak disdainfully of family, staff, or guests at Grossinger's, no matter what she may have felt, and she implored me to follow her example. She brought me up in an environment where I came under the influence of a never-ending array of interesting people, and I thrived under their tutelage. By raising me to be independent, she demonstrated her confidence in me. It is time to stop blaming her and take responsibility for some of my own choices. Karla wanted to be a good mother, that I truly believe. It may not have worked out that way from my perspective, but I'm sure she thought she did the best she could.

"Desperate. No one to turn to in moments of elation, in moments of despondence; yet life is so beautiful. My daughter wants me far away." My mother wrote at length in her last years of our alienation, of her despair at finding herself alone, of not having a daughter who cared. I couldn't stand, and still can't, to read those entries. I didn't want to know. I knew that in many ways she was right. In my early thirties I was resentful and put off by her emotional demands, but today, as I grow older and potentially face a parallel situation when it comes finding oneself alone, I wish I had been unselfish enough to have at least shown some compassion. I didn't do a damn thing, and for that, had it ever been possible, I would have asked forgiveness.

We both deserved better than that.

Looking Back: Childless by Choice

Knowing this will be my last letter to you, Natasha, saddens me more than I anticipated. Through this one-sided correspondence, I've made an attempt to share and make sense of my life, only to discover that lives may not be meant to be made sense of. Truth, I've learned, wears many costumes and speaks in many tongues. It does not automatically set one free, no matter how desperately one wishes it to. Memories can be tricks we play on ourselves, and reexamining my past has proven more complicated and challenging than I imagined. At times it's been as if I'm writing about someone I'm meeting for the first time. I've been so many different people in so many different situations in so many different places that one needs the skills of a magician, which I most definitely am not, to pull it all together. I didn't have a life; I've had lives. I've been many Tanias, some daring, some controversial, some exemplary, others embarrassing, but altogether it's been one incredible ride, one on which I look back with amusement and pride.

Without doubt the most important choice I made was not to have a child. The desire to create a life, to bring a new person into the world who might make it a better place, to give love in undreamed of ways—that feeling never went away. In my house of wishful thinking I always pictured a gaggle of kids. Our home would overflow with laughter and love; holidays would be filled with family and friends. Everyone is entitled to their version of Oz. Oz was beyond my reach.

Having my mother for a mother, as you know, is the prime reason I never became one myself. Fear can be a very powerful force. Fear of turning out like my her, fear of turning into her. Motherly love. Unconditional love. So many questions. What if, because I was my mother's daughter, I wasn't capable? What if I didn't do motherhood right? Would I learn from her mistakes or unwittingly repeat them? My mother wanted to have a daughter she could love, who would be her friend, but neither seemed to come naturally to her. What if I turned out the same way? If, as experience showed, my mother didn't trust me, maybe my daughter wouldn't, either. Would I go overboard and fight too problematically for her love, as my mother in later life did with me? Would she follow my lead and turn away? Reject me as I rejected Karla? I didn't mind making mistakes or taking chances with my own life, but I had no right to gamble with a child's. A friend once suggested that the only way to prove I could be a better mother than my own was to have a baby of my own. Motherhood as a competitive sport? What if I lost?

Memory cheats children. Most psychologists agree that our brain cells don't permit us to remember the very early years when, if lucky, we were coddled, cuddled, and cajoled and at the center of our parents' universe. I have no idea how I was treated when I was a baby. How desperately I wish I could have had at least one parent to whom I could say, "I learned about love from you."

I never bought into the myths that unless I had a child I could never be a complete woman, that having kids was the meaning of life, that I had a social responsibility to reproduce for the good of the world, or even that children were good insurance for a parent's future. It is the child's responsibility, even before being born, to fulfill her mother, make her complete, and give meaning to her life? How frightening. I never believed that the act of intercourse suddenly bequeaths nobility, that fertilization of an egg by a random sperm automatically confers maternal wisdom. I cringed when the singer Rihanna said to her fans via *Access Hollywood,* "We're reproductive machines; that's what we're here for." Or when, in an episode of *All in the Family,* Archie Bunker's wife, Edith, asked by her daughter, Gloria, what she would have done if she hadn't had a baby, replies, "I don't know. I can't imagine. That's what woman was meant to do. That makes her useful."

Giving birth is the ultimate act of faith. No baby comes out of the womb with a returnable/refundable guarantee of "happily ever after" stapled on its bellybutton. Assurances are not automatic that he or she will grow up to be healthy, successful, thoughtful, kind, loving, and able to satisfy the parents' as well as the child's own needs. I actually love being around children. Maybe because I have nothing at stake, I am totally open to their innocence, spontaneity, emotional honesty, and purity of expression. When I'm alone, I do my best, if not always successfully, to nurture the child within, the one who views the outside world with trust and a sense of wonder, who sees both the forest and the trees and accepts the need to embrace both.

I feel such warmth watching parents interact with their children, especially when I see fathers cradle their baby girls. I wonder how old the baby is; is she less than six months? Did my own father hold me that close to his heart? I wish my mother had saved one photo of us together. Something I could hold on to *in loco parentis.* When I see families, I wonder what kind of father Neil would have been. We didn't make a good husband and wife, but I have never doubted that he would have been a fine dad . . . with someone else. Art was the only other man I could have seen as the father of my child. He was the one man with whom I felt complete, who loved and embraced me so wholeheartedly that, had our situation been different, I might have even considered taking the chance. Easy enough to say, because I wasn't called upon to make the commitment.

A life well lived does not mean not having made mistakes or wishing certain things had been different. I would not have married Neil as quickly as I did, if at all. I'm sorry I wasn't mature enough to pay attention to the warnings, to see things as they were rather than as I would have liked them to be. We should have gone for premarital guidance, we should have slept together before we married, but social mores were different then. And so was I. I still carry the hurt I caused Neil, that I verbally confirmed his deepest fear, that I told him he was unable to love. Even in dreams where he periodically appears, I try to apologize, and he pushes me away. I always believed, as I've related before, that unless he forgave me, I would never be able to have a viable relationship with another man, and until I met Art, my suspicions were justified. If Art hadn't come into my life, I can't bear to think what it, what I, would have been like.

I still believe I made the right choice by not having a child. Weren't there times I would have loved to have a family, loved ones with whom I could share my life? Of course. But I made a conscious decision to forgo that possibility and rarely looked back. Life is a series of trade-offs. Other people's lives often seem more rewarding than our own. While I envied friends' family get-togethers, they conceivably coveted my independence and freedom. There is no right or wrong. We often wish for what others have. It's very simple; we can't always have those things. What we can do is make the best of what we have. That I believe I have done with a vengeance!

I do regret not giving enough thought, financially and emotionally, to what might happen when I reached a "certain" age. Until recently, age was only a number: forty, fifty, sixty, sixty-five, seventy. But now that I've reached that "certain" age, I'm not quite sure how to see myself. I'm not sure how others see me. My mind is more agile than fragile, my sense of humor is intact, but my seventy-five-year-old body is taking on a life of its own. Parts of it can't be trusted (unstable knee, basal cell carcinomas here and there) and are attempting to dominate me. It takes more energy than I'd like to fight back. It hurts me that my body can't be trusted. Like when one realizes one can't trust a lover. Or a friend. One can hopefully find a new friend, maybe even a loved one. But where will I find a new body? I inhabit it every day, every night. I hate it! Whoever coined the phrase "Golden Years" should be forced to live them.

My circumstances are different from those of my mother. I live surrounded by books, music, and memories in a rent-controlled apartment in the heart of Greenwich Village. It has been my home, workplace, and protective cocoon for more than five decades. My Facebook profile lists me as author, consultant, talk show guest, travel writer, and troublemaker, all of which I attest to with pride. I accept that being alone was my choice, and, please, take me at my word—the words "If only I had had a child" do not for a moment apply. I am not second-guessing my life. It is wishful thinking, as unfortunately many people I know have discovered, that as long as one has family, someone will always be there for them. If only! I have had the good fortune at different stages of my life to be surrounded by treasured friends. I've lived through some painful deaths and was there when needed. I don't want anyone to have to go through such traumas with me. My close circle diminishes as time goes by, and I've come to realize that there are fewer and fewer people I can depend on. I'm not sure what the answer is, but hopefully I have time to figure it out.

I am also somberly aware that I am at the end of the line. No survivors to acknowledge in my obituary. My father and his family are long gone, as is my mother and hers. I stand as a testament to their being; no one stands to mine. My limited circle of life. *Fini.* I write these letters to have something of value to leave behind, to pass on, to leave my mark. And I look back on who I am.

And what kind of person am I? It is timely that I write this now, at the beginning of the Jewish High Holy Days, Rosh Hashanah and Yom Kippur. Ten days of penitence. Days of awe. The one holiday that even secular Jews like myself observe. According to tradition, on the eve of the first night of Rosh Hashanah, the Book of Life is opened, and at the end of ten days, the fate of Jews all over the world are inscribed by God for the coming year. On the last day, Yom Kippur, the Book is sealed. Between those days, one looks into one's self, prays for redemption and renewal, asks personal forgiveness of those one has offended, and seeks forgiveness of God. On the first day many perform the act of *Tashlich*, symbolically casting their sins (via nuggets of bread) upon the waters, in hopes they will be forgiven. Yesterday morning, the first day of the Jewish New Year, I took the subway to Brighton Beach in Brooklyn. In my pocket was a baggie of my multigrain sins. I had never done this before and found the symbolic cleansing of the soul rewarding.

I consider myself to be a decent human being. I try not to hurt others and apologize when I have. Whatever grievous sins I've committed this past year, I've committed against myself and will seek my own forgiveness. I will fast on Yom Kippur, I will attend services, and I will say memorial prayers in honor of both my parents. "Thou hast gone from me, but the bond which unites our souls can never be severed; thine image lives within my heart," reads the Jewish prayer recited in memory of a deceased mother. The meaning is inescapable; I will do my best to respect it.

As I walked on the beach toward the breaking waves, a few resolutions came to mind:

I will act on my instincts.

I will be more understanding of others' dispositions—we all harbor
   demons.

I will check tendencies toward being petty and judgmental.

I will try not to disappoint others.

I will try not to disappoint myself.

I will try to not take it to heart when others disappoint.

I will try to not be so impatient.

I will not expect more from others than they can realistically give.

I will remember, as Art taught me, that it is the journey, not the
   destination, that counts.

I will keep in mind that if I'm not living on the edge, I'm taking
   up too much space.

I will not waste time I don't have.

I will always drink the good wine first!

And so, Natasha, it is time to take my leave. I will miss you probably more than I know. Letting go has never been my strong suit. I'm
not sure I'm ready to say goodbye.

Thank you for being my partner. Thank you for letting me open
my heart.

Your appearance has made a difference in my life.

With love,

Tania

Acknowledgments

I count myself fortunate to be surrounded by friends who have my best interests at heart. This book could not have become a reality without the extraordinary support of Skyhorse Publishing, especially Associate Publisher Bill Wolfsthal whose insights made this book stronger and Jennifer McCartney whose editing skills were truly remarkable and deeply appreciated. I thank Jen Hobbs, the former publicity director, for prodding me to make the submission and especially Dermot McEvoy who, out of deep friendship, is singularly responsible for my introduction to Skyhorse. My cousins Rose Grossinger and Mary Ann Grossinger were there when I needed them most. I will never forget. Mary Ann, Pat Strongin, Patricia Mescall, Maureen McCafferty, Linda DeRefler, Joyce Walkwitz, and Emily Rosen served as first readers when I was grappling with various sections. Without their feedback I doubt I would have had the confidence to continue. Dr. Burt D'Lugoff, Michael Fink, Bernard Sucher, my exemplary website designer Richard O'Brien, Zoya Bitici, Arlyn Blake. Marguerite Martin, Eugene May, you have brought joy to my life.

I thank you one and all!

DATE DUE